Harold Pinter Collected Screenplays One

Harold Pinter was born in London in 1930. He lived with Antonia Fraser from 1975 and they married in 1980. In 1995 he won the David Cohen British Literature Prize, awarded for a lifetime's achievement in literature. In 1996 he was given the Laurence Olivier Award for a lifetime's achievement in theatre. In 2002 he was made a Companion of Honour for services to literature. In 2005 he was awarded the Nobel Prize for Literature and, in the same year, the Wilfred Owen Award for Poetry and the Franz Kafka Award (Prague). In 2006 he was awarded the Europe Theatre Prize and, in 2007, the highest French honour, the Légion d'honneur. He died in December 2008.

by the same author
plays
ASHES TO ASHES
BETRAYAL
THE BIRTHDAY PARTY
THE CARETAKER
THE COLLECTION and THE LOVER
THE HOMECOMING
THE HOTHOUSE
LANDSCAPE and SILENCE
MOUNTAIN LANGUAGE
MOONLIGHT
NO MAN'S LAND
OLD TIMES
ONE FOR THE ROAD
OTHER PLACES
(A Kind of Alaska, Victoria Station, Family Voices)
PARTY TIME
THE ROOM and THE DUMB WAITER
A SLIGHT ACHE and other plays
TEA PARTY and other plays

PLAYS ONE
(The Birthday Party, The Room, The Dumb Waiter, A Slight Ache, The Hothouse, A
Night Out, The Black and White, The Examination)

PLAYS TWO
(The Caretaker, The Dwarfs, The Collection, The Lover, Night School, Trouble in the
Works, The Black and White, Request Stop, Last to Go, Special Offer)

PLAYS THREE
(The Homecoming, Tea Party, The Basement, Landscape, Silence, Night, That's Your
Trouble, That's All, Applicant, Interview, Dialogue for Three, Tea Party (*short story*),
Old Times, No Man's Land)

PLAYS FOUR
(Betrayal, Monologue, One for the Road, Mountain Language, Family Voices, A Kind
of Alaska, Victoria Station, Precisely, The New World Order, Party Time, Moonlight,
Ashes to Ashes, Remembrance of Things Past (*with Di Trevis*))

screenplays
HAROLD PINTER COLLECTED SCREENPLAYS TWO
(The Go-Between, The Proust Screenplay, Victory, Turtle Diary, Reunion)

HAROLD PINTER COLLECTED SCREENPLAYS THREE
(The French Lieutenant's Woman, The Heat of the Day, The Comfort of Strangers, The
Trial, The Dreaming Child)

prose, poetry and politics
COLLECTED POEMS AND PROSE
THE DWARFS (a novel)
100 POEMS BY 100 POETS (an anthology)
99 POEMS IN TRANSLATION (an anthology)
VARIOUS VOICES: Prose, Poetry, Politics 1948–2008
WAR

HAROLD PINTER

Collected Screenplays One

The Servant

The Pumpkin Eater

The Quiller Memorandum

Accident

The Last Tycoon

Langrishe, Go Down

Introduced by the author

faber and faber

First published in 2000 by Faber and Faber Limited
Bloomsbury House, 74-77 Great Russell Street, London, WC1B 3DA

Photoset by Parker Typesetting Service, Leicester
Printed and bound by CPI Group (UK) Ltd, Croydon, CR0 4YY

This collection © Harold Pinter, 2000
Introduction © Harold Pinter, 2000

Copyright in the screenplays is as follows:

The Servant ©1971 by Associated British Press Productions Ltd
The Pumpkin Eater ©1971 by Columbia Pictures Corporation
The Quiller Memorandum © by Ivan Foxwell Productions Ltd
Accident ©1971 by London Independent Producers (Distribution) Ltd
The Last Tycoon © 1977 Horizon Pictures Inc.
Langrishe, Go Down © 1978 Dynamite Entertainment Inc.

Copyright in the original works is as follows:

The Servant © 1948, 1964 by Robin Maugham
The Pumpkin Eater © 1962 by Penelope Mortimer
The Berlin Memorandum © 1965 by Jonquil Trevor
Accident © 1965 by Nicholas Mosley
The Last Tycoon © 1941 by F. Scott Fitzgerald
Langrishe, Go Down © 1966 by Aidan Higgins

The original works were published as follows:

The Servant by William Heinemann, Ltd
The Pumpkin Eater by Hutchinson & Co Ltd
The Berlin Memorandum by William Collins, Sons and Co. Ltd
Accident by Hodder & Stoughton Ltd
The Last Tycoon by Scribners
Langrishe, Go Down by John Calder

The right of Harold Pinter to be identified as author of this work
has been asserted in accordance with Section 77 of the
Copyright, Designs and Patents Act 1988

A CIP record for this book is available from the British Library

ISBN 978-0-571-20319-2

CONTENTS

INTRODUCTION

I wrote the screenplay of Robin Maugham's *The Servant* for
Michael Anderson in 1962 but he wasn't able to find finance
for the film. The script found its way to Joseph Losey. I went
to see him in his house in Chelsea. 'I like the script,' he said.
'Thanks,' I said. 'But there are a number of things I don't
like about it.' 'What things?' I asked. He told me. 'Well, why
don't you make another movie?' I said, and left the house.

Two days later he called me. 'Shall we try again?' he said.
I said 'Okay.' I went back to his house, we did further work
on the script and over the next twenty-five years we worked
on three more screenplays and never had another cross
word. It's strange to think that *The Servant* was written
almost forty years ago. The film still seems as fresh as a daisy
to me, whilst stinking of moral corruption. I think Joe Losey
and the cameraman Douglas Slocombe did a superb job and
Dirk Bogarde and James Fox made a wonderful couple.

For some obscure reason, *The Pumpkin Eater* has never
been released as a video and only very occasionally shown on
television, so it is little known. This is sad because Jack
Clayton was a director of great distinction. The book, by
Penelope Mortimer, was the story of a woman with many
children, a very successful husband, all material comforts,
but who nevertheless inhabits a desert island of the mind.
She is totally and irrevocably alone. Anne Bancroft gave a
fine performance and James Mason one of unforgettable
viciousness.

The Quiller Memorandum, based on a spy story by Adam
Hall, fell, I think, between two stools: one, the Bond films
and the other, *The Spy Who Came In From The Cold*. In other
words the film never quite made up its mind as to which
path it was taking. It *was* seriously intended but at the same

time couldn't resist received ideas of the 'spy movie', too often resorting to melodrama. Nevertheless the neo-Nazi theme was, I believe, treated quite boldly and in some respects (the character of Inge) with subtlety. When it was shown in West Germany and dubbed into German the distributors changed the neo-Nazis to Communists.

Sam Spiegel financed the writing of *Accident* on which I worked with Joe Losey. When I had finished the script Spiegel read it and asked us to meet him in his office. He sat behind his classic producer's desk, the script in his hand, and stared at us.

'You call this a screenplay?' he said. 'I don't know who these people are, I don't know what their background is, I don't know what they're doing, I don't know who's doing what and why, I don't know what they want, I have absolutely no idea what is going on, how can you call this a screenplay?'

Joe and I sat in silence. Joe finally said, 'I know what's going on.' 'So do I,' I said. 'You two might know what's going on,' Spiegel said, 'but what about all the millions of peasants in China?'

We took the screenplay elsewhere.

The novel by Nicholas Moseley was a first person narrative, highly subjective, incorporating 'streams of consciousness'. I tried to go with that in an early draft but very quickly realized that 'streams of consciousness' are fatal in the cinema. I settled for a hard, spare, tight, objective scrutiny and Joe Losey carried that scrutiny through in the shooting of the film. In consequence, I think it's a film of great economy and poise and a truly chilly beauty.

Mike Nichols was originally going to direct *The Last Tycoon* but he withdrew after some months work on the script because he couldn't get on with Sam Spiegel in his capacity as producer. Elia Kazan took over. My own relationship with Sam had changed, indeed mellowed, over the years and I didn't find working with him too difficult. He could be testing but he was without question shrewd, knowledgeable and imaginative.

The film itself I found disappointing. I thought it too romantic and the casting of the central female role was underpowered. Monroe Stahr was one of Robert de Niro's first leading parts. He was impressive.

An independent producer called Max Rosenberg came to me with *Langrishe, Go Down*, a novel by Aidan Higgins, on which he had taken an option. It was a brilliant, haunting book and I much enjoyed adapting it. Naturally, the finance could not easily be found and it languished as a project for some years. Finally, David Jones at the BBC came across the script and was determined to direct it. He did, in Ireland, in 1978. The film was true to both the script and the book and I thought it tough and delicate. Jeremy Irons scored a bull's-eye with his portrait of the unscrupulous German student. The film was shown once on television and hasn't been seen since.

I have never written an original film. But I've enjoyed adapting other people's books very much. Altogether, I have written twenty-four screenplays. Two were never shot. Three were rewritten by others. Two have not yet been filmed. Seventeen (including four adaptations of my own plays) were filmed as written. I think that's unusual. I certainly understand adapting novels for the screen to be a serious and fascinating craft.

Harold Pinter
13 September, 2000

The Servant

The Servant was first presented by Elstree Distributors Ltd on 14th November 1963 with the following cast:

BARRETT Dirk Bogarde
TONY James Fox
SUSAN Wendy Craig
HEAD WAITER Derek Tansley
GIRL IN PHONE BOX Dorothy Bromiley
SOCIETY WOMAN Ann Firbank
SOCIETY MAN Harold Pinter
VERA Sarah Miles
BISHOP Patrick Magee
OLDER WOMAN Doris Knox
YOUNGER WOMAN Jill Melford
CURATE Alun Owen
LORD MOUNTSET Richard Vernon
LADY MOUNTSET Catherine Lacey
CASHIER IN COFFEE BAR Chris Williams
MAN IN PUB Brian Phelan
GIRL IN PUB Alison Seebohm
WOMAN IN BEDROOM Hazel Terry
GIRL IN BEDROOM Philippa Hare

Directed by Joseph Losey

EXT. KNIGHTSBRIDGE SQUARE. OCTOBER. DAY.

A quiet square off Knightsbridge. Winter sun. Bare trees. Numerous parked cars.

At the far side of the square Barrett appears. From high, see him approach. He stops at the kerb. Cars pass. He crosses the road. His steps are sharp on the pavement. Looking for a number he passes houses. He stops at a house, slightly shabbier than the others, discerns number and goes up the steps.

The door is open. He looks into the dark hall. Silence. There is no doorknocker. He finds a bell, rings. A faint uncertain ring.

INT. HALL. TONY'S HOUSE. DAY.

From inside the hall see Barrett enter and stand. The hall wallpaper is dark, of a faded grape design. There are no carpets, no sign of occupation. Silence. He crosses to the drawing-room door, knocks.

INT. DRAWING-ROOM. DAY.

From conservatory end of the large empty room see Barrett look round the door. He walks into the room and peers into the conservatory. Low down in an old deckchair lies a body.

INT. CONSERVATORY. DAY.

Barrett approaches, stops a little way from the body, regards it. He bends over Tony.

BARRETT

Excuse me . . .

(*Tony starts up.*)

My name's Barrett, sir.

Tony stares at him, clicks his fingers.

TONY

Oh God, of course. I'm so sorry, I fell asleep. We've got an appointment.

BARRETT

Yes, sir.

TONY

What time?

BARRETT

Three o'clock sir.

TONY

Well what time is it now?

BARRETT

Three o'clock, sir.

TONY

Too many beers at lunch, that's what it is. Do you drink beer?

BARRETT

No I don't, sir.

Tony stands.

TONY

Come upstairs. We can sit down.

They move to the door.

INT. HALL. STAIRS. DAY.

They walk up the stairs.

4

TONY

I'm just back from Africa. I'm quite liking it. What do you think of the house?

BARRETT

It's very nice, sir.

TONY

Needs a lot done to it of course.

INT. TONY'S BEDROOM. FIRST FLOOR. DAY.

Winter sun striking across floorboards. The room is empty but for two chairs. The door is flung open. Tony comes in, followed by Barrett. His words gain a slight echo in the room.

TONY

Damn lucky to get this place, actually. Little bit of wet rot, but not much. Sit down.

BARRETT

Thank you, sir.

Barrett sits. Barret's chair is in the centre of the room. Tony, while speaking, moves about the room, almost circling the seated figure.

TONY

Well now, this post. What's happening is this . . . I'll be moving into this house in about . . . two or three weeks and I'm all alone at the moment, so I'll be needing a manservant, you see. I've seen one or two chaps already but they didn't seem very suitable to me somehow. What . . . you've had experience at this kind of work have you?

BARRETT

I've been in service for the last thirteen years, sir. The last few years I've acted as personal manservant to various members of the peerage.

TONY

Oh.

BARRETT

I was with Viscount Barr until about five weeks ago.

TONY

Oh Lord Barr? My father knew him well. They died
within a week of each other as a matter of fact. So you're
free?

BARRETT

I am sir.

Tony stands at the front window.

EXT. GARDENS IN THE SQUARE. DAY.

*The gardens in the square, seen by Tony from the window.
Barrett's reflection in the pane.*

INT. BEDROOM. DAY.

Tony turns.

TONY

Do you like the work?

BARRETT

Oh I do, sir. I do very much.

TONY

Can you cook?

BARRETT

Well it's . . . if I might put it this way, sir, cooking is
something in which I take a great deal of pride.

TONY

Any dish in particular?

BARRETT

Well, my . . . my soufflés have always received a great deal of praise in the past, sir.

TONY

Do you know anything about Indian dishes?

BARRETT

A little, sir.

TONY

Well, I know a hell of a lot.

Tony sits in the other chair.

You'd have to do all the cooking here.

BARRETT

That would give me great pleasure, sir.

TONY

I could have got a housekeeper of course, to look after the place and run the kitchen, but quite honestly the thought of some old woman running about the house telling me what to do . . . rather put me off.

BARRETT

Quite, sir.

TONY

Now apart from the cooking, I'll need . . . well, everything . . .
                    (*He laughs.*)
General looking after . . . you know.

BARRETT

Yes, I do, sir.

INT. RESTAURANT. NIGHT.

Small, elegant restaurant with dance floor. The band playing. Dancers. Susan swings into close shot over Tony's shoulder.

SUSAN
(*laughing*)

Brazil?

TONY

Yes. In the jungle.

The music stops. They go back to the table.

TONY

Waiter! We've got to clear the jungle first.

SUSAN

What? just you?

TONY

No! It's a giant development. They're going to build
three cities.

SUSAN

Are they?

TONY

Mm. Gigantic project. Matter of clearing hundreds of
miles of jungle.

HEAD WAITER

Sir?

TONY

I'll have another bottle, and by the way, this one's corked.

HEAD WAITER

I'm very sorry, sir.

SUSAN

You're corked.

TONY

Now listen, I'm telling you. . . . First we have to build
the cities. Then we've got to find the people to go and
live in the cities.

SUSAN

Where are you going to find them?

TONY

From Asia Minor. Thousands of peasants, you see.
They're having a pretty rough time of it in Asia Minor
and this'll mean a new life for them. Anyway he wants
me to help arrange the whole thing. It's going to cost
millions, millions.

Head waiter returns with bottle. Pours. Tony sips.

TONY

Fine. I'm having lunch with him next week.

SUSAN

Where? In the jungle?

TONY

Either here or in Paris, actually. Anyway there's no
hurry. I could do with a rest.

SUSAN
(*laughing*)

A rest from what?

TONY

No. Seriously, what do you think of the idea?

SUSAN
(*lifts her glass*)

Cosy.

INT. DRAWING-ROOM. BARE FLOORS. NIGHT.

*Tony and Susan lying on the floor, coats as a pillow, a rug over
them. A small electric fire plugged in. Night light from window.
They kiss.*

TONY

Want to go there?

9

SUSAN

Where?

TONY

The jungle.

SUSAN

Not now.

TONY

No, not now.

He kisses her.

SUSAN

Bachelor.

She kisses him.

TONY

Oh by the way, I forgot to tell you. I've found a
manservant.

SUSAN
(*laughing*)

What?

INT. HALL AND STAIRS. DAY.

*Looking from top of stairs down into empty hall. Voices ascend
from kitchen.*

BARRETT

Very good idea, sir.

They appear in hall, look up the stairs.

What about the landing, sir?

TONY

White.

They begin to walk up the stairs.

INT. FIRST LANDING. DAY.

Tony and Barrett come up the stairs.

> TONY
> Well perhaps a little blue here and there . . . but I think the overall colour should be white.

> BARRETT
> Mandarin red and fuchsia is a very chic combination this year, sir.

> TONY
> Not overall, surely?

> BARRETT
> No, no, no. Not overall.

> TONY
> Just a wall?

> BARRETT
> Oh yes, just a wall, sir, here and there.

INT. BEDROOM. DAY.

They enter and look about. Tony's personal bathroom and dressing-room in background.

> TONY
> You're very knowledgeable about decoration, Barrett.

> BARRETT
> Well, it makes all the difference to life, sir.

> TONY
> Oh. What does?

> BARRETT
> Tasteful and pleasant surroundings.

> TONY

Quite right.

INT. TOP LANDING. DAY.

Tony and Barrett arrive on landing.

> TONY
> (*pointing*)

That's your room. Wait a minute, what's that?

They open door of a small room.

INT. BOX ROOM. DAY

They enter. It is small, ill-lit.

> TONY

Box room.

> BARRETT

Always do for a maid, sir.

> TONY

Oh we'll have a cleaning woman. D'you think we'll need a maid?

> BARRETT

They can be useful, sir.

INT. HALL. DAY.

Decorators all over the house, plasterers, painters, etc. The workmen set up plank on two ladders. Barrett coming downstairs passes them on his way to the kitchen.

> BARRETT

Mind the paintwork.

He looks in through the dining-room door.

INT. DINING-ROOM. DAY.

Sheets on the floor. Painters on ladders.

> **BARRETT**
> Is everything going all right?

> **WORKMAN**
> Yes, thank you.

> **BARRETT**
> Yes, well I'll be glad if you'll tell me of any problem so
> we can correct it before it becomes a fault.

The two painters look at him, then at each other. Barrett exits.

INT. CONSERVATORY. DAY.

*Tony, smoking, is sketching a design for the garden. Barrett enters
from drawing-room and puts tray down.*

> **BARRETT**
> Lunch, sir.

> **TONY**
> Ah that's nice.

> **BARRETT**
> No trouble, sir.

> **TONY**
> How are they getting on?

> **BARRETT**
> I'm keeping an eye on them.

> **TONY**
> Are you? You might bring me a lager.

> **BARRETT**
> I was just about to, sir.

13

TONY
(*sitting to salad*)

I'm ready for it.

BARRETT

Sir . . .

Barrett goes, leaving Tony eating.

EXT. TONY'S HOUSE. NIGHT.

High shot of sports car slowing to halt, Tony and Susan get out, go up steps.

INT. HALL. NIGHT.

House well lit and carpeted. Furniture rather too large for the rooms. It has come from Tony's family house. Barrett opens the door, inclines his head.

TONY

This is Barrett, Susan, Barrett . . . my fiancée . . . Miss Stewart.

SUSAN

Hallo.

BARRETT

Good evening, Miss Stewart. Shall I take your coat?

SUSAN

No, I'll keep it on, thanks.

TONY

In here.

INT. DRAWING-ROOM. NIGHT.

They come in. She looks about.

14

TONY

Do you like it?

SUSAN

Mm. It's beautiful.

BARRETT

The simple and classic is always the best, Miss.

She looks at a heavy ornament.

SUSAN

Is this classic? This isn't classic, it's prehistoric.

TONY

We've always had it and I like it. Barrett, let's have a drink.

BARRETT

Yes, sir.

SUSAN

Vodka on the rocks.

BARRETT

The usual, sir?

TONY

Thank you. Which one d'you want?

He gestures to armchairs.

SUSAN

This one.

TONY

My mother's favourite.

Barrett serves the drinks and exits.

He's been a wonderful help, that chap. Wait till you taste the food. Honestly, I've never been more comfortable.

SUSAN

Never?

TONY

I don't have to think of a thing.

SUSAN

Does he give you breakfast in bed?

TONY

Of course.

She smiles faintly, stands, walks about.

SUSAN

Have you checked his criminal record?

Barrett appears at the door.

TONY

Yes, Barrett?

BARRETT

You will ring, sir, when you'd like dinner served.

TONY

Yes, I will.

Barrett goes.

SUSAN

Why didn't you get a housekeeper?

TONY

Oh, women are no damn good. They can't cook.

He seizes her, kisses her, pulls her on to sofa.

INT. DINING-ROOM. NIGHT.

Tony and Susan sitting at dinner. Barrett with wine. He wears white cotton gloves.

16

SUSAN

The whole place needs brightening . . . more variety
you know . . . colour.

TONY

Oh. Do you think so?

SUSAN

Yes, and tomorrow I'm going to organize a proper spice
shelf for the kitchen.

BARRETT

Would you like to taste the wine, sir?

TONY

Thank you.

SUSAN

What ducky gloves.

TONY

Barrett's idea. I like it.

BARRETT

It's Italian, miss. They're used in Italy.

SUSAN

Who by?

Tony tastes wine.

TONY

Excellent.

BARRETT

Just a Beaujolais sir, but a good bottler.

SUSAN

A good what?

TONY

Bottler.

Barrett slightly inclines his head and goes.

INT. KITCHEN. NIGHT.

Barrett sitting alone on chair in kitchen, smoking, picking his teeth.

EXT. HOUSE. DAY.

Tony running in pouring rain up steps of house.

INT. HALL. DAY.

Tony's wet feet. He takes off his raincoat.

INT. KITCHEN. DAY.

Barrett pouring salt into bowl of warm water.

INT. DRAWING-ROOM. DAY.

Tony sitting in library alcove. Barrett undoes his shoes, takes socks off. Tony puts feet in bowl.

> TONY
> Oh, is this necessary?

> BARRETT
> Better to be safe than sorry, sir.

> TONY
> You're too skinny to be a nanny, Barrett.

Barrett looks at him.

> Oh, come on, don't sulk, I didn't mean it.

He squiggles his feet.

> Oh . . . oh . . . splendid!

INT. DRAWING-ROOM. NIGHT.

Close shot of Susan's feet. Pull back to show Tony lying on carpet, smoking long, thin cigar. Susan sitting in chair. Record player on. The record plays throughout the scene.

GIRL SINGING ON RECORD
Now while I love you alone
Now while I love you alone
Now while I love you
Can't love without you
Must love without you . . . alone.

SUSAN
Any news from your new frontier?

TONY
No, no, there isn't actually. Well, as a matter of fact he had to go over there and do various things, you know, make various arrangements. Heads of Government and all that.

SUSAN
Heard from him?

TONY
Yes, I mean of course the whole idea's in a very preliminary stage.

He puffs. Silence.

Still I'm quite happy at the moment, . . . aren't you?

SUSAN
Mm.

TONY
I can manage for a good few months. Oh, Barrett has installed my new abstract in the garden. Looks very chic doesn't it?

Susan stands, looking through the conservatory into garden.
Turns back, goes to him, kisses him. He pulls her to the floor with
him, kisses her. The record continues.

GIRL SINGING

. . . Leave it alone
It's all gone
Leave it alone
It's all gone
Don't stay to see me
Turn from your arms
Leave it alone
It's all gone
Give me my death
Close my mouth
Give me my breath
Close my mouth
How can I bear
The ghost of you here
Can't love without you
Must love without you . . .

. . . Now while I love you alone
Now while I love you
Can't love without you
Must love without you
Now while I love you alone
Now while I love you alone
Now while I love you
Can't love without you
Must love without you . . . alone.

TONY

That mouth!
            (*She kisses him.*)
Why don't you come and stay?

SUSAN

For a weekend? . . . A long weekend? . . . Or a couple of weeks . . .?

TONY

Marry me.

They embrace. She rolls on top of him. A concealed door opens in the library alcove. Barrett comes in.

They look up.

Music ends.

BARRETT
(*withdrawing*)

I'm so sorry to disturb you, sir.

He closes the door. Susan lies still. Tony stands.

TONY

I'm sorry.

SUSAN

Why didn't he knock?

TONY

He made a mistake.

Pause.

SUSAN

Mistake! Well for God's sake, restrict him to quarters.

Pause.

Couldn't he live out?

TONY

Out? No he couldn't.

SUSAN

Well he doesn't have to be here after he's washed up the dinner things, does he?

He looks at her blankly.

TONY

He's got to lock up!

Pause.

SUSAN

Well I think I should go anyway.

TONY

Why?

SUSAN

I'm just going.

TONY

This is ridiculous.

She goes to the door, hesitates.

SUSAN

Come home and stay with me.

TONY

Oh look, . . . stay here.

She goes out.

INT. HALL. NIGHT.

Susan collects her coat, Tony helps her on with it. Barrett appears, opens front door for her. She looks at him.

SUSAN

A little late for you, Barrett, isn't it? About time you were tucked up in bed.

Tony gestures to Barrett, who goes.

TONY

I'll drive you back.

SUSAN

No.

TONY

I'll walk along with you.

SUSAN
(*gently*)

No.

She takes his face with her hands, kisses him, goes. Tony stands, then goes into drawing-room.

INT. DRAWING-ROOM. NIGHT.

Barrett enters.

BARRETT

I do apologize for the intrusion, sir. I had no idea . . .

TONY

Don't do it again!

BARRETT

I did knock, sir.

TONY

Oh get to bed . . .

Tony puts his hand to his head.

Have you got an aspirin?

BARRETT

Yes, sir. I expect you caught a bit of a chill the other day in the rain, sir.

INT. TONY'S BEDROOM. DAY.

Tony in bed. Susan drawing curtains, opens windows.

SUSAN

You need more air.

TONY

Oh I don't know.

SUSAN

No, you don't.

She turns, goes to door, goes out.

INT. LANDING. DAY.

Barrett is there as Susan comes out and takes vase of flowers from table, then returns to bedroom.

INT. BEDROOM. DAY.

Susan comes back with a vase of flowers, places them.

TONY

Oh God! I'm so sorry. I completely forgot. They're beautiful. Thanks very much.

SUSAN

Every time you open a door in this house that man's outside. He's a Peeping Tom.

TONY

He's a vampire too on his Sundays off.

SUSAN

Why didn't you have them in your room?

TONY

Well as a matter of fact he was saying that they're bad in a sick room at night . . .

A knock on the door.

. . . come in.

Barrett comes in.

BARRETT
Your medicine, sir. And the post.

TONY
Oh thank you.

Barrett gives Tony the capsules and a glass of water. Tony takes them.

Barrett leaves the mail on the bedside table. An uneasy silence.

SUSAN
What did the Doctor say yesterday?

TONY
Oh nothing much. Virus.

Barrett picks up the vase to move it to another position in the room.

SUSAN
Put that down!

Pause.

TONY
Oh put it down, Barrett.

BARRETT
(*doing so*)
I beg your pardon, sir.

Barrett goes.

TONY
I do wish you'd stop yapping at Barrett all the time. It'll be a bastard if he leaves.

SUSAN
What the hell would that matter?

TONY

What would it matter? Well, you try and find another like him.

SUSAN

I'm sorry I was rude to your servant.

TONY

Look, he may be a servant but he's still a human being!

She turns, leaves the room.

INT. HALL. DAY.

Barrett, beating Susan to the front door, opens it for her.

BARRETT

I'm afraid it's not very encouraging miss . . . the weather forecast.

She looks at him for a moment steadily, and then goes down the steps. Barrett closes the door behind her.

EXT. TONY'S HOUSE. KNIGHTSBRIDGE SQUARE. DAY.

Susan stops at the base of the steps. Suddenly looking lost. A wind is blowing through the square.

EXT. KNIGHTSBRIDGE SQUARE. EARLY EVENING.

The wind has now grown in force. The streets are wet.

INT. PUBLIC PHONE BOX. KNIGHTSBRIDGE SQUARE. EARLY EVENING.

Barrett stands in the phone box.

BARRETT

Yes. Bolton 62545.

He waits. A group of girls collect outside the box, talking, giggling. The skirt of one of the girls blows up. Barrett observes this blankly. Another girl remarks on his gaze. The girls laugh. The operator tells him to go ahead.

> VERA'S VOICE

Hallo.

> BARRETT

Vera?

> VERA'S VOICE

Yes.

> BARRETT

Are you ready?

> VERA'S VOICE

Yes, I'm ready . . .

> BARRETT

All right then, tomorrow.

> VERA'S VOICE

All right. I've bought something new.

> BARRETT

Mm?

Barrett's attention goes again to the group of girls. The same girl is trying to keep her skirt down in the wind.

> VERA'S VOICE

. . . I'm wearing it now.

> BARRETT

Oh.

> VERA'S VOICE

I'll show it to you if you're being a good boy.

> BARRETT

I am. Are you being a good girl?

THE SERVANT

VERA'S VOICE

What?

He grits his teeth.

BARRETT

I said are you being a good girl?

VERA'S VOICE

I am.

BARRETT

I'll be at the station.
You got my last letter, didn't you?

VERA'S VOICE

Oh yes, I got that all right.

BARRETT

All right then. At the station. Tara.

VERA'S VOICE

Bye.

Barrett goes out of box. The girl squeezes past him. Barrett jabs her away.

BARRETT

Get out of it, you filthy bitch.

INT. DINING-ROOM. TONY'S HOUSE. NIGHT.

Barrett has made certain changes in this room too, as throughout the house.

Tony is at the table. Barrett standing by.

TONY

You've mulled some delicious claret, Barrett.
(*He laughs.*)
I say, that's rather good, isn't it? Claretty Barrett.

28

BARRETT

In the army they used to call me Basher Barrett, sir.

TONY

Oh really? Why?

BARRETT

I was a very good driller.

TONY

Ah!

(*Pause.*)

I like the changes you've been making in the house.
You've been enjoying yourself, haven't you? . . .

Barrett clears a little.

BARRETT

I have, sir . . . thank you very much, sir. Oh by the way,
sir, I took the liberty of removing those er chintz frills of
Miss Stewart's off the dressing table. Not very practical.

(*Tony grunts.*)

Haven't seen very much of Miss Stewart recently have
we sir?

TONY

Mmmmn? No.

BARRETT

My sister's arriving tomorrow sir, as you agreed.

TONY

Oh yes. Fine.

BARRETT

She's very happy about the arrangement, if you are.

TONY

Well, we might keep her, if she's any good.

EUSTON STATION. DAY.

Barrett standing on platform. A train draws in.

COCKTAIL BAR IN SOHO FRENCH RESTAURANT. DAY.

Tony is standing at bar. A man and girl talking.

> GIRL
>
> He's a wonderful wit.

> MAN
>
> Terribly funny.

> GIRL
>
> Terribly.

> MAN
>
> Cheers.

> GIRL
>
> Cheers. I'm dying to see him again. I haven't seen him for ages.

> MAN
>
> You won't for some time.

> GIRL
>
> Oh. Why?

> MAN
>
> He's in prison.

Susan enters the restaurant.

> TONY
>
> Hello.

> SUSAN
>
> Hello.

> HEAD WAITER
>
> Good morning, Miss Stewart.

SUSAN

Good morning.

HEAD WAITER

Good morning, sir.

TONY

Good morning.

HEAD WAITER

Very nice to see you here again.

SUSAN

Thank you.

They sit. Head Waiter hands them menus.

HEAD WAITER

I can recommend the Roast Duck.

TONY

What are you having?

SUSAN

Are you better?

TONY

Yes thanks.

They look at each other.

SUSAN

I've brought you a present.

She hands him a package.

TONY

What for?

SUSAN

Because I wanted to.

31

THE SERVANT

EUSTON PLATFORM. DAY.

Vera running down platform towards Barrett.

INT. SOHO RESTAURANT. DAY.

Tony and Susan eating. The restaurant is packed. Hors d'oeuvres. A Bishop and a Curate enter the restaurant.

                    HEAD WAITER
Good morning, Bishop.

                    BISHOP
Good morning.

EUSTON STATION. PLATFORM. DAY.

From high, see Vera and Barrett walk down platform, not speaking. He carries her bag.

INT. SOHO RESTAURANT. DAY.

Tony and Susan eating main course, with wine. Silence. Camera passes them to middle-aged woman and young woman sitting at table.

                    OLDER WOMAN
What did she say to you?

                    YOUNGER WOMAN
Nothing.

                    OLDER WOMAN
Oh yes she did. She said something to you.

                    YOUNGER WOMAN
She didn't. She didn't really.

                    OLDER WOMAN
She did. I saw her mouth move. She whispered something to you, didn't she? What was it? What did she whisper to you?

YOUNGER WOMAN

She didn't whisper anything to me. She didn't whisper anything!

SUSAN

Why don't we go away . . . for a few days . . . mm?

TONY

Where?

SUSAN

Anywhere.

TONY

Agatha and Willy Mountset have invited us down actually.

SUSAN

Well why don't we go there?

TONY

Yes, we could I suppose.

EXT. LONDON STREET. INT. TAXI. DAY.

Inside the taxi Vera and Barrett are sitting, not touching. Vera is looking out of the window.

INT. SOHO RESTAURANT. DAY.

Tony and Susan with coffee. A constrained silence between them. Bishop and Curate drinking.

CURATE

I hear Father O'Flaherty won't be at the Cork Convocation.

BISHOP

Flaherty? For the love of God don't be a child. Sure the man wouldn't miss a trip like that, you can bet your pound on that.

Didn't they have to carry him out last time?

Ah for God's sake who didn't they have to carry out?

Cut to Tony and Susan, girl and man in background.

I just don't like him.

You don't know him.
(*Pause.*)
I mean surely you can take my word for the fact.

Don't trust him.

Why?

I don't know.

It's the snow. It's the snow I like.

He looks like a fish with red lips I admit. But apart from that, what's the matter with him? You're making him so bloody important. I mean it seems to me you've got the whole thing absurdly out of proportion.

Yes, perhaps.

They pick up glasses.

Bishop and Curate get up.

34

BISHOP
And where are you creeping off to now, my son . . . ah?

CURATE
Nowhere Your Grace, nowhere . . . Nowhere at all.

BISHOP
Is that a fact?

SUSAN
Why don't you just tell him to go?

TONY
You must be mad.
(*Pause.*)
You just don't care about my . . . and what it amounts to is it's my judgement you're criticizing. It's not only ridiculous it's bloody hurtful.

GIRL
(*at other table*)
They were gorgeous – absolutely gorgeous.

MAN
Were they really?

TONY
I'm sorry. I'm a fool.

SUSAN
You are.

TONY
Well . . . I mean . . .

GIRL
Divine, but I simply couldn't get them on.

MAN
Pity!

Pause. Susan touches Tony's hand.

35

SUSAN

Look . . . I'm sorry.

TONY

Well . . . well I wouldn't . . .

He touches her hand, frowning, unsure.

INT. TONY'S HOUSE. FIRST LANDING. DAY.

Barrett showing Vera up the stairs. On the first landing she looks into Tony's bedroom and at Barrett. He guides her away and up further flight to her room.

INT. TONY'S HOUSE. TOP LANDING AND SMALL ROOM. DAY.

Barrett showing Vera to her bedroom. She looks round the room and then at him. He regards her, expressionless.

INT. HALL. DAY.

Tony is by front door.

TONY

Barrett!

He goes into drawing-room.

INT. DRAWING-ROOM. DAY.

Tony enters.

TONY

Barrett!

He unwraps package and takes out a short black silk dressing gown. He hears Barrett and throws it on the sofa.

BARRETT

Did you call, sir?

TONY

Yes. Damn awful lunch. Where were you? Get me a
brandy.

BARRETT

Yes sir.

Barrett pours brandy and notices gown.

It's very handsome, sir.

Tony drinks.

Oh . . . might I introduce my sister to you, sir? She's
arrived . . . she's very excited at the prospect of being
with us.

TONY

Oh is she?

Barrett turns to door.

BARRETT

Vera.

INT. KITCHEN. DAY.

*Boiling water into teapot from kettle. Camera pulls back to show
Barrett checking the tea tray. He passes it into Vera's hands. She
exits.*

INT. DRAWING-ROOM. DAY.

*Tony lying in an armchair. His feet rest on a foot stool. A side
table by his chair. Vera comes in, places tea tray on side table
with great care, bending over Tony to do so.*

INT. DRAWING-ROOM. TWILIGHT.

*Tony still lying, dozing, a book on the floor, the tea tray empty.
Vera and Barrett enter with flowers. They arrange the flowers on*

37

a table by the window. Tony watches through half-open eyes. He sees Vera's face and throat through the flowers, her body, in her short black maid's uniform, moving under the table, her legs.

INT. LORD AND LADY MOUNTSET'S COUNTRY HOUSE. LATE AFTERNOON.

Lord and Lady Mountset, Tony and Susan.

> LADY MOUNTSET
> Well I'm absolutely certain you'll be fascinated by Brazil.

> LORD MOUNTSET
> Oh yes.

> LADY MOUNTSET
> I was in the Argentine of course, briefly, as a girl. . . . I was certainly fascinated by the Argentine.

> TONY
> It should be very interesting.

> LADY MOUNTSET
> Fascinating, Tony darling.

> LORD MOUNTSET
> How many cities are you going to build?

> SUSAN
> Three.

> TONY
> Yes, it's – quite a big development.

> LORD MOUNTSET
> In the jungle?

> TONY
> Not exactly in the jungle, no sir. On the plain.

SUSAN

Oh but some of the jungle will have to be cleared, won't it?

TONY

Some of the jungle, yes. A little bit.

LADY MOUNTSET

That's where the Ponchos are, of course, on the plains.

SUSAN

Ponchos?

LORD MOUNTSET

South American cowboys.

SUSAN

Are they called Ponchos?

LORD MOUNTSET

They were in my day.

SUSAN

Aren't they those things they wear? You know, with the slit in the middle for the head to go through?

LORD MOUNTSET

What do you mean?

SUSAN

Well, you know . . . hanging down in front and behind . . . the cowboy.

LADY MOUNTSET

They're called cloaks, dear.

INT. FIRST LANDING. MORNING.

Very close shot of Tony's bedroom door. Vera's hand comes into shot and knocks on it.

TONY'S VOICE

Come in.

INT. TONY'S BEDROOM. MORNING.

Tony sits in bed, no pyjamas. Vera comes in with breakfast, sets it down.

VERA

Good morning, sir.

TONY

Morning . . . Where's Barrett?

VERA

He's gone out shopping sir.

She opens the curtains and arranges them.

Anything else, sir?

TONY

No thank you.

She picks up about the room. Tony watches. She goes.

INT. KITCHEN. DAY.

Barrett comes in through the kitchen door from the garden. Vera enters from hall. They look at each other. She goes to the sideboard and pours tea, crosses to the table and sits on it. Her skirt is above her knees. As Barrett approaches she begins to grin. Her grin fades to an expression of intense anticipation. As he draws closer to her her head is suddenly flung back in a soundless sexual laugh, mouth open.

INT. TONY'S BEDROOM. DAY.

Close shot of silent valet. Barrett's hand taking jacket off it, helping Tony into it.

Pause.

TONY

For God's sake look at this. That's not much good, Barrett!

BARRETT

I beg your pardon, sir.

Barrett brushes the jacket gently.

TONY

Pull your socks up now. Come on, come on, come on, give it a good brush, you won't hurt me.

BARRETT

Perhaps you'd like to take the jacket off, sir?

TONY

No, damn it. Do it on. I haven't got time to mess about.

Barrett brushes vigorously.

BARRETT

Would you turn round sir.

TONY

No. All right, all right.
(*Sulkily.*)
All right, it'll have to do.

He goes to the mirror.

BARRETT

We heard this morning that our mother's ill up in Manchester, sir. Apparently she's been asking for us. It might be dangerous. Would you mind if we took the night off and came back tomorrow late?

TONY

Both of you?

41

BARRETT

Well it is touch and go, sir.

TONY

Well that's bloody inconvenient.

BARRETT

I appreciate that, sir, I do appreciate that. But we could leave you a cold buffet and salad.

TONY

I wanted something hot! Couldn't you make it tomorrow?

BARRETT

I suppose we could, sir.

TONY

Make it tomorrow. It'll give us time to get organized.

BARRETT

Right, sir.

TONY

Well I'm off.

BARRETT

Oh there's one other thing I'd like a brief word with you, sir, about, before you go.

TONY

Well what is it? – Where's my Cologne?

BARRETT

It's about Vera.

TONY

What about her?

BARRETT

Well it's her skirts, sir. They rather worry me.

TONY

Her skirts? What's the matter with them?

BARRETT

Well, might I suggest that they're a little short, sir?

Silence.

TONY

A little short?

BARRETT

I should say so.

Pause.

TONY

Well what the hell do you want me to do about it? She's your sister, tell her yourself. Where's my Cologne? . . .

He crosses through dressing-room, to bathroom door.

VERA'S VOICE

Don't come in. I'm naked! Who is it?

Tony stops still. The door remains ajar.

VERA'S VOICE

Oh, I am sorry, I forgot to lock the door.

TONY

I want my Cologne.

VERA

Your what?

TONY

The bottle . . .

VERA

It's all right, I've got a towel on now.

Tony grasps the door handle and holds the door firmly towards him.

43

TONY

I just want my Cologne.

He waits, his face set.

VERA

What, the one with your initials on?

TONY

Yes.

The door is pulled. Tony resists the pull, holds the door tight, slightly ajar. Her arm comes through with the Cologne.

VERA

I'm sorry sir, I thought everyone was out.

For a moment he watches her hand move, searching for him. He then takes the bottle, goes back into his room and dabs Cologne on his handkerchief.

TONY

D'you know Vera's in my bathroom?

BARRETT

I beg your pardon, sir?

TONY

She's having a bath in my bathroom. Well, I mean to say . . . I mean . . . after all . . . you've got one of your own upstairs.

He gives Barrett the Cologne.

Have a word with her.

Tony exits. Barrett crosses to bathroom and enters.

INT. BATHROOM. DAY.

Barrett and Vera. Vera in towel. He holds the bottle of Cologne.

44

BARRETT

Who told you to take a bath in his bathroom? Who said you could use his bathroom? A gentleman doesn't want a naked girl bouncing about all over his bathroom.

VERA

You told me to, didn't you?

BARRETT

Me? Why would I tell you a thing like that?

He closes the door.

I'll tell you what I'm going to do now.

VERA

What?

BARRETT

I'm going to have a bath in his bathroom.

Vera turns the tap.

VERA

You're terrible.

He gives her the Cologne.

BARRETT

And I want that . . . all over me.

He takes off his jacket. She watches him. The water boils into the bath.

INT. BEDROOM. DAY.

The square is seen through the window. Barrett and Vera walking, with bags. Tony comes into foreground, watches, turns, heavy. Telephone rings.

TONY

Hallo.

45

SUSAN'S VOICE

It's me.

TONY

Oh hello.

SUSAN'S VOICE

I've been worried about you.

TONY

Er – can I ring you back?

SUSAN'S VOICE

Well yes – but when?

TONY

Are you at the office?

SUSAN'S VOICE

Yes, but I'm just going out. Are you in tonight?

TONY

Er . . . Yes. Ring me then, would you?

SUSAN'S VOICE

All right, good-bye.

TONY

Bye . . . bye.

INT. CHELSEA COFFEE BAR. NIGHT.

It is crowded. Guitarist. Tony at table signalling to waitress. She eventually comes to his table and clears some dirty crockery. As she bends over table she momentarily resembles Vera. Tony vaguely holds menu.

WAITRESS

Back in a moment, sir.

She goes. He is left. She comes back towards him but is waylaid

46

by another table. He starts tapping knife, suddenly rises, goes to the door. The cashier looks at him.

CASHIER

Yes, sir. Can I help you?

TONY

No I haven't had anything.

He goes out.

EXT. BROMPTON ROAD. NIGHT.

Snow. Late at night. Distant storm approaching. Tony walking along the road, alone.

EXT. TONY'S HOUSE. KNIGHTSBRIDGE SQUARE. NIGHT.

Snow. Tony walking to house. He goes slowly up the steps.

INT. HALL. TONY'S HOUSE. NIGHT.

Tony switches on light, throws coat onto hall stand, stands irresolute. He looks at mail, throws it down unopened, goes to the kitchen.

INT. KITCHEN. TONY'S HOUSE. NIGHT.

Tony comes in, turns on the light, pours a glass of water, puts ice in it, sips it. He puts glass down on the sink, sits down, picks up paper, stares at it. He looks for glass, puts down paper, stands, collects glass, drinks, standing. Suddenly he turns round sharply. Vera is at the door.

VERA

Oh! . . . I wondered who it was.

TONY

What are you . . . what are you doing here?

VERA

I was just going to bed and – I thought I heard a noise.

TONY

But you went to Manchester.

VERA

I didn't feel too well at the station, so he sent me back in a taxi.

Silence. The tap is dripping.

TONY

Sent you back?

VERA

Yes . . .

Tap dripping.

TONY

How do you feel now?

VERA

I feel a bit better.

He stares at her. She smiles.

TONY

Shall I get you a glass of water?

VERA

I'm glad it was you. I thought it might have been him coming back.

TONY

Has he gone?

VERA

Oh yes – yes he went. I'm glad I'm not alone. I didn't fancy being alone by myself in this house.

Tap dripping. Tony turns the tap off, turns. Silence.

VERA

Can I get you anything, sir?

TONY

No . . . no . . .

Phone rings. They look at it. Tony does not move. It stops.

Vera perches on the table.

VERA

. . . Oh . . . isn't it hot in here . . . Isn't it? . . .

The saucepan and crockery glisten on the shelves.

So hot.

The kitchen glistens, the gas stove, the pans. Vera's body inclines backward on the table, her skirt halfway up her thighs.

TONY

Your skirt's too short.

VERA
(*looking down at her legs*)
My what? That's how all the girls are wearing them. Well that's how they all wear them . . . Why? do you think it's too short?

He comes close to the table. She gestures to his face.

You hot?

A sudden savage embrace.

Oh that's nice that's nice oh that's nice.

Two figures seen distorted in shining saucepans.

INT. HALL. EVENING.

Barrett enters, examines mail, walks to kitchen.

49

INT. KITCHEN.

Barrett studies two plates on table, chicken bones on them. Tony appears in the kitchen door.

                    TONY
    Oh, hello Barrett, how's your Mother?

                    BARRETT
    On the mend, sir.

                    TONY
    Oh, good. Good. Little Vera wasn't very well then?

Barrett takes plates to the sink.

                    BARRETT
    Well no. She looked so poorly at the railway station, sir.
    I thought it wasn't wise to let her travel. I hope she
    hasn't been any inconvenience to you.

                    TONY
    Oh not at all. No, she hasn't at all.

                    BARRETT
    Did she manage to do anything for you, sir?

Tony looks at him sharply.

                    TONY
    I beg your pardon.

                    BARRETT
    I hope she was well enough to see to your meals.

                    TONY
    Oh yes, yes, we . . . I had lunch.

                    BARRETT
    I notice she didn't do the washing up.

                    TONY
    Still under the weather, I suppose.

BARRETT

Under the what, sir?

TONY

The weather.

BARRETT

Oh yes.

TONY

Oh Barrett, you wouldn't like to go to the off-licence for me would you, for a quart of beer? I've got rather a thirst.

BARRETT

There's plenty of beer, sir.

TONY

Yes I know that, but I want some plain brown ale.

BARRETT

Certainly, sir.

Barrett exits.

INT. HALL. EVENING.

Barrett goes out front door. Tony appears immediately and calls.

TONY

Vera!

VERA

Yes sir?

TONY

Come down a minute.

VERA

I'm coming. Where are you?

TONY

Down here. He's back.

He steps into library door. She comes down the stairs. As she passes him, he grasps her from behind. She screams, wheels round, giggling.

VERA

Oh you . . . what are you doing?

He pulls her into the library.

INT. LIBRARY ALCOVE.

He seats Vera in the leather chair.

VERA

I've got to wash up.

TONY

I've sent him to the pub, he'll be back in a minute.

VERA

Who cares about him?

TONY

Well, he's your brother.

VERA

What are you doing?
                    (*Giggles.*)

EXT. KNIGHTSBRIDGE SQUARE. EVENING.

Barrett approaching Tony's house steadily.

EXT. LIBRARY. EVENING.

Vera and Tony in embrace.

EXT. TONY'S HOUSE.

Barrett up the front steps, opens the door.

INT. LIBRARY. EVENING.

Tony and Vera half lying on the table. Tony hears the door.

> **TONY**
> Come down at twelve o'clock.

He goes quickly through the library door into the garden.

INT. HALL. EVENING.

Vera meets Barrett at foot of stairs. She looks at him.

> **VERA**
> I'm going to bed, I'm tired.

He watches her go upstairs and goes into drawing-room.

INT. KITCHEN. NIGHT.

Barrett pouring a glass of brown ale. Tony comes in through kitchen door from garden.

> **TONY**
> Oh hullo Barrett. Just getting a bit of air in the garden.

> **BARRETT**
> Rather cold sir.

> **TONY**
> Got the beer? Oh good.

> **BARRETT**
> Anything else you want, sir?

> **TONY**
> No thanks, I'll be going out soon but I'll be back before
> . . . midnight. There'll be no need for you to wait up for
> me. I'll lock up myself.

BARRETT

Right, sir.

Tony picks up glass of ale, sips, grimaces.

INT. DRAWING-ROOM. NIGHT.

Later. Near midnight. Tony drinking whisky. He jumps up, looks at watch, goes out.

INT. HALL. NIGHT.

Tony comes out of the drawing-room and goes up the stairs.

INT. FIRST LANDING. NIGHT.

Tony comes up from the hall and continues up the stairs to the top landing.

INT. TOP LANDING. NIGHT.

It is dark. Tony comes up stairs, looks warily at Barrett's door, then taps very lightly on Vera's door. After a few seconds her voice is heard through the keyhole.

VERA

All right, I'm coming. Go down.

Tony goes downstairs.

There is a pause and the light goes on in Vera's room. She opens the door carefully and looks out.

INT. VERA'S ROOM. NIGHT.

A low angled shot from the stairs. As Vera opens the door further to come out, Barrett can be seen in her bed reaching for a newspaper which he picks up and reads. She exits.

INT. DRAWING-ROOM. NIGHT.

Tony pulls Vera to him in the half darkness.

> TONY
>
> Are you cold?

> VERA
>
> No.

> TONY
>
> What about him? Is he asleep?

> VERA
>
> His room's dark.

He stares at her. He lowers her into the leather chair, swings the chair so that she faces him. Her legs stretch out across the arms of the chair.

INT. FIRST LANDING. DAY.

Vera knocks on Tony's door.

> TONY
>
> Come in.

> VERA
>
> Can I have your tray, sir?

She goes in. Camera stays on closed door.

INT. HALL. DAY.

Barrett comes from kitchen to alcove under the stairs and hides there.

INT. FIRST LANDING. DAY.

Vera slips out of Tony's door, flushed, and goes downstairs carrying the tray.

INT. HALL. DAY.

Vera comes downstairs, puts tray down on hall table and looks at herself in mirror. Suddenly Barrett's hands reach for her. He pulls her back out of sight. A sharp gasp from her, a grating 'Aaaaahhh' from him. A phone can be heard ringing off screen. Stay on empty hall.

INT. TONY'S BEDROOM. DAY.

Tony still in bed. He is on the telephone.

TONY

Hallo.

SUSAN'S VOICE

Hallo.

TONY

Oh hullo, Susan.

SUSAN'S VOICE

Did you get my note? I expect you've been rather busy?

TONY

Yes. I have been rather busy, actually, with one thing and another.

SUSAN'S VOICE

Well what time will you call then?

TONY

Oh about two-thirty. Should give us time enough to get down there. I'm having lunch with my father's solicitor.

SUSAN'S VOICE

All right. Well see you then.

TONY

Right. Bye.

56

SUSAN

Bye.

INT. HALL. DAY.

Tony runs up from below and opens the door of Vera's bedroom.

INT. VERA'S BEDROOM. DAY.

Vera is in bed. She is pale, trembling, exhausted. Tony goes in.

TONY

What's the matter?

Vera looks like a child, trembling continually.

TONY

What's the matter? What is it?

VERA

I'm not well.

He sits on the bed.

TONY

What is it?

No answer. He touches her hand.

He's gone out . . . I . . .

She looks at him with a tense distrustful smile. She speaks suddenly and harshly, with a bitter reined hysteria.

VERA

Come on then.

INT. HALL. DAY.

Barrett opens front door to Susan. She carries flowers.

BARRETT

I'm afraid the master's not at home.

SUSAN

I know. Collect my things from the taxi please.

Barrett goes out of the house to collect parcel from taxi. Susan moves into the drawing-room.

INT. DRAWING-ROOM.

Susan picks up a vase. Barrett comes in.

SUSAN

Fill this with water. Where's the parcel?

BARRETT

It's in the hall, Miss.

SUSAN

Bring it to me.

Barrett collects the parcel and brings it in. He goes out with vase. Re-enters with it. Susan arranges flowers in the vase.

SUSAN

How do you like them, Barrett?

BARRETT

I'm not certain that the flowers wouldn't be better in a different jar, Miss.

SUSAN

I thought you'd be uncertain, Barrett.
(She opens the parcel and throws a number of small cushions from it on to the sofa.)
What do you think of them?

BARRETT

I beg your pardon?

SUSAN

What do you think of the cushions?

BARRETT

It's difficult to say what I think of them, Miss.

SUSAN

Shall I tell you the truth, Barrett?

BARRETT

Yes, Miss.

SUSAN

The truth is, I don't care what you think.

Pause.

I want some lunch. A salad will do. Use the tarragon I bought on Wednesday.

BARRETT

Yes, Miss.

She takes a cigarette.

SUSAN

Light . . . Put that coat down and give me a light.

Barrett lights her cigarette. Moves to the door.

SUSAN

Barrett! Come here.

He goes to her.

Do you use a deodorant?

He stares at her.

Tell me. Do you think you go well with the colour scheme?

BARRETT

I think the Master's satisfied.

SUSAN

What do you want from this house?

59

BARRETT

Want?

SUSAN

Yes, want.

BARRETT

I'm the servant, Miss.

SUSAN

Get my lunch.

EXT. LORD MOUNTSET'S ESTATE. DAY.

Gracious turreted house. Lawns and arbours. Undulating fields sweep down to lake. Poplars. Two figures far down by the lake. Keep on them for some seconds in the distance. They are throwing snowballs.

EXT. THE LAKE. DAY.

Tony and Susan running. They stop and kiss.

SUSAN

Why don't you come up to my room? There's a wonderful view from there. Or what about your room? What's it like from yours?

TONY

It's not very good from mine.

Susan laughs.

TONY

The best view . . . is from our room . . . at the house. What about leaving tonight?

SUSAN

Wouldn't that be a little rude?

TONY

No . . . no . . . they won't mind.

INT. TONY'S CAR. EVENING.

Tony driving. Susan huddled close to him.

EXT. THE SQUARE. NIGHT.

The car coming into the square, drawing up to the house. It slows.

INT. CAR. NIGHT.

TONY

There's a light on in my room. Quarter to twelve. Who
the hell's in my room?

INT. HALL. TONY'S HOUSE. NIGHT.

*The dark hall. Tony opens the front door softly. He walks
carefully to the stairs, treads halfway up and halts. Susan remains
at the bottom.*

A light comes through his bedroom door, which is ajar. Voices:

BARRETT

Give us one over.

VERA

You've only just had one.

BARRETT

Well I want another one.

Pause.

VERA

All this bloody smoking, it drives you mad.

BARRETT

You're driving me mad.

Pause.

> VERA
>
> Come on . . . oh come on for Christ's sake, put it down.

> BARRETT
>
> I've only had one puff.

> VERA
>
> Oh come on put it down.

> BARRETT
>
> I'm worn out. What's the matter with you?

> VERA
>
> I know someone who wouldn't say no.

> BARRETT
>
> Him? He'd be on the floor.

Bedcreak. Rustle.

> Let me finish this fag. You're like a bloody machine.

> VERA
>
> I know I am but I can't help it.

Tony rests his head against the wall.

> SUSAN
>
> It's your servants.

There is a sudden silence in the house. Barrett's voice.

> BARRETT
>
> There's someone there.

> VERA
>
> No, there isn't.

> BARRETT
>
> Did you lock up?

VERA

Of course I did.

BARRETT

What about the bolt?

VERA

Oh no . . . well I didn't bolt.

BARRETT

You bloody little idiot!

A silence. Tony and Susan remain still. Barrett's naked shadow appears at the top of the stairs.

Tony turns and looks up. A long silent stare between them.

Suddenly, harshly, raucously, Vera's voice.

VERA

There's no one there. I told you. Oh come on, Hugo. You'll catch your death of cold out there. I'm waiting for you. Come and look at me, I'm all here waiting for you! Come on, what's the matter with you? I'm all rosy lying here. I'm rosyyyyy! What the bloody hell are you doing?

Barrett turns and goes back.

INT. DRAWING-ROOM. NIGHT.

Tony enters the dark room, covers his face. Susan follows, switching on lights.

SUSAN

What are you going to do?

He does not answer.

SUSAN

This is your house.

Silence.

SUSAN

They're in your room, in your bed.

Pause.

Did you know this was going on?

Pause.

Tony abruptly shivers, clenches his fist and goes to the door.

TONY

Barrett! Barrett! Come down here.

He comes back. A tense silence.

I think I should see him alone.

SUSAN

Why?

Barrett appears at the foot of the stairs and stops at the drawing-room door.

TONY

Come here.

He steps into the room.

I want an explanation.

BARRETT

Might I speak to you alone, sir?

TONY

Do you realize you've committed a criminal offence?

BARRETT

Criminal, sir?

TONY

She's your sister, you bastard!

Barrett looks at him.

BARRETT

She's not my sister, sir.
> (*Pause.*)

And if I might say so we're both rather in the same boat.

Silence. Barrett looks at Susan.

He knows precisely what I mean . . .

She stares at Tony.

BARRETT

. . . In any case, apart from the error of being in your room I'm perfectly within my rights. Vera's my fiancée.

TONY

What!?
> (*dully*)

Barrett goes to the door.

BARRETT

Vera.

They wait. She comes down to door.

BARRETT

Owing to this unfortunate incident, Vera, we shall have to tell our little secret to Mister Tony. Come on . . . don't be shy. Go and tell him, go on.

VERA

Hugo and I are going to be married.
Well, you've done all right, what are you worrying about? You can't have it on a plate for ever, can you? Oh come on Hugo!

Barrett inclines his head slightly and they both go.

TONY

Get out! Both of you!

Susan is sitting. Tony sits on the arm of a chair. Sounds of drawers being pulled out, cases banging, from upstairs. Tony rises and pours a drink, drinks it, pours another. They do not look at each other. He stands, goes to record player, puts on a record. 'All gone.'

GIRL SINGING

. . . my mouth
How can I bear

       (Door slams.)

The ghost of you here
Can't love without you . . .
. . . must love without you
Now while I love you alone
Now while I love you alone
Now while I love you
Can't love without you
Must love without you – alone
Now while I love you
Can't love without you
Can't love without you alone.

Silence between them. Sounds of Barrett and Vera descending stairs. The front door slams. Tony turns and looks at Susan. They look at each other. Eventually Tony in a half-appeal, half-demand, whispers:

TONY

Come to bed.

She slowly stands. He half moves to her. She turns, goes out of the door and out of the house.

He stands, alone. Switches off record. Looks at door, slowly moves out of room.

INT. STAIRS. NIGHT.

Tony slowly ascending stairs.

INT. VERA'S BEDROOM. NIGHT.

Tony enters room, looks at disordered bed. He goes to it, lies flat out on it.

INT. HALL. DAY.

Tony is alone in the house. He treads unsteadily down the stairs and goes into kitchen.

INT. KITCHEN. DAY.

The kitchen is very untidy. He rummages amid the unwashed plates for a can of fruit juice. It is empty. He throws it away. He fumbles in a corner for a bottle of squash. It has only dregs in it. He unscrews the top and puts it to his nose, grimaces, looks into the bottle. The orange flakes appear atrophied in the stagnant juice. He screws the top and lifts up the lid of the waste bin. The bin is full to bursting with rubbish, its top covered with fish-bones. He tries to lodge the bottle between two piles of crockery on the draining board, the bottle slips and falls with a bang. He kicks it viciously.

EXT. LONDON STREET. NIGHT.

Tony, quite aimless, walking spasmodically. He is drooped. He stops to watch the buses and taxis go by. His face in the passing lights is haggard, blank.

INT. PUBLIC PHONE BOX. NIGHT.

Tony dialling number. He listens.

SUSAN'S VOICE
Hello. Who's that? Tony? Hello who is it? Hello.

He replaces the receiver.

INT. DRAWING-ROOM. NIGHT.

Tony in room, which is also in some disarray. He is unshaven, drinking a large whisky. He goes to record player and with slightly trembling hands puts a record on the turn-table. He lifts the head and attempts to place it in the groove. Three times he fails, the needle sheering off the side of the record. Suddenly his trembling hand jerks the head which scrapes in a grating scratch across the record. He stands hunched.

INT. FIRST PUB. EVENING.

Tony wanders into the saloon bar of a pub which is half empty. He goes to the bar, orders whisky, sits next to a man. Beyond the man is a partition that separates the saloon bar from the private bar. Both bars are visible in full mirror behind the barman. Barrett is sitting up at the private bar just beyond the partition. Tony has not seen him. He drinks half his whisky in a gulp and is then conscious of being watched. He looks into the mirror, sees Barrett. He looks away. Then half back, then away again. For some minutes there is a quiet in the pub, the only sounds being the bell on the cash register and the spasmodic sound of conversation. At the bar, Barrett and Tony, with the third man between them, look into their glasses intently, glance up at the bottles on the shelves. Neither of them moves. The third man, an oldish man, stands gloomily. The third man suddenly speaks to no one in particular.

MAN
I had a bit of bad luck today.

There is no response. The Barman appears, polishing some glasses, looks vaguely for any further orders, withdraws.

I really had a bit of bad luck.

Silence.

It'll take me a good few days to get over it, I can tell you.

Pause. The man turns to Tony as if Tony had spoken.

Eh?

Tony is blank. The man finishes his drink and turns to go.

You're right, there.

He goes. Silence. Barrett and Tony look at each other. Tony non-committal. Barrett seems shabbier, uneasy, his breath is laboured.

BARRETT

Might I buy you a drink?

Tony does not answer. Barrett signals nervously to the Barman, points to Tony's glass.

BARRETT

Scotch. Large scotch.

The drink arrives and he pays for it. Tony sips it immediately, with no gesture. Barrett begins to speak, in a low voice, very quickly, stuttering, compulsive.

I wanted to come and call round on you . . . but . . . I tell you what though . . . I was led up the garden path. I couldn't be more sorry, honest. I was besotted by her long before I came to you. I was simply besotted by her. I thought she was keen on me too – we were saving up money to get married . . . her father was a brute. You see I . . . I couldn't bear to see her . . . suffering . . . . . . but I had to pay him like – you know, to pay him to get his consent to take her away. I had to find her a home somewhere that – that's why I told you she was my sister – I thought she was devoted to me . . . anyway – you see I . . . I didn't know a thing about what was going on between you two until that night. That night I got it out of her . . . I twigged she was just a scrubber . . . She

69

never intended to marry me, and d'you know what she's done now? Gone off with my money . . . she's living with a bookie in Wandsworth – listen, give me – give me another chance, sir . . . I was so happy there with you . . . it was like bliss . . . we can turn over the page . . . I'm with an old lady now in Paultons Square – ringing the bell all day long – up and down those stairs – all day long – I'm skin and bone . . . I deceived you – I played you false – I admit that – but she was to blame – it was her fault. She done us both . . . if you can find it in your heart sir . . . give me another chance.

He stops, looking down at his glass, biting his nails. Tony is still, expressionless.

EXT. SQUARE. WINTER.

Some weeks have passed. A wind blows through the square.

INT. HALL. TONY'S HOUSE. DAY.

The house is changed. It is airless, dark, oppressive. Curtains and blinds are almost constantly drawn. There are no longer any flowers. The log fire has been replaced by illuminated gas logs. The sleek television in the bedroom has been replaced by a heavy Console, now in the drawing-room. Cheap sex magazines replace the expensive monthlies. There is an overlay of Barrett everywhere. Photos of footballers sellotaped to mirrors. Pornographic calendars. Nudes stuck in oil paintings. The furniture has subtly changed, the rooms no longer possess composition. Elegant pornographic books have been yanked from Tony's bookshelves and are strewn about. The bookshelves are left disordered and heavy with dust. Barrett's brown paper obscene books are piled about, and cellophaned piles of photos. The ashtrays are crammed full, glasses half empty and empty beer bottles are on the liquor trolley. Barrett is now dressed in a rough sweater, corduroy trousers and heavy boots.

THE SERVANT

INT. DRAWING-ROOM. DAY.

Tony is sitting at a table, doing a crossword puzzle. He is in his pyjama jacket. Barrett enters, dressed in sweater and tight trousers.

> **BARRETT**
>
> You still sitting there?

> **TONY**
>
> What's this? 'It's waxed so will soon wane', five letters.

> **BARRETT**
>
> I haven't got time for all that.

> **TONY**
>
> Well you ask me soon enough when you want some help.

> **BARRETT**
>
> Look at all this muck and slime. It makes you feel sick.

> **TONY**
>
> Well do something about it. You're supposed to be the bloody servant!

> **BARRETT**
>
> You expect me to cope with all this muck and filth everywhere, all your leavings all over the place, without a maid, do you? I need a maid to give me a helping hand. I'm not used to working in such squalor. Look what I've got on my hands, you! As soon as I get the Hoover going you're straight up it. You're in everybody's way.

> **TONY**
>
> Oh why don't you leave me alone?

Tony gulps some beer. Barrett lights a cigarette, and pensively flips the pages of a leather-bound book.

. . . What's this? 'It's waxed so will wane soon?' Five letters.

BARRETT

Look, why don't you get yourself a job instead of moping around here all day? Here I am scraping and skimping trying to make ends meet . . . getting worse and worse . . . and you're no bloody help . . . d'you know that butter's gone up twopence a pound?

TONY

As a matter of fact I'll be meeting a man very shortly.

BARRETT

What man? The man from Brazil? What's he going to do for you? Come down by helicopter on the roof? Eh?

TONY

Oh why don't you shut up!

INT. HALL. DAY

Tony storms out of the drawing-room.

TONY

Barrett!

He goes up the stairs.

Barrett!

INT. BARRETT'S BEDROOM. DAY.

Barrett is in bed. Tony enters and pulls the clothes off him.

BARRETT

What's the matter with you?

TONY

Get out of it!

72

BARRETT

What you doing?

TONY

There's tea dregs on the carpet.

BARRETT

Where?

TONY

In the drawing-room.

BARRETT

Well I didn't put them there.

Tony holds a damp rag to Barrett's face.

TONY

Now here you are. Use it.

BARRETT

Don't do that to me.

TONY

Clear it up!

BARRETT

Not my fault – them tea dregs.

TONY

You filthy bastard!

BARRETT

Right. I'm leaving!

Barrett gets out of bed. Their voices clash and rise.

TONY

That's exactly what I want.

BARRETT

You talk to me like that . . .

TONY

Now leave my house alone . . .

BARRETT

. . . after all I've done for you.

TONY

. . . Get down and clear it up.

Barrett goes out.

INT. STAIRS AND LANDING. DAY.

Barrett comes briskly down the stairs, followed by Tony.

BARRETT

I won't stand for any more of this.

TONY

Take your pigsty somewhere else.

BARRETT

It's not my pigsty, it's yours.

TONY

You creep!

BARRETT

Nobody talks to me like that!

TONY

D'you know what you are? I'll tell you.

BARRETT

I know all about your sort.

TONY

You're a peasant.

BARRETT

I'll tell you what I am, I'll tell you what I am. I'm a gentleman's gentleman. And you're no bloody gentleman!

74

> **TONY**
> You think I'm past it? I haven't had a drink all morning.
> I'm through with it. I'll knock your head off.

> **BARRETT**
> Violence will get you nowhere.

> **TONY**
> If you don't get down and wipe those tea dregs up I'll
> stick your nose in them.

> **BARRETT**
> (*laughing*)
> You're funny.

INT. DINING-ROOM. DAY.

*Morning. Tony and Barrett in the dining-room. Barrett is
smoking, sitting, doing a crossword puzzle. Tony is looking out
into the garden. Long silence. Children's voices outside.*

> **TONY**
> I wouldn't mind going out for a walk.
> It must be quite nice out.

He remains still.

Barrett continues his crossword.

Silence.

INT. HALL. STAIRS AND LANDINGS. EVENING.

*Tony is at the top of the stairs, Barrett at the foot. They are
playing a game of ball, in which, according to their own rules, the
ball must be bounced off the wall or on the stairs past the
opponent. A point is scored for each pass. Twenty-one is game.*

*A longish rally is in progress. Both breathe hard, concentrating
intently. Finally, Barrett skids the ball past Tony.*

BARRETT

Watch it!

TONY

No, out of play – out of play!

BARRETT

Right – got you!

TONY

Bit wild!

(*Laughs.*)

BARRETT

Nearly got you then . . .
Hah! . . . thirteen ten . . . ?
. . . counting . . . ?

TONY

Well I can't do it any more. I have to bend all the time.

BARRETT

What about me? I'm in the inferior position. I'm playing uphill.

TONY

I need a drink.

BARRETT

That's the point of the game, the bending. You're getting as fat as a pig. You need the exercise.

TONY

Right. Service!
(*He smashes the ball past Barrett.*)
Fourteen twelve!

BARRETT

That wasn't fair, I wasn't ready.

TONY

I said service, didn't I?

BARRETT
(*picking up the ball*)
I'm not having that point counted.

TONY

What do you mean? That's a perfectly fair point. What about the other night? You did about six of them like that.

BARRETT

There's no need to take advantage of the fact that you're in the best position.

TONY

My dear . . .

BARRETT

. . . you ought to be able to play the game according to the rules.

TONY

My dear Barrett, you're just a little upset because you're losing the game.

BARRETT

Oh! . . . take your ball!

He throws the ball hard at Tony, who catches it.

TONY

Take it yourself!

Tony throws the ball back viciously. It hits Barrett on the nose.

BARRETT

Aaahhh!

He clutches his nose. Tony runs down.

77

TONY

Well, what's the matter?

BARRETT

I'm going.

TONY

It couldn't have hurt.

BARRETT

Get out of it. I'm off. I'm not staying in a place where they just chuck balls in your face!

TONY

Oh don't be silly! Come on, let's have a drop of brandy. I'll tell you what we'll do, we'll call that game a draw. Now here you are. Isn't that fair?

BARRETT

Stuff your brandy.

TONY

Don't talk to me like that!

BARRETT

Stuff you and your brandy! Get back to your coal-heap and leave me alone for Christ's sake.

TONY

Now look, Barrett, don't you forget your place. You're nothing but a servant in this house!

BARRETT

Servant! I'm nobody's servant. Who furnished the whole place for you? Who painted it for you? Who does the cooking? Who washes your pants? Who cleans out the bath after you? I do! I run the whole bloody place – and what do I get out of it? Nothing!

TONY

Now listen, Barrett –

BARRETT

I know all about you, sonny . . .

TONY

Now look . . . Listen, I am grateful, honestly . . . don't
be daft. You know I am. I don't know what I'd do
without you.

BARRETT

Well go and pour me a glass of brandy.

TONY

Well that's what I suggested in the first place.

BARRETT

Well don't just stand there! Go and do it!

*Tony runs into the drawing-room and pours Barrett a large
brandy. Barrett watches him from the hall.*

INT. DRAWING-ROOM. EVENING.

*The same evening. Tony and Barrett eating dinner. Black
candles. Black ceiling.*

TONY

Fabulous.

BARRETT

Not bad.

TONY

It's fabulous.

BARRETT

Bit salty.

TONY

No, no. It's marvellous.

Silence. They eat.

79

I don't know how you do it.

BARRETT

It's nice to know it's appreciated. It makes all the difference.

TONY

Well, I do appreciate it.

Pause.

BARRETT

You know sometimes I get the feeling that we're old pals.

TONY

That's funny.

BARRETT

Why?

TONY

I get the same feeling myself.

Pause.

BARRETT

I've only had that same feeling once before.

TONY

When was that?

BARRETT

Once in the army.

TONY

That's funny. I had the same feeling myself there, too. Once.

INT. HALL. STAIRS AND LANDING. NIGHT.

Barrett stands inside the drawing-room door. His hands are over his eyes. He is counting aloud.

BARRETT

Forty-seven, forty-eight, forty-nine, fifty.

He takes his hands from his eyes and goes into the hall. Here, he stands and talks aloud, to a listener.

I've got a tiny feeling that you're not downstairs at all. I think you're up there, aren't you? Now I'm on my way up to get you.

He races up the stairs. At the top he speaks:

Where's your little lair this time?
Puss, puss, puss, puss, pussy, puss, puss, puss, puss, puss, puss.

He opens his own bedroom door violently and looks in, comes out. He does the same in Vera's room, and then runs downstairs to Tony's room at a very great pace and pulls the door open.

INT. TONY'S BEDROOM. NIGHT.

Barrett enters, creeps about, looking.

BARRETT

I'm getting warm! You're hiding but you'll be caught. You've got a guilty secret, you've got a guilty secret, but you'll be caught. I'm coming to get you, I'm creeping up on you!

INT. BATHROOM. NIGHT.

Tony is jammed in the corner behind the door. (The bathroom is in complete disorder.) His eyes are staring with excitement. Barrett's voice comes nearer.

BARRETT

I'm getting warm, I can smell a rat, I can smell a rat . . .

Tony shivers. The door bursts open. Barrett charges in and confronts him. Barrett utters a terrifying maniacal bellow. Tony faints.

81

INT. HALL AND FRONT DOOR. NIGHT.

Barrett comes down the hall, opens the door. Vera.

BARRETT
What do you want?

VERA
I want to speak to him.

BARRETT
Clear off out of it.

VERA
I want to speak to him.

BARRETT
Out of it. Quick.

Tony appears in the hall. She darts in. Barrett puts out a foot. She falls.

Come on out! Come on.

TONY
(*rising to Tony*)
Look I want . . . please . . .

TONY
I'll speak to her, leave her.

He goes into the drawing-room. She follows.

VERA
Eh . . . now listen here . . . look . . . I'm not making a go of it, see? . . . I'm ill.

She looks as though she might fall. Tony does not offer her a chair.

I come to you.

He looks at her, says nothing.

I'm broke . . . I'm ill, you see, that's what it is . . .

82

Silence.

So I come to you, you see.

Silence.

TONY
Go to your bookmaker.

VERA
What?

TONY
Go to your bookie.

VERA
What bookie?

TONY
The one you ran off with.

VERA
Run off? Who ran off? What's he told you, eh? He chucked me out, soon as we left. He chucked me out. He's finished me. Listen, I got to go to hospital, they're taking me in . . . give me a few quid . . . just . . . go on . . . just . . .

TONY
What about what you did to me?

VERA
It was him. He made me. I loved you though. I still love you.

She goes into Tony's arms. He holds her, uncertain. Barrett comes in, looks.

BARRETT
Tch, tch, tch. Playing games with little Sis again, are you? That won't get you anywhere, Tone.

83

Tony hesitantly lets her go, blinks, goes out.

INT. HALL. NIGHT.

Barrett escorting Vera from room into hall to door. Tony is standing at the back of the hall.

> BARRETT
>
> Come on, little sister, out of it.

> VERA
> (*to Tony*)
> It was him. He done it.

She breaks away. Barrett grabs her and pulls her to the door.

> BARRETT
>
> Come here, stinking the place out.

Tony goes back into drawing-room.

> VERA
> (*calling after him*)
> I love you!

> BARRETT
>
> Get back to your ponce. Move out of it.

He pushes her out of the door.

INT. DRAWING-ROOM. NIGHT.

Tony is pouring whisky. Barrett comes in. Tony looks at him.

> TONY
>
> Slut.

INT. DRAWING-ROOM. EVENING.

Barrett handing Tony a bottle with no label.

84

BARRETT

I've got something special for you, from a little man in Jermyn Street.

Tony looks at bottle.

TONY

Not for me.

Barrett pours a glass.

BARRETT

Oh come on. Have a little sip, see what it tastes like.

TONY

I told you, I'm not drinking.

BARRETT

Just have a little sip, that's all, just a sip.

Tony looks sulkily at the glass, picks it up and sips.

TONY

Mmmmmm. Ooh, it's marvellous.

BARRETT

There you are, you see. I can still think of things that'll please you, can't I? You won't get any better than me you know. What do you want? An old hag running round the house, getting you up in the morning, at the crack of dawn, telling you what to do? My only ambition is to serve you, you know that don't you?

TONY

I'm sorry. I've been a bit edgy lately.

BARRETT

Oh well I mean, I admit, I make mistakes, but, well after all I'm only human aren't I? You wouldn't like me if I wasn't human, would you?

TONY

The place could be cleaner, that's all.

BARRETT

I know, I know it could be a bit cleaner. That's what I've been going on about for days.

TONY

(*with sudden intensity*)

Listen . . .

The intensity fades. He loses track of his thought.

Listen . . .

With great concentration he forces the words out.

Perhaps we could . . . both . . . make . . . an extra effort.

He looks up suddenly at Barrett, the expression on his face one of entreaty. Barrett smiles.

BARRETT

You're right there, Tone, you're dead right. That's what we ought to do.

Tony's face is at once confused, irritated. He suddenly begins to rake his hair violently, scratching his skull with his fist, his elbow raised, his posture resembling that of a chimpanzee.

INT. BEDROOM. NIGHT.

Portable record player. Tony listening, with glass. Chime of front door bell. Barrett enters.

BARRETT

Hey! Your other one's here.

TONY

What?

BARRETT

Your old flame. One yesterday, one tonight. You are popular aren't you. She's waiting.

TONY

Did you tell her we were expecting visitors?

BARRETT

I did. But I also took the liberty of showing her into the drawing-room. After all – she is a lady, isn't she?

Tony goes down.

INT. DRAWING-ROOM. NIGHT.

Susan is gazing at the changes of the room. Tony comes in, slams the door.

TONY

Hello.

He stands smiling, slightly swaying.

SUSAN

Vera's been to see me. She says you owe her some money.

Tony bends forward in a fit of soundless laughter. She watches him.

SUSAN

I think you owe her some kind of compensation.

TONY

She's a liar, they're all liars. You didn't come here because of Vera. It's all gone. Leave it alone.

He goes closer to her.

You don't want to . . . come here . . .

SUSAN
(*dully*)

I love you.

The front door is heard opening. Girls' voices. Barrett's voice. Giggling, going down the passage.

SUSAN

Who's that?

The record in the bedroom is turned louder.

TONY

Friends.

A Woman's voice is heard.

VOICE

Where's Tony?

SUSAN

Don't you . . . like me at all?

TONY
(*non-committal*)

Yes . . .

WOMAN'S VOICE

Where's that Tony?

SUSAN

Well what's wrong with me then?

BARRETT'S VOICE

Hey come on, we're waiting for you.

TONY

Nothing's wrong with you.
(*Laughs.*)
Come and join the party.

He takes her by the hand. She does not resist.

INT. BEDROOM. NIGHT.

Barrett and four women including Vera are in the room.

RECORD
Give me my death
Close my mouth
Give me my breath
Close my mouth etc.

TONY
Where's my drink?

BARRETT
It's here.
(*To Susan.*)
Do you want one, love, eh?

Susan stands still inside the door. Tony gulps his drink.

GIRL SINGING
Now while I love you alone . . .
Now while I love you alone.

A girl pulls Tony gently away.

TONY
What are you doing?

She takes him in a corner and whispers to him. Another girl joins them. They bend over him, whispering. He staggers away. A woman in a large black hat pulls him down on the bed and kisses him.

BARRETT
(*to Susan*)
Do you know where we're going in the morning?

Pause.

We're going to Brazil in the morning.
(*He grins.*)

Aren't we Tone?

> (*To Susan.*)

Have a fag.

Tony lies on the bed staring glazed at Susan. Susan moves to Barrett and kisses him. He laughs and holds her. She looks at Tony. His mouth is open, he moves from the bed. One of the girls touches him. He shivers, stumbles, falls and collapsing, brings tablecloth, glasses, bottles down with him.

BARRETT

Tch, tch, tch.

Tony sits a second, glass-eyed. The record player still plays. He suddenly reaches up to the shelf and sweeps it on the floor. There is a smash and grate of record and pick-up head.

TONY

> (*in a sudden dazed childish horror, in a monotone*)

Get out, get out. Get 'em all out.

His hand swinging knocks a bottle over.

Get out.

BARRETT

Come on then, out.

> (*He nudges Susan.*)

You too. Come on.

The women go to the door. Barrett whispers to them.

Make it tomorrow night.

> (*Confidential.*)

And bring John.

INT. HALL AND STAIRS. NIGHT.

The women go down and out. Barrett halfway down stairs, turns. Susan is still at bedroom door. Tony sits on floor, head drooping. She stares at him, expressionless. Barrett calls up stairs.

Eh you! Come on!

He emits a piercing whistle. No response.

OY!

She turns, walks slowly downstairs. She stops and looks at him, and then hits him with all her might, with closed fist, across the face. He staggers, his fists clench. He looks at her. She is still. Slowly he recovers his composure. He turns, goes to the front door, holds it wide open. With a smile, he inclines his head towards her. She leaves the house.

EXT. HOUSE. NIGHT.

Susan walks across the dark square. She looks back at the house, turns, walks on. The camera holds on the house and closes slowly in toward the door.

INT. LANDING. NIGHT.

Barrett locks door and bolts it. He walks slowly up the stairs.

INT. HALL. NIGHT.

Tony crawls onto the landing and sits in a corner.

INT. STAIRS. NIGHT.

Close up of Barrett's hand trailing the banister, as he climbs the stairs.

The Pumpkin Eater

The Pumpkin Eater was first presented by Columbia Pictures Corporation on 15th July 1964 with the following cast:

JO Anne Bancroft
JAKE Peter Finch
GILES Richard Johnson
DINAH Francis White, Kate Nicholls
FERGUS Fergus McClelland, Christopher Ellis
SHARON Sharon Maxwell, Mimosa Annis
MARK Kash Dewar
ELIZABETH Elizabeth Dear, Sarah Nicholls
PETE Gregory Phillips, Rupert Osborn
JACK Michael Ridgeway, Martin Norton
MR ARMITAGE Alan Webb
MR JAMES Cedric Hardwicke
PHILPOT Maggie Smith
YOUNGEST CHILD Mark Crader
NANNY Faith Kent
DOCTOR Cyril Luckham
INGRAM Eric Porter
WOMAN IN HAIRDRESSERS Yootha Joyce
CONWAY James Mason
MAN AT PARTY Gerald Sim
BETH Janine Gray
MRS JAMES Rosalind Atkinson
UNDERTAKER John Junkin
SURGEON Anthony Nicholls
WAITRESS AT ZOO Leslie Nunnerley
THE KING OF ISRAEL Frank Singuineau
PARSON John Franklin Robbins

Directed by Jack Clayton

EXT. LARGE HOUSE IN ST JOHN'S WOOD, LONDON. SUMMER DAY. PRESENT DAY.

Bonnet of a Jaguar foreground. Jo is standing at the window, looking out. Reflected in the window pane demolition of buildings, tall skeletons of new constructions.

INT. SITTING-ROOM.

Jo at window, looking out.

Another angle: Jo.

She turns, stares at the room.

INT. SITTING-ROOM.

We see the room. It is large, expensively furnished. Bookshelves, a piano, pictures, numerous thick rugs, etc. On a small table, tea for one is laid.

Another angle.

Jo goes to table, pours tea into the cup.

Close on Jo's hands.

She holds the cup tightly in its saucer, does not pick it up.

INT. HALL.

Jo comes quickly out of living room. As she turns into hall, letters thud on to carpet through the letter box.

Another angle: Jo.

She looks at them for a moment, makes no attempt to pick them up.

Another angle: Jo.

Footsteps above. She looks up. Through bannisters along first landing, a man's legs walking quickly.

Another angle: Jo.

She stands still. Water heard rushing into a basin from above.

EXT. GARAGE OF ST JOHN'S WOOD. HOUSE. DAY. PRESENT DAY.

Brilliant sunlight, heat haze. Pool of petrol. The Jaguar, the Floride, the child's scooter. Jo bends to pick up scooter.

The shining Jaguar, from her eye level as she bends. Sunlight. Jo's face.

Sun on wheelcaps.

Jo.

She straightens, scooter half held.

Another angle.

Her hands drop scooter. She moves swiftly towards garage.

EXT. SIDE DOOR OF HOUSE. DAY

Jake appears at side door. Stands looking left and right. Jo is not there. He gets into the Jaguar.

INT. JAGUAR. DAY.

Jake sits, adjusts his tie in the mirror, lights a cigarette, starts motor. Suddenly catches sight of Jo in the mirror.

The mirror. Reflecting interior garage.

Jo in the corner of the dark garage. Still, amid junk.

Another angle, Jaguar.

Jake gets out of car and crosses to garage.

INT. GARAGE. DAY.

> JAKE
> What are you doing?
> > (*Jo looks at him.*)
> What are you doing?

> JO
> Nothing.

Jake crosses to her, touches her arm.

> JAKE
> I thought you were going shopping.

Silence.

> It's late. I've got to go.
> > (*Pause.*)
> How are you feeling?

Pause.

> JO
> All right.

Pause.

> JAKE
> Look, I've got to go out to dinner . . . I'm sorry.

> JO
> All right.

Jake kisses her tenderly, speaks with a smile.

> JAKE
> Do you think you're going to get over this period in
> your life, because I find it very depressing.

He turns away, moves back to Jaguar, gets in and drives off.

Another angle: Jo watching car disappearing. She walks down path to front gate and into street. The car has disappeared. She turns, looks at the house.

INT. BARN. DAY. TEN YEARS EARLIER.

A large room, sub-divided by numerous home-made partitions. It is sparsely furnished but crowded with children. Jo is at a table making pastry. Some of the children are playing on the floor with train sets and home-made constructions of roads and stations. The smallest girl apart, examining a doll's house.

Another angle towards door.

It opens. Giles and Jake enter. A child (Dinah) rushes up to them.

CHILD ONE

Daddy – I was going to be the signal-box man and now look!

GILES

All right.
(To Jo.)
Darling, this is Jake.
(To children.)
What is it?

JO
(to Jake)

Hullo.

CHILD TWO

Dinah's got no right to open the gates until the express has been through.

JAKE
(to Jo)

Glad to meet you.

98

CHILD THREE

You can't stop a non-stop express.

Jo and Jake shaking hands. Her hands covered with flour.

Jake playing bricks with children.

JAKE

What's this bit going to be?

CHILD TWO

The ladies' lavatory.

JAKE

Where's the ticket office?

Another angle: Jo and Elizabeth.

ELIZABETH

Who's that?

JO

A friend of Daddy's.

CHILD TWO

These are oil pipes. They take the oil.

Another angle: Jake looking at Jo over bricks, as –

CHILD THREE

We don't want any oil. There are no diesels on this line.

Another angle: Giles coming from makeshift kitchen with tray of tea.

JAKE

Where's the control tower?

CHILD TWO

This isn't an airport, it's a station.

JAKE

You could have a helicopter.

Another angle: the two oldest boys chasing each other.

CHILD TWO

That's my diesel!

CHILD THREE

It's broken down.

CHILD TWO

Give it to me!

JO

Pete!

Child (Jack) climbs over partition.

GILES

Jack!

Another angle: the partition.

As child (Pete) clambers after Jack. It collapses.

Another angle: Giles at partition with hammer and nails.

CHILD TWO

He had my diesel!

GILES

This is about the sixth time.

Another angle. Jo moving away to light cigarette.

Close-up. Jake looking at her.

Close up. Jo.

Back to Giles holding up three planks of partition, examining them. One plank falls.

Plank falling.

Large close-up.

Jake kissing Jo's ear.

(No background noise.)

INT. STUDY IN JAKE'S FATHER'S HOUSE. EVENING. APPROX.
TEN YEARS EARLIER.

*Jake's father (Mr Armitage). He, Jo, and Jake sit, with drinks,
eating cheese straws.*

MR ARMITAGE
But why on earth do you want to marry Jake?

Short pause. Jo giggles.

JAKE
Why not?

MR ARMITAGE
It's incomprehensible.

JAKE
What is?

MR ARMITAGE
He'll be an impossible husband.

JAKE
Oh now, wait a minute –

MR ARMITAGE
I assure you. I mean, he's got no money. He's bone
lazy. He drinks too much. He's quite useless.

JAKE
Oh thanks.

MR ARMITAGE
What do the children say?

JAKE
We haven't exactly discussed it with them.

JO
They . . . don't mind.

MR ARMITAGE
(*to Jake*)

Do you like children?

JAKE

Of course I like them. Of course I do.

MR ARMITAGE

Have you actually known any?

INT. LIVING-ROOM. JO'S FATHER'S HOUSE. DAY. SAME
PERIOD.

Jo's father (Mr James). Jo and Jake.

MR JAMES

Do you realize what you're saddling yourself with?

JAKE

Er . . . Yes . . . yes . . .

MR JAMES

A zoo. A children's zoo. And their keeper. Are you
reconciled to having to keep the zoo and its keeper?

JAKE

Yes . . . of course . . . I mean . . .

MR JAMES

Are you fit?

JAKE

Well . . .

MR JAMES

I take it you know something of my daughter's record?

JO

My what?

Jake laughs.

> JAKE

Yes, I know.

> (*Pause.*)

I want to marry her.

> MR JAMES

You're a fool. Still, the least I can do is to give you some kind of a start, I suppose. You think that's fair?

> JAKE

Fair?

> MR JAMES

I think you're a fool, but I'll give you a start. A start. Do you think that's fair?

> JAKE

Oh yes, that's fair . . . quite . . . very fair.

> MR JAMES

Right. Well, first of all we've got to shed the load. There's too many children.

> JO

What do you mean?

> MR JAMES

I suggest we send the eldest two to boarding school. That will be two off your hands.

> JO

No! That's ridiculous.

> MR JAMES

Now listen, this is Jake's business, not yours. It's the burden on him that's ridiculous.

> JO

But I don't want them to go away to school.

103

MR JAMES

Look, be sensible. They'd love it.

JO

They wouldn't love it.

MR JAMES

I'd love it. Jake'd love it. And they can come to stay with us in the holidays.

JO

Why don't we just give them away?

JAKE

It's only the first two. I mean, there are others.

MR JAMES

Now listen. I'm not going to have you trailing home with half a dozen more children in five years' time and another messed up marriage on your hands. You're not going to be allowed to crush this poor boy before he starts. He's going to have to work like a slave as it is.

JO

But we can't afford to send them to school.

MR JAMES

I'm paying.

JAKE

Oh . . . thanks. Thanks very much.

MR JAMES

And I've managed to buy you a fairly good lease on a house in London. Quite reasonable. It's an old one but it should suit you – it'll pretty well clean me out, but you might as well have the money now as when I'm dead.

INT. KITCHEN – ST JOHN'S WOOD. HOUSE. DAY. PRESENT
DAY.

*Close on tray. With tea being set on draining board, with a sharp
sound.*

Another angle: Jo stands, does not touch crockery.

Another angle: at window.

Glimpses of demolition through window.

Another angle: Jo.

*She turns away, clutching her arms, walks vaguely about the
kitchen, her heels clicking on the tiled floor. An immaculate,
gleaming modern kitchen, spotless, nothing out of place.*

Another angle: Jo.

*As she moves, we see: new dishwasher, new refrigerator, new
washing machine and spin dryer, new electric oven, racks of
gleaming crockery, photograph on teak wood wall, a large photo
pinned from a magazine of Mr Jake Armitage, Mrs Armitage
and their children.*

Jo.

She glances at it.

*Another angle: She continues walking, her fingers tracing on the
worktop.*

EXT. HOUSE IN ST JOHN'S WOOD. DAY. APPROX. TEN YEARS
EARLIER.

*The house is considerably more shabby, both inside and out, than
in the present day sequences.*

*A furniture van is parked outside. Men are carrying furniture
from it into the house. Objects, furniture, heaped and strewn about
outside, through the ground floor, up stairs. We see certain*

recognizable objects from the barn. In foreground, a child's bike and scooter.

The Morris Minor turns the corner and draws up. Children fall out, followed by Jake and Jo. Again, we hear no sound until:

CHILD
They've got here before us!

The children rush up the path.

INT. HALL.

Through open door, we can see the empty kitchen. Jo is confronted with a piece of furniture.

JO
(*to removal men*)
Mmm . . . upstairs. The first floor front . . . left . . .

Children rush up and down stairs.

Don't get in the way.

She stands in the chaos. Jake appears, kisses her.

INT. LANDING (THAT NIGHT).

Silence. Nightlight through windows. Open doors. Their voices heard. There is certain junk (odd pieces) on landing, rolls of carpeting.

JO
My first marriage. You're my first husband.

JAKE
You've been married three times.

JO
No. You're the first.

106

JAKE

Are the children asleep?

JO

Yes.

JAKE

I'll close the door.

Jake moves to door and closes it.

JO

I want to go away with you . . . and come back with you
. . . and live with you.

JAKE

You will.

JO

You'll never go from me . . . we'll have the same life.
Do you want anything else?

JAKE

No. I don't want anything else.

INT. BATHROOM. EVENING. APPROX. EIGHT YEARS
EARLIER.

*Bathroom, small, crowded and full of steam. Dinah in bath, Jo
washing her ears and neck. Jake is drying a smaller Boy with a
large towel.*

BOY
(*to Jake*)

Can I tell you a story?

DINAH
(*to Jo*)

Do you like living in this house?

JO

Why? Don't you?

DINAH

Yes.

BOY

A story about a killer whale.

Jo leaves Dinah to wash herself and takes the boy's pyjamas from towel rail.

DINAH

How long are we going to live here?

JAKE

We're moving in the morning.

DINAH

We're not! Where?

JAKE

Building a big house on top of that hill.

DINAH

What hill?

Jo reaches for the Boy with his pyjamas.

JAKE

I haven't done his feet. Lift your foot.

Boy lifts his foot. Jake dries it.

BOY

It's about this whale . . .

DINAH

What hill?

JO

By the barn.

> DINAH

What, in the morning?

> JAKE

Well, we'll have lunch first.

> JO
> (*to Jake*)

Hurry up.

> BOY

It's a story about two whales and a shark.

> DINAH

What sort of house?

> JAKE

With eight bathrooms. All for me.

INT. SITTING-ROOM. MORNING. APPROX. SEVEN YEARS EARLIER.

Jo is putting a sweater on a small boy, who is struggling in her arms, trying to join the other children whom we can see beyond Jo, playing in the garden. Jo is pregnant.

> JAKE'S VOICE
> (*calling*)

Where's the opener?

> JO
> (*calling back*)

Just a minute –

INT. KITCHEN. MORNING.

It is filled with steam. We hear sounds of children. Jake is holding two cans of beer and searching for the opener. He regards the steaming pans on the gas stove, looks into the oven at the joint, closes oven door, his face blank.

109

INT. SITTING-ROOM.

Jake enters. He stops centre of room and reacts for a second to the children thudding about upstairs, and their shouts from the garden. He comes to table, finds opener.

Jo finishes inserting the Small Boy into his sweater, sets him down. He rushes out to the garden.

Jake, with a grimace, opens can. It spurts over the wall, where we can already see the stains from previous moments of this kind.

JAKE

Want one?

JO

Yes, I'll have one.

He hands her opened can. She takes it. Jake opens second can. It also spurts over wall.

JAKE

Aaaahh!

JO

It's all right, it'll wipe off.

JAKE
(*looking at can*)

It's ridiculous.

Jake sits at table on which are sheets of writing paper. He looks at them and throughout the ensuing dialogue vaguely scratches out words with his pen.

Shouts and thuds from garden and upstairs. Jo drinks from can.

JO

Let's go out today.

JAKE

Umm? Where?

JO

I don't know. Take them out.

JAKE

All of them?

Two Children rush in from garden, through the room and upstairs. Jake looks at Jo, chuckles shortly, dryly.

JO

I'll take them out, if you like, this afternoon. You can have a rest.

JAKE

No, no, don't be silly.

JO
(*touching him*)

No, really, I will. I will.

JAKE

No, no, I wouldn't dream of it. After all, it's Saturday, we can go out.

Loud crash from above.

What are they *doing* up there?

Pause.

JO

Do you want turnips or swedes?

JAKE

Turnips or swedes?

JO

Yes. Or both if you like.

He looks at her blankly.

JAKE
(*with sudden concentration*)

Turnips or swedes. Wait a minute. Just a minute. Let
me think about it.

INT. KITCHEN. DAY. APPROX. FIVE YEARS EARLIER.

*A young woman (Philpot) is sitting on the old-fashioned sink
cleaning saucepan lids with steel wool, slowly, as she speaks
towards the open doorway into the hall, where Jo is visible in the
foreground using an old Hoover.*

PHILPOT
(*above Hoover noise*)

Wives don't usually like me. I like them. That's the
funny thing. But I seem to worry them somehow. I
don't know. They get so ratty, people's wives. The
funny thing is that I like them better than their
husbands, do you think that's funny or not? Perhaps I'm
not normal. I'm quite normal really, I'm sure I am.

Jo has finished Hoovering and switched off. She enters kitchen as:

But perhaps it's just that I'm *ab*normal. I can't see how I
can be, can you? I mean . . . I've been told that I'm
frigid, but I don't see how you can tell, I mean –
honestly, how can you tell?

JO

I shouldn't think you are. Just a minute.

Jo moves to get hot water. Philpot sits on old-fashioned icebox.

You don't look it anyway.

PHILPOT

I think you're marvellous – I really do, I think you're
absolutely marvellous. You're so capable. All you do, all
the children and everything, the way you cope. Of
course, Jake's the most fabulous husband and father.

He's *the* most fabulous –

Jo touches Philpot's leg.

JO

Can I get in the . . .

Philpot moves her legs. Jo opens icebox.

PHILPOT

– *the* most fabulous father. How many are his?

JO

Er . . . one . . .

PHILPOT

One. One is his. And the others aren't his?

JO

No, they're not.

PHILPOT

But he's a wonderful father to them all, isn't he?

EXT. HAMPSTEAD HEATH FIVE YEARS EARLIER. DAY.

A damp, drizzly day. Jo and the Children. Hill. Running.

CHILD ONE

Why does Philpot have to stay with us?

JO

She's been turned out of her flat.

CHILD TWO

But why does she have to stay with us? We've got
enough people.

JO

She's looking for another one.

CHILD TWO

I've never seen her look.

CHILD ONE

Who is she?

JO

She's a friend of a friend of Daddy's.

CHILD ONE

Why does she have to sleep in my bed? Why can't I sleep in my bed?

They run downhill. In the background, we see girls playing netball. Dinah stands alone. They go to her.

DINAH

I've got a pain.

MISTRESS
(*calling*)

Dinah!

Dinah goes towards game. Game continues. Damp, muddy. Jo and Children watch game vaguely from the rise.

CHILD ONE

Why doesn't Philpot go home?

JO

She hasn't got a home.

CHILD THREE

She smells of fish.

CHILD TWO

She doesn't. She smells of onions.

CHILD THREE

Fish.

CHILD ONE

She had a spot on her chin yesterday, but this morning she'd squeezed it.

CHILD THREE

She stinks of fish.

JO

She doesn't stink at all. Now stop it.

CHILD TWO

What's the difference . . .

JO

Anyway, it's just perfume.

CHILD THREE

What is?

JO

Anyway, I like her.

CHILD ONE

Dad had to catch her yesterday when she fainted. It
must have been awful, the smell.

JO

Fainted?

CHILD THREE
(*falling*)
Do you faint like this? Is this how you faint?

CHILD TWO

She fainted. Dad caught her.

JO
(*to Child Three*)
Oh for goodness sake get up! You're smothered in mud,
look at it.

The limp netball game.

MISTRESS

Come on, keep moving, keep moving. Keep at it. Keep
at it. Come on, pass the ball. Keep moving. Keep at it.

The Girls move in the drizzle.

EXT. GROUP ON HILL. SHOOTING UP FROM GAME.

Prams moving across upper field. Jo and Children move away.

INT. PHILPOT'S BEDROOM. MORNING.

It is obviously a child's room, although Philpot's belongings are scattered around – clothing, ribbons, hairpins, a pair of laddered stockings, a shawl . . .

Jo with tray. Philpot in bed.

> PHILPOT
>
> He's a brilliant writer. It must be wonderful to have a man working in the house, mustn't it, working at home, you shouldn't have brought me tea, really, I should get up, I mustn't have tea in bed, really, it's bad for me, but honestly it must be so challenging to write for films, don't you think, it's so challenging, don't you think, the cinema is, wouldn't you say, but of course his understanding is so extraordinary, his innate . . . the way he draws his characters . . . swift strokes . . . so swift . . . and for you of course after all your struggles to suddenly have success on the doorstep, after all those husbands you've had and everything, but of course you're so intelligent and everything and of course so beautiful, do you help him much with his work?

> JO
>
> Not much.

Pause.

> Are you feeling any better?

> PHILPOT
>
> Better?

JO

You weren't too well the other day.

PHILPOT

I'm perfect. It's so warm here. *Real.* You know, so *real.*
I've never felt such a sense of *reality*, as there is here. Do
you know what I mean?

INT. KITCHEN FIVE YEARS EARLIER. AFTERNOON.

Jo vaguely washing. Jake making tea.

JO

Does Philpot faint much?

JAKE

What?

JO

Philpot. Does she do a lot of fainting?

JAKE

How the hell would I know?

Pause.

I mean, why should she faint? What's she got to faint
about?

JO

The children said she fainted yesterday.

JAKE

I don't know. Did she?

JO

They said you caught her.

JAKE

Me?

JO

Yes.

JAKE

Why would I catch her?

JO

To stop her . . . banging her head on the . . .

JAKE

What head? What are you talking about?

JO

Did you catch her when she fainted?

JAKE
(*a shout*)

How do I know?

He bangs the table.

INT. KITCHEN. LONDON HOUSE. DAY. PRESENT TIME.

Water running. Tea tray set for one. Jo turns off tap. Goes out of kitchen into hall.

INT. HALL FIVE YEARS EARLIER. NIGHT

As the front door closes softly.

INT. SITTING-ROOM FIVE YEARS EARLIER. NIGHT.

JO

Where's she gone?
(*Pause.*)
She's just gone out the front door.

JAKE

Has she?

JO

That's a bit odd, isn't it?

JAKE

What?

JO

I mean, we've just come in, haven't we? Now she's gone
out.

Jake yawns.

JAKE

Probably gone for a walk. Why don't you take off your
coat?

Pause.

JO

What?

(*Pause.*)

Why has she gone?

(*Pause.*)

She's . . . Do you want some coffee?

JAKE

No thanks.

Pause.

JO

What did you think of the film?

Jake grimaces.

What did you think of the bloody film?

JAKE

Nothing! I didn't think anything of it!

JO

Is your film going to be better, the one you're writing,
do you think it's going to be better?

He stands.

JAKE

Listen –

JO

Do you like sitting between two women? Does that thrill you? Does it give you a thrill?

JAKE

Yes, it does. It really does. What do you think I should do about it? What shall I do, go and see a psychiatrist about it?

He sits. Pause.

JO

All right, what –

JAKE

Look. Listen –

Pause.

It was nothing, nothing. Don't you understand?

JO

What do you mean, it was nothing?

Pause.

What do you mean, nothing?

JAKE

What do you think I mean?

JO

What did you catch her for?

JAKE

I didn't catch her!

JO

She fainted.

JAKE

What does it matter if I caught her or not? I didn't catch
her, it doesn't matter, can't you understand? Who cares?

JO

I care.

JAKE

What about? What's it all about?

JO

I care about you. Who else?

JAKE

Me? You don't care about me. All you care about is that
bloody great army of children I'm supposed to work my
guts out for. That's all you care about. Where the hell
do I come in?

Pause.

I can't even take a bath in peace, I can't . . . I can't even
go to bed with you without one of them comes barging
in in the middle, but so what, you just . . . I'm sick of
living in a bloody nursery. Where the damn hell do I
come in?

She giggles.

What are you sniggering about? It's funny when I tell
you the truth for once, I suppose.

JO

The truth?

JAKE

That I'm capable of fancying someone else. I'm a perfectly
normal man who's capable of fancying someone else.

121

They look at each other. He goes to table and pours a drink. He sits near her, pulls her on to his lap. She regards his face calmly.

JO

Aaah.

JAKE

She was just here, that's all. I was bored with the script, that's all. It was nothing. Forget it.

JO

Did you sleep with her?

JAKE

Don't be silly.

JO

You didn't?

JAKE

No.

JO

You promise?

JAKE

Yes.

She kisses him.

JO

Do you still want to?

He laughs.

JAKE

Yes.

He laughs again, kisses her.

INT. PHILPOT'S ROOM. NIGHT.

Jo pushing all Philpot's belongings into a shawl.

EXT. BY DUSTBINS. NIGHT.

Jo piling all stuff by the dustbins. She stands still in the night, becomes cold, turns.

INT. STAIRWAY. NIGHT.

Jo ascends stairs, stands still at top. Sound of a child muttering in its sleep.

INT. MAIN BEDROOM. NIGHT.

Moonlight. Jo enters, moves to bed, stops, looks at Jake asleep. She sits on the dressing table stool watching him, her hands tightly clenched.

Eventually she gets into bed. Jake turns, snores. Jo retreats to the edge of the bed, away from him, staring at him with eyes open, clutching the pillow between them.

SERIES OF SHOTS. PRESENT TIME.

Jo as we follow her. The street backgrounds change. She enters a large department store (Harrods).

INT. HARRODS. AFTERNOON.

We follow Jo as she walks through various departments. See:

Row of gleaming refrigerators.

Row of beds.

Shoppers hustling by. A salesman demonstrating a very efficient Hoover.

Jo wandering through store.

Children's clothing, bottles of scent, children's toys, handkerchiefs.

INT. LINEN DEPARTMENT. JO.

She suddenly stops and stands there in the centre of the floor, crying.

Another angle: shoppers passing, glancing at Jo curiously.

Another angle: Jo standing quite still, crying soundlessly.

Long shot: Jo standing there, crying. The many shoppers, still looking at her, have moved away, leaving her standing isolated and motionless. Eventually a Saleslady approaches, takes her arm and guides her away.

EXT. HOUSE IN ST JOHN'S WOOD. LATE AFTERNOON.

A taxi draws up outside. Jo is helped out by a uniformed nurse. The front door of the house opens. Certain Children in school uniform appear from inside the house and stand watching. Silence. The Nurse and Jo walk up the path.

INT. HALL.

Silent Children, including the Smallest Child with the Nanny. Jo and the Nurse enter. Dinah comes to them.

DINAH
(to her mother)

I couldn't find Daddy. I called the studio but he wasn't there. I left a message.

As Nurse, Jo and Dinah move upstairs, one child pushes another, and a crying row breaks out.

INT. FIRST FLOOR LANDING AND STAIRS. NIGHT.

The Doctor is descending the stairs. Jake can be seen waiting in the hall.

JAKE

Let's go in here, shall we?

DOCTOR

Yes.

They go into the sitting-room. The door is pushed to, but it swings back a little.

INT. LANDING. NIGHT.

We see the door of the sitting-room below, ajar. Light through chink. Hear murmurs. Jo's bedroom door opens. Jo slips out. Looks down.

INT. STAIRWAY. NIGHT.

Jo moves silently, halfway down the stairs, crouches there, listening. Sound of a soda syphon. The voices of Jake and the Doctor are only occasionally heard clearly. The Doctor appears to be at the far end of the room. His voice is low, his tone grave.

Jake is clearly walking about, his shadow sometimes appearing through the chink. Only when he is close to the door do we hear his words. These are interspersed with murmured questions and comments from the Doctor.

Jo sits crouched on the stairs, listening.

JAKE

Would you like a drink?

DOCTOR

Er, no, not for me, thanks.

JAKE

I should have got in touch with you before. It's been getting worse all the time. Going on for ages. There was a girl friend of hers staying with us for a time, then she left . . . Mmmm . . . yes, it was round that period, but it's been . . . getting worse all the time.

DOCTOR

What exactly?

JAKE

I don't know. I . . . I can't get near her. She, she thinks
everybody's . . . against her, keeps finding fault all the
time. You know the sort of thing.

DOCTOR

Haven't you any idea why?

JAKE

No. I mean, breaking down in Harrods like that.
Harrods of all places!

DOCTOR

Has there been any . . . kind of trouble between you?

JAKE

No.

DOCTOR

There's nothing particular, no specific problem?

JAKE

No. Nothing at all.

DOCTOR

I think perhaps she should see a psychiatrist.

JAKE

Should she?

DOCTOR

It might be a good idea.

JAKE

All right. If she wants to.

DOCTOR

He might want to see you too.

JAKE

Me?

DOCTOR

Yes. After all, you are her husband.

JAKE

I don't really see what I . . . She probably wants to have
another child. That's what it is.

DOCTOR

Oh. Well, why doesn't she? She's a perfectly . . . healthy
woman.

JAKE

We've got enough! Have you counted them? Well, any
sane person would know we've got enough. When is she
going to face facts? I mean she's a beautiful woman, she
could . . . join in . . . live . . . all she wants to do is to sit
in a corner and give birth.

*Jo stands, retreats. The door opens. She stands at the top of the
stairs.*

Another angle: stairway.

*Jo standing at top, by her bedroom door, in the shadows. Jake
comes out of sitting-room below with Doctor, looks up, does not see
her. He gets the Doctor's coat. Jo steps back into:*

INT. MAIN BEDROOM.

Jo stands in doorway, listening, as:

DOCTOR'S VOICE

I'll give you a ring about it. Be kind to her.

JAKE'S VOICE

. . . Kind? I'm always kind.

DOCTOR'S VOICE

Good night.

JAKE'S VOICE

Good night.

Sound of front door closing. Jo gets into bed, glances at door expectantly. But Jake does not come up the stairs.

Another angle: Jo in bed, listening. She hears the whirr of the telephone dial. Jake's voice speaks softly. Jo looks at bedside telephone, stares, does not pick it up.

Another angle: Jo in bed eyes open. The ting of the receiver, from downstairs. Silence.

Footsteps.

Jake comes in. Jo's eyes are closed.

JAKE
(*sitting on bed*)

Asleep?

JO

No.

He caresses her.

JAKE

You'll be all right.

JO

I am.

Pause.

When are they going to finish the house?

JAKE

Soon.

Pause. She closes her eyes. He strokes her hair.

128

INT. SITTING-ROOM. EVENING.

Jo and Jake sitting. He is reading a book. She has a magazine on her lap. Silence.

                    JAKE
We've finished the script.

Pause.

We're going . . . to Morocco for a couple of weeks.

                    JO
Mmm-hmm.

Pause.

                    JAKE
Would you like to come?

Pause.

I mean . . .

                    JO
Oh, I . . .

Pause.

                    JAKE
It'd mean living in tents and all that . . . but . . . if you felt like it . . .

                    JO
Couldn't just . . . sit in a tent . . .

                    JAKE
You wouldn't have to stay in the tent.

Silence.

                    JO
Timothy loved the train.

JAKE

What train?

JO

Your birthday present. The one your secretary sent for you.

JAKE

Well, anyway . . . the Doctor . . . we've arranged for a very good man for you to go and see.

Silence.

Why don't you come down to the studio tomorrow?

JO

What for?

JAKE

Meet everyone. They all want to meet you. Watch the work. It might interest you.

JO

I don't want to come to the studio.

Pause.

JAKE

You're not interested . . . in what I do.

Pause.

JO

You never ask me.

JAKE

I've just asked you. I've asked you dozens of times.

JO

You don't want me to come.

JAKE

That's silly.

130

JO

No. It's not what you want.

Pause.

JAKE

You've never shown the slightest interest . . .

JO

Why are we talking about it?

Pause.

JAKE

You're just not interested in what I do, are you?

JO

You leave me. You're never with me.

JAKE

I have to work! It's my life.

JO

Where's mine? Where's my life?

Pause.

JAKE

With me.

She laughs.

I've worked, haven't I? What's wrong with that? I've had
to work, haven't I? What did you expect me to do? The
children go to good schools –

JO

Do you love me?

JAKE

I wouldn't be here if I didn't.

131

JO

You'd always be here if you did.

JAKE

Oh that's ridiculous.

JO

Always.

Pause.

JAKE

You resent the money, don't you? That's what you resent.

JO

Money? It's nothing to do with the money.

JAKE

Look at that damn kitchen! Look at all this! What about the new house? You wanted it. I've done it for you. But all you want now, I suppose, is just to go back and live in that barn!

JO

It's nothing to do with the kitchen, it's nothing to do with the money – it's nothing to do with any of it!

JAKE

Well, *what*? What is it? What *do* you want? What?

She does not reply. He stands.

JO

You're going out.

JAKE

I have to.

JO

Don't go out now. Why are you going out now?

JAKE

I've got to. You know that. I can't not go.

JO

Stay. Not for long.

JAKE

I'm late. I'm late. It's business, it's not friends, it's business. If it were friends you could come.

JO

What friends? We haven't got any friends. The only friend I ever had was Philpot, but she was more your friend, wasn't she, than mine? But of course you've had lots of friends since Philpot, haven't you? Lots of nice friends. For years.

JAKE

You're quite wrong.

Pause.

JO

I don't want to come to the studio. I don't want to meet your . . . people. Never. Never.

The young Nanny enters.

NANNY

They're ready to say good night to you, Mrs Armitage.

No response.

Mrs Armitage –

Jo lifts her head, smiles. Silence. Jake stands.

JAKE

Are they . . . out of the bath?

NANNY

Yes.

Jake goes out and upstairs with Nanny. Jo sits still.

INT. ST JOHN'S WOOD. HOUSE. DAY.

Jake is getting into a large car outside house.

Chauffeur holding door. Children running, shouting. Jake waving. Jo standing holding a Child by its hand. Jake waves, she waves. Car door slams; car drives off. Children run to wave. Jo waves, Jake waves out of window.

INT. PSYCHIATRIST'S OFFICE. DAY.

Darkened, soft lights. Jo sitting in armchair. Psychiatrist, (Ingram) at desk.

> INGRAM
> Do you like children, Mrs Armitage?

She giggles.

> JO
> They don't do you any harm.

> INGRAM
> You have a remarkable number.

> JO
> I had them of my own free will.

> INGRAM
> Of course.

> JO
> Nobody forced me to have them.

Pause.

> INGRAM
> Your two eldest boys have been at boarding school for some years.

JO

Some years, yes.

INGRAM

You agreed to their going away.

JO

Yes.

INGRAM

Have you seen them recently?

JO

Not recently.

INGRAM

Do you want to see them?

Pause.

JO

I believe they're doing terribly well.

Pause.

INGRAM

Tell me about your first husband.

JO

Oh . . . I can't remember.

INGRAM

Really? You were married to him for two years.

JO

He was . . . sweet . . . quite sweet . . . Drank a bit, I
think . . . second one died, he was killed . . . he was
nice . . . third one was a violinist . . . Giles . . . he was
nice . . . we lived in this barn with the children . . .
hardly went out, really . . . some years, I think . . .

INGRAM

Why did you leave him? What happened?

JO

Happened? Nothing happened. Nothing happened at all.

INT. MAIN BEDROOM. DAY.

Jo drinking hot milk. Dinah with her.

DINAH

What about this book? Do you want to read it?

JO

Which one's that?

DINAH

It's the one about Trotsky.

JO

Oh yes.

DINAH

It's pretty marvellous. He was assassinated you know.

JO

Was he?

DINAH

Didn't you *know*? They killed him. They assassinated him.

JO

Who did?

DINAH

God, it's a fantastic story. They sent this man, you see.

JO

I'll read it downstairs.

DINAH

You getting up?

JO

Yes, I feel better now.

DINAH

Don't you cry any more?

JO

No.

DINAH

Why do you cry like that?

JO

I don't. I feel better.

DINAH

Do you miss him? Is that it?

JO

Who?

DINAH

Daddy.

Jo smiles, gets out of bed.

Anyway . . . you know . . . read that book . . . it'll cheer you up.

JO

Yes, I will.

INT. PSYCHIATRIST'S OFFICE. DAY.

Jo and Ingram.

JO

What has Jake got to do with me? Why do you keep asking me about Jake? I come here and all you ask me

137

about is Jake. Why the hell don't you see Jake? Perhaps it's him you should be seeing, not me. There's nothing to *say* . . . about him.

INGRAM

Do you like him?

JO

No.

INGRAM

Do you love him?

JO

. . . Yes, so what? You don't –

INGRAM

What?

JO

I've forgotten what I was going to say.

Pause.

INGRAM

Do you think Jake is liable to change?

JO

I'm no match for him.

INGRAM

You're no match for him?

JO

No.

INGRAM

What do you mean?

Pause.

Do you think he's liable to change?

JO

No.

INGRAM

What would you say was the difference between Jake and your previous husbands?

JO

They weren't necessary.

Pause.

INGRAM

When you say –

JO

You should have a bowl in front of that gas fire.

INGRAM

A bowl?

JO

Of water – a bowl of water.

INGRAM

Ah, yes.

JO

You need it, for Christ's sake.

INGRAM

Mmm . . .

JO

The trouble is, if you have a bowl of water people throw matchsticks into it, and they float about for days, and become soggy; the water becomes black, and then anyway, it all dries up anyway. So perhaps you're better off without it.

Pause.

INGRAM

Do you find the thought of sex without children
obscene, Mrs Armitage?

JO

No.

INGRAM

Really? Are you sure the idea doesn't disgust you? I
mean, don't you find the idea messy? Isn't sex
something you must sanctify, as it were, by incessant
reproduction?

Pause.

JO

I shall have to give that question a little thought.

INGRAM

You would do well to, I think.

Pause.

I won't be seeing you for a couple of weeks. Just chew it
over, and take the pills of course.

JO

Couple of weeks?

INGRAM

Oh, I'm sorry, haven't I told you? We're off to Gstaadt
on Friday for a spot of skiing. It's my great passion, I'm
afraid.

JO

Skiing?

INGRAM

Oh, and cut down on liquids as much as you can. Can
we make an appointment for the . . . 19th.

JO

Can't make it. No . . . can't make the 19th.

INGRAM

The 20th?

JO

Can't make it.

INGRAM

Oh come now . . .

JO

What liquids?

INGRAM

Liquids.

JO

Yes, but what liquids? Listen, why are you going to Gstaadt? Where is Gstaadt? Why the hell don't you go to Cortina? Or Kitzbuhel?

INT. HAIRDRESSING SALON. DAY.

Rows of chairs, all occupied. Hair dryers. Jo sitting under dryer, looking at a magazine. The Woman next to her is looking at her. She is middle-aged. The Woman leans over, Jo looks up, sees the large face of the Woman close to her. The Woman is smiling, talking, her mouth moves. Jo lifts her dryer to hear.

WOMAN

I hope you don't mind, I've just been looking at your photo in one of these magazines, you know, a photo of you all, all your family, all your wonderful children and your wonderful husband, I thought you must be the same person.

JO

Oh . . . yes.

WOMAN

I think you're much lovelier than your photo. I really
do. I was . . . I had a . . . Do you mind me speaking to
you?

JO

Er . . . no . . .

WOMAN

To tell you the honest truth, my life is an empty place,
to tell you the dog's honest truth. Your eyes are more
beautiful than in that picture. I bet you didn't always
have things so good, that's why you appreciate, don't
you? I never dreamed I'd meet you like this and I mean
you're so kind, you're so full of sympathy for me. My
husband doesn't come near me any more, no, nowhere
near me. Don't you think I'm attractive any more? I
think I'm still attractive.

JO

Of course you are.

WOMAN

I'm not as attractive as you. But in a different way I am.
That's one thing I do know. I had a hysterectomy
operation four months ago. Yes, a hysterectomy. You
know, they take it all away. But you should see the way
men look at me. The way they still look at me. My word
of honour. You can tell by that, you see. I'm desirable.
I'm not old. I know. But he doesn't seem to care about
cheering me up any more . . . Oooh, I'm so thirsty.

Pause.

JO

Would you . . . like a cup of tea?

WOMAN

I'm off liquids.

Pause.

JO

Well, I . . . I am sorry . . .

WOMAN

It's no bloody use being sorry, chum. What are you
going to do about it? I've just told you my life is an
empty place.

JO

What do you want me to do?

WOMAN

I don't want any favours, for a start. Don't patronize
me, for a start.

JO

I'm really not. I'm really not.

WOMAN

'I'm really not. I'm really not.' God! I thought you'd be
different. I thought you'd be a different woman to the
one you are, Miss. I thought you'd be a very different
woman.

JO

I'm sorry . . .

WOMAN

You're what? I do a weekly wash in a copper boiler!
Oh, you've got such wonderful children, wonderful,
wonderful, wonderful, wonderful. You're wonderful
too. You must be a lovely woman. You must be such a
lovely woman. I think women are the only ones . . .
They're the only ones. I can see your grace and your
sweetness just sitting here. What does your husband
think of you, eh? Does he find you attractive? Eh, I've
been wondering, do you think your husband would find
me desirable? Eh?

JO
Look . . . I don't actually feel very . . .

WOMAN
I'd show him some tricks, I'd show him some tricks.
Heh! You want to bet? . . . I'd show him a few things I
bet you don't know. My love. My little darling. Anyone
ever clawed your skin off? You see these claws? Ever had
your skin clawed off?

An Assistant comes to the Woman. She looks curiously at them both.

You're going to give me two curls there, this time? Over
the ears, two curls, one either side, two lovely curls at
each side, are you? Are you?

INT. HALL AND STAIRS. MORNING.

Children rushing down the stairs, shouting.

EXT. HOUSE IN ST JOHN'S WOOD. MORNING.

Jake getting out of chauffeur-driven car at the front gate.

INT. HALL.

Children flinging themselves at Jake.

JAKE
Hullo . . . hullo . . . hullo . . . Good God, – who's this?
Ha-ha-ha . . . (etc.) . . . Where's Mum?

Shout from Child.

CHILD
Here she is!

INT. SITTING-ROOM.

Silent, empty. Shouts from hall. (Dialogue from previous scene repeated.)

> JAKE'S VOICE
>
> Hullo . . . hullo . . . hullo . . . Good God, – who's this?
> Ha-ha-ha . . . (etc.) . . . Where's Mum?

> CHILD'S VOICE
> (*shouting*)
>
> Here she is!

Sitting-room door is flung open.

EXT. FRONT PATH.

Children struggling with cases.

INT. SITTING-ROOM. MORNING.

Jake and Jo. Children. Jake gives Jo a Moorish dressing gown.

> JAKE
>
> It's meant to bring you luck.

Children are opening cases with cries, unwrapping presents. Jake claps his hands.

> Come on, come on, where's that drink? None of these are for you, you haven't been good enough.

> CHILD ONE
>
> We have!

> CHILD TWO
>
> They've got our names on!

A Child takes Jake a drink. He sips.

> JAKE
>
> Who put all that soda in?

CHILD ONE

I got a green star for spelling.

CHILD FOUR

Where's mine?

CHILD TWO

What's this?

JAKE

What do you think?

Jo helps them unwrap packages.

CHILD THREE

Did you see any lions?

CHILD FIVE

We went to the circus.

CHILD SIX

We went to the pictures.

CHILD THREE

Did you see any camels?

CHILD TWO

That's where I fell down.

CHILD FOUR

Was it a jet?

CHILD THREE

What about hyenas?

CHILD ONE

I've got a new book.

CHILD TWO

I had a bandage.

INT. SITTING-ROOM. LATER SAME MORNING.

*Jo and Jake with drinks. Paper and packages all over room.
Sounds of children playing, from upstairs. A record playing. Jake
smiles, touches her.*

> JAKE

Darling . . .

She smiles.

> JO

I'm all right now.

> JAKE

Wish you'd been there. Marvellous place.

> JO

Was it?

> JAKE

Come here.

She sits with him. He kisses her. He settles down comfortably.

Of course, Hurst and Betty hated each other on sight.

> JO

Did they?

> JAKE

Well, first of all, there was some ridiculous business
about a camel, he got her up on this camel, pure spite of
course, anyway, she must have been dead drunk at the
time, anyway –

A sudden crash from outside the door. A cry.

*Jo stands. Door bursts open. Three Children run through, one
crying. The crying Child chases the other two through window to
garden.*

JO

Hey!

EXT. THE GARDEN. THEIR POINT OF VIEW.

In garden, we see the first Two Children turn running, shooting at Third.

Back to scene.

Sudden silence in room.

A radio and gramophone suddenly blurt together from above. Shouts.

CHILD'S VOICE
(*shouting*)

I'm playing mine!

CHLD'S VOICE
(*shouting*)

I told you just now!

Jake sinks in chair, blankly chuckles.

JO

What happened?

JAKE

Mmmmm? Well, what was so funny . . . you see . . . it was really what she was wearing, really . . . that's what was so funny . . .

JO

On the camel?

A scream from the garden. They look out of window.

THE GARDEN. THEIR POINT OF VIEW.

A Child lies prone on the grass.

                    JO
              (*through window*)
Tim! What are you doing?

                    CHILD (TIM)
     Nothing!

BACK TO SCENE.

Silence in room.

                    JO
     We've got lunch . . . ready soon . . . for you.

                    JAKE
     Ah.

Music from upstairs.

                    JO
     Bit of a racket.

                    JAKE
     Saturday morning.

He yawns, sits. She goes to the door.

                    JO
                  (*calling*)
     Turn one of those off!

                    CHILD'S VOICE
     I had mine on first.

                    JO
     I said turn one of them off, at once, now.

                    CHILD'S VOICE
     Which one?

                    JO
     Turn them both off!

                    149

JAKE

It doesn't matter, it doesn't matter.

She goes to him.

JO

What happened? Tell me.

JAKE

What?

JO

About . . . the camel . . . and . . .

JAKE

Oh, it's . . . all . . .

Closes his eyes.

. . . pretty uninteresting.

Opens his eyes.

What's the matter? What are you crying about?

JO

No.

JAKE

Nothing to cry about.

She rests against him.

Is there?

Pause.

JO

Look. Why don't we ask them round?

JAKE

Who?

150

JO

All of them. Tonight.

JAKE

Tonight?

JO

Yes. Why not? All of them.

JAKE

Who?

JO

Oh . . . the Conways, Hurst, all of them. Then I could
hear all about it. Properly. Come on, why not?

JAKE

But why do you want all that lot round here tonight!
They might not be free anyway.

JO

Ring and find out.

JAKE

But . . . do you want to . . .?

JO

Yes, I do. I'll ring. What's the Conways' number?

JAKE

Have you been having an affair with that doctor or
something?

JO

Yes. How did you know?

JAKE

What are you up to?

She seizes his head. She kisses him hard.

INT. SITTING-ROOM. NIGHT.

*The party. The glass doors between sitting-room and dining-room
are open. Both rooms are crowded with people. Concentrated
party noise. Jo's face. Conway is hemming her into a corner,
talking.*

CONWAY

Professional people are all a lot of bloody parasites, the
lot of them. Doctors, lawyers – you know what I mean –
parsons, the whole bloody crew of them. I call myself a
tradesman because it's the only thing left to respect in
my honest opinion. In my honest opinion, an honest
tradesman is the only thing left to respect in this world.
A man like me, for instance. The rest of them are just a
bunch of lousy frauds.

*Dinah signals to Jo from another corner of the room. As Conway
turns, Dinah smiles radiantly. Conway turns back to Jo, nudges
her, leans closer.*

What do you think? Come on, what do you think?

JO

Excuse me a second, I must . . .
            (*She catches sight of Jake.*)
Jake, I think Mr Conway wants another drink.

*Conway drains his glass. Jo moves away. Camera follows her as
she moves. Snatches of conversation overheard:*

GUEST ONE

Well, there was this man, you see, there was this man,
and all his life, the one thing he wanted more than
anything else was to beat a woman, you see. No it's
quite true, really. It's a true story. It was the one thing
he really wanted to do. But he never met anyone who
wanted him to do it . . .

GUEST TWO

But it's got nothing to do with you, darling.

GUEST ONE

He was a very nice chap, you see, very quiet sort of
bloke . . .

GUEST THREE

It has absolutely everything to do with me as a matter of
fact.

GUEST ONE

Well, one night at a party he met a woman. He was
telling her about it, you see, and she said what a
wonderful coincidence, there's nothing I'd love more in
the whole world. Well, he couldn't believe his ears . . .

GUEST FOUR

He stands to make at least fifteen grand out of it, so
what's the matter?

GUEST FIVE

Who said anything was the matter?

GUEST ONE

No, it's really true, really. She took him home to her
flat. He was so excited he could hardly get up the stairs.

GUEST SIX

I had three showers a day – absolutely every single day.

GUEST SEVEN

What were the peasants like?

GUEST EIGHT

Extraordinarily interesting. Fascinating faces.

GUEST SEVEN

Lots of character, I suppose.

GUEST EIGHT

Oh lots, lots.

Jo joins Dinah.

JO

How's things?

DINAH

Marvellous. Dad's really with it tonight, isn't he? I
didn't know Beth Conway had red hair. I thought it was
sort of blonde. She's lovely, isn't she? Isn't she smiling
at you? Have you spoken to her?

*Beth. Dinah's point of view, lying on couch, talking to Jake and
surrounded by people.*

Back to scene.

Man comes up with a drink for Dinah.

MAN

Here you are, my dear.

He peers at Jo, smiling.

Who's this?

DINAH

She's my mother.

MAN

Really?

JO

Hullo. Just a minute.

She moves away, camera with her. Snatches of conversation:

GUEST ONE

(*trying to make himself heard above laughter*)

. . . No, well, anyway, after all that, at last, at last, they stood there stark naked, looking at each other. He had the cane in his hand . . .

GUEST NINE

It'll be a smash, and believe me, when I say smash . . .

GUEST TEN

Who knows if you don't.

GUEST ONE

Suddenly, to his amazement . . . suddenly to his horror and amazement . . .

GUEST ELEVEN

How's your new house, Mr Gross?

GUEST TWELVE

Which one?

GUEST ONE

He saw that she was holding a cane too. 'What's all this?' he said.

GUEST THIRTEEN

Actually, you really are terribly masculine.

GUEST FOURTEEN

Am I really?

GUEST ONE

Suddenly she whacked him with all her might. 'Oww!' he screamed.

Jo joins Beth, Jake and Conway and the group around the couch.

JAKE

Beth wants your advice. I've told her you know all about children.

JO

I wouldn't say that.

CONWAY

What my wife needs is another half-dozen and quick.

JO
(*to Beth*)

Did you like Morocco?

BETH

Oh, it was quite fun. Quite fun really.

All the noise of the party dies away, as we dissolve to:

INT. SITTING-ROOM. LATER SAME NIGHT.

The room dishevelled, full of smoke, overflowing ashtrays, bottles, glasses, but empty of people except for Conway, Beth, Jake and Jo.

CONWAY
(*his voice coming out of the silence*)

I call myself a tradesman, because it's the only thing left to respect, in my honest opinion. In my honest opinion, an honest tradesman is the only thing left to respect in this world. That's my honest opinion.

JAKE

You'd say that in all honesty, would you?

CONWAY

In all honesty, Jake. In complete honesty, boy. Ask Beth. Ask Beth if I mean what I say.
(*Pause.*)

Ask her!

They look at Beth.

BETH

Oh, my husband always . . . means what he says.

156

(*To Jo.*)

Does yours?

JO

You'd better ask him.

Jake laughs.

BETH

He writes film scripts beautifully, anyway, doesn't he?
He's got such extraordinary understanding, such . . .
swift . . . you know . . . kind of illumination of people.
Some of the scenes with John actually made me really
cry.

JAKE

That was just the sand in your eyes.

CONWAY

Lots of sand in Morocco, was there?

JAKE

Uh.

Pause.

JO

Another drink?

BETH

I'm fine.

JO

Mr Conway?

CONWAY

No, I don't think I'll have another one, thank you very
much.

JAKE

I'll have one.

157

Jo gets it.

> CONWAY
>
> I looked after our baby girl while Beth was away.

> JAKE
>
> How did she respond to that?

> CONWAY
>
> How did she respond to it? I'm her father!

Pause.

> Intelligent woman, your wife.

They all look at Jo.

> JO
>
> Oh no. I'm not at all.

> BETH
>
> I think he's right. I think you look very intelligent.

> CONWAY
>
> I like intelligent women. They're stimulating, they're
> vital . . . vital . . . that's what makes them intelligent, I
> suppose.

> JAKE
>
> Yes, it depends which way you look at it.

> BETH
>
> Jake's got an idea for a new film, it takes place on the
> Italian Riviera. We could all go, all of us together, the
> four of us, think what fun we could have.

Silence. They all sit. Staring.

INT. MAIN BEDROOM. LATE NIGHT.

After the party. Jo and Jake are undressing.

JO

They've nearly finished the house.

JAKE

Have they? Oh, good, good.

Pause.

JO

You're a marvellous colour.

JAKE

It was hot.

Pause.

JO

Do you think she's attractive?

JAKE

Who?

JO

Beth.

JAKE

Mmmm-hmmm. I suppose so.

She pulls him on to the bed, caresses him, tracing his body. Jake murmurs:

I need you.

JO

What about the Arab women?

JAKE

Oh, I couldn't begin to tell you.

JO

Did they like you?

JAKE

Wouldn't leave me alone.

JO

Did they touch you like that?

He suddenly turns her over on her back and stares down at her.

What is it?

Silence. He looks at her, as if about to speak, then kisses her suddenly.

EXT. HILLSIDE. DAY.

We see the new house in the background. It is of very modern design, startling against the skyline.

Jake and Four Children are cycling up the path towards the house. One of the smaller children is on a tricycle. When they near the house, the Child on the tricycle begins to slide back down the hill. Jake gets off his bike, pushes Child till they reach the straight, then remounts and rides on.

The other Children ride in circles around large picnic rugs on the grass. Dinah is there with the Smallest Child.

Another angle: the picnic laid out on the grass.

DINAH

Mummy's looking for some plates upstairs.

CHILD

Where's the big red ball?

JAKE

After tea.

Jake goes towards house, goes in door. Child shouts up to top window:

CHILD

Mummy! Can I have the big red ball?

Jo appears at window.

JO
(calling down)

What?

CHILD

I just want to put it on the grass. I won't play with it.

INT. UPPER FLOOR OF NEW HOUSE.

It is empty of furniture. Jo at window. Jake enters.

JO
(to Jake)

Give me the ball.

He does so. She throws it out of window, leans on sill, smiling, as:

JO

Here it is.

CHILD

I'm going to throw it at Dinah.

JO

You'd better not.

Jake picks up a pile of dusty plates. Jo glances at him and smiles. He comes to her. They both look out of window.

Another angle: at window.

Jo and Jake looking down over fields. Suddenly focus on barn, low down, broken, overgrown. (A momentary shot.)

Jo and Jake looking at each other.

JAKE

I love you.

INT. BEDROOM. JO'S FATHER'S HOUSE. DAY.

Mr James in bed, Jo beside him. Her Mother sobbing by window. Mr James's hands reach for Jo's, grasp them, draw them to his eyes, hold them to his eyes. Hold them. Drop them. Stillness. Silence. Jo's face. Mother sobs at window. Bed still. Body.

INT. STAIRCASE. FATHER'S HOUSE. DAY.

Sheets and blankets being carried up by two old women.

INT. LIVING-ROOM. FATHER'S HOUSE. EVENING.

Jo and Mother drinking brandy.

MOTHER

He was such a good man. Nobody knew how good he was. Have you told Jake yet? He was very fond of George. He was, I know. And George was fond of him. George really was fond of him.

JO

I know.

MOTHER

He didn't care for any of the others much, but I don't know . . . he was really *fond* of Jake.

JO

Jake was fond of him, too.

MOTHER

I know he was.

(*Pause.*)

I'll never see him again. I'm glad he wanted to be cremated. I wish I could believe I'd see him again. But I'm glad he'll be cremated. I couldn't bear to think of him buried . . . The thought of him under that . . . I mean just the thought . . .

JO

Mother . . .

MOTHER

Just to think, just to think of him . . .

JO

Mother, listen, I want to tell you something.

*Mother turns, looks at Jo. Silence. Jo goes over to table, picks up
bottle of sedative and spoon.*

I'm . . .

MOTHER

What? No! You can't! You're not! You're not! You
can't!

JO

Well, there it is . . .

MOTHER

But . . . but . . . what can Jake be thinking of?

Jo pours sedative into spoon, gives it to Mother, as:

JO

He doesn't know. Nobody knows.

MOTHER

You must be mad! Aren't you ever going to get any rest?

JO

It'll be all right, really.

MOTHER

How can you be so careless, so thoughtless! It's lunacy!
How can you want to start all that over again?

INT. LIVING-ROOM. JO'S FATHER'S HOUSE. DAY.

Jake, Jo, Dinah and Jo's Mother. They all wear coats.

163

MOTHER
(*to Jake*)

He was so fond of you. He was. He was so proud of you
too. He really was. Only the other night he said we must
go and see your new film. He did. Of course, he
couldn't go . . .

JAKE

No . . .

MOTHER

No, oh no, he couldn't go.

FRONT DRIVE OF HOUSE. THEIR POINT OF VIEW THROUGH
WINDOW.

The hearse draws up.

Back to scene.

MOTHER

Oh dear, there they are. There they are.

She holds Jo's hand.

The Undertaker comes through the front door.

UNDERTAKER

We can't . . . quite . . . get to the front door. Could the
gentleman please move his car?

JAKE
(*to Mother*)

You go into the garden. I'll . . .

EXT. GARDEN. JO'S FATHER'S HOUSE.

Jo, Dinah and Jo's Mother, walking.

MOTHER

He loved his vegetables. We never bought a single

vegetable until last winter. He just couldn't manage it any more. Remember the strawberries, Dinah? You loved his strawberries.

DINAH

Yes, they were marvellous.

MOTHER

I know you did.

Jake appears.

JAKE

A few minutes.

They all walk.

JO

How's things at home?

JAKE

Fine.

DINAH

Chaos.

JAKE

Of course it isn't. All in control.

MOTHER

Oh, I don't know what George would have said if he knew.

JAKE

Mmmm? About what?

JO

You could let this off for allotments, couldn't you?

MOTHER

He loved the children, but he always thought there were too many. Always. I don't know what you're thinking of, Jake, really.

JAKE

What do you mean?

JO

Are they ready yet?

MOTHER

It's too much. I'm glad he didn't live to see it.

JO
(*to Dinah*)

Go and find out if they're ready.

JAKE

What do you mean? See what?

DINAH

Won't they tell us when they're ready?

JO

No, they won't. They might be waiting, or something.
Go on, please.

DINAH

O.K.

Dinah goes.

MOTHER

At least he's going to be cremated. I'm so glad about
that.

Jake looks at Jo.

JAKE

Live to see what?

Pause.

MOTHER

On top of everything else. As if she hasn't got enough.
Mind you, he loved them, he loved the children.

166

Jake stands still and stares at Jo.

Dinah appears around the corner.

EXT. FRONT OF JO'S FATHER'S HOUSE.

Two Teenage Boys, gawky, standing in school uniform. The hearse.

The group appears from the garden. Jake walks apart, smoking.

> MOTHER
> Oh, look, the boys are here. The boys have come.

She goes to them, Jo stays a moment with Dinah.

> DINAH
> Who are they?

> JO
> Your brothers.

> DINAH
> Good God!

Dinah goes to them. Jo looks round to Jake.

Close-up of Jo.

Close-up of Jake not looking, collar up.

Another angle: Jo walks towards the group.

Another angle: The Boys watch her come.

Close-up of Jake.

The group.

> PETE
> Hullo, Mum.

> JO
> Hullo.

JACK

Hullo.

JO

Hullo.

Pause.

Mother brings her handkerchief to her mouth.

                    (*to Dinah, indicating her Mother.*)
     Dinah . . .

DINAH
(*looking at boys*)
I wouldn't have believed it.

She draws Mother away.

JO
(*to boys*)
What do you think of your sister?

JACK

Pretty good.

Pause.

JO
Are you . . . everything all right?

JACK

Fine.

Pause.

PETE

Yes. Fine.

Pause.

JO

Good.

EXT. FRONT OF JO'S FATHER'S HOUSE. ANOTHER ANGLE.

All getting into cars. Jake alone, in Jaguar, moves swiftly away.

> MOTHER
> (*to Jo*)
> Poor Jake – he's so upset. He was always so very fond of
> George.

INT. DINAH'S BEDROOM. ST JOHN'S WOOD. HOUSE. NIGHT.

Dinah, dressed, on floor with book. Jo.

> DINAH
> It was when the coffin went in, when they pushed it in,
> you know, I think that's when it was. I suddenly
> thought, well, it might be possible. You know . . . God
> might be possible. Have you ever read Thomas
> Aquinas? I'm reading this book, it's marvellous. 'That
> the Divine Being cannot be specified by the Addition of
> a Substantial Difference.' See what I mean?

INT. LANDING OUTSIDE DINAH'S ROOM.

*Jo comes out of Dinah's room, closes door, starts down stairs –
then suddenly changes her mind, turns.*

INT. TOP STAIRCASE.

Jo climbing up stairs to:

INT. ATTIC.

*Jo enters. Junk everywhere. Jo looks around, and walks slowly
over to corner. She reaches out and pulls down a cot, a rubber
bath.*

The rubber bath is perished. She stands looking at it, looks up.

A high chair, a pair of scales, stuck up in corner, out of reach.

Jo begins to clamber over suitcases to reach them – stops, as she hears the front door slam, footsteps. She turns in sudden panic, throws bath back on to pile, makes for the door.

INT. STAIRWAY.

Jo descending stairs to hall.

INT. SITTING-ROOM. NIGHT.

Fire in grate. Jake, having just come in, settling himself by it. Jo enters.

JO

You look awful.

JAKE

I feel awful.

She sits on other side of fire. They look into it. She kicks her shoes off.

You must be tired.

JO

Mmmm.

Pause.

And you.

JAKE

Mmmm.

Pause.

JO

I'm sorry.

Pause.

JAKE

Sorry?

Pause.

                         JO
    I know you don't want it.
                    (*Pause.*)
    I know . . . you don't want the baby.

                         JAKE
    Do you?

Pause.

                         JO
    I'm sorry . . . I'm sorry . . .

Pause.

                         JAKE
    It can't be helped.

                         JO
    It'll be all right, it will . . . I mean, you'll like it . . . I
    mean, perhaps it'll be a boy . . . you haven't got nearly
    enough boys. When we get the house ready we can
    spend the summer there. We can spread out a bit . . . I
    mean, you won't notice.

                         JAKE
    All right. It doesn't matter.

                         JO
    It does. It does matter.
                    (*Pause.*)
    You mean you . . . you really don't want it?

                         JAKE
    No.

She stands, walks.

                         JO
    What do you want then?

                        171

JAKE

It doesn't matter, does it?

Pause.

JO

Why?

Pause.

JAKE

I don't want it. That's why.
(*Pause.*)
I wanted us to change. Now we can't change. You see?
It's my fault. It's because of me, I know that. But I
thought we could change . . . branch out . . . be free.
(*Pause.*)
Now there's no chance.
(*Pause.*)
We're back where we were.

She goes to him, holds him.

I'm not blaming you, I'm blaming myself. It's my fault,
I know that. We haven't . . . lived together. But it's just
that I've suddenly realized . . . that we could lead a
more sensible life. It was possible. We haven't lived.
(*Pause.*)
We don't need it. It'll kill us. We could begin, you see,
we could really begin . . . I know it . . . you know, to
. . . You know what I mean. I mean there is a world,
there is a world apart from birth, there's a world apart
from . . . we don't want any more . . . how can we have
any more?

Silence.

I know the idea of abortion is repellant to you, I know
that. It is to me, too. You must admit I've never
suggested it.

172

Silence.

It's ghastly, the idea of abortion, I know that. Ghastly.
(*Silence.*)
I wouldn't dream of suggesting it.
(*Silence.*)
But after all, it would be perfectly legal, you've just been
treated for depression, I mean the Doctor said . . . there
wouldn't be anything underhand about it.

Close-up of Jake.

After all, I got you into this. I just want to make you
happy. All those boring months, the pain at the end. I
just want to get you out of it. I want to get us both out
of it while there's still time, that's all.

INT. SURGEON'S OFFICE. NURSING HOME. DAY.

Surgeon and Jo.

SURGEON
(*with papers*)
Now, Mrs Armitage . . . I've had a talk with your
husband . . . and I did suggest to him that . . . in your
case . . . we might consider going somewhat further
than this . . . operation. I recommend pursuing, shall
we say, a more sensible, long-term policy. Has he
spoken to you about it?

JO
I . . . don't think so.

SURGEON
No. Good. I thought it would be better to speak to you
myself.

JO
What do you mean?

173

SURGEON

The reasons for recommending that this pregnancy be
terminated, you see, would seem to apply with equal
validity to any future pregnancy. Do you see what I
mean?

(*Pause.*)

You've had a considerable number of children. Perhaps
it would be wise for you not to have any more.

JO

How do you do that?

SURGEON

It's a matter of sterilization. Quite simple. You can lead
a completely normal married life, but you'll never
conceive.

JO

Oh.

(*Pause.*)

What did my husband say?

SURGEON

Oh, he left the decision entirely to you, of course. As we
do.

INT. JO'S ROOM IN NURSING HOME. NIGHT

Jo is lying in bed, silent, alone, eyes open, still.

INT. JO'S ROOM IN NURSING HOME. DAY. CLOSE-UP OF JO.

*In nightdress, head flung back on pillow, laughing. She is still in
bed. Jake sits on chair.*

JAKE

Be careful. You'll hurt yourself.

JO

I'm so happy.

174

JAKE

Good.

JO

You don't know what it's like to be sterilized. You've never been sterilized.

JAKE

Never.

JO

It's wonderful. I'm free, you see, free. Aren't I? Completely free.

JAKE

Yes. I know.

JO

We don't have to worry about it any more, you see. It'll just never happen again. We just don't have to worry about all that ever again.

He kisses her, leaning.

JAKE

No. Never.

JO

I'm going to get rid of that Nanny for a start. I've always hated her. In the summer, we'll be able to move to the country, won't we?

JAKE

Yes.

JO

We can live with the children again, properly, and then we can go away, just do anything, just do anything.

JAKE

Yes.

He takes her hand and kisses it.

Close-up of Jake's face smiling, gentle.

INT. JO'S ROOM IN NURSING HOME. EVENING.

The room is full of flowers. Jo in bed. Dinah with a small bunch of violets.

> DINAH
>
> I brought you these.

> JO
>
> Oh . . . thank you.

> DINAH
>
> They don't stand much of a chance with all these others.

> JO
>
> Oh yes they do.

> DINAH
> *(examining flowers)*
> Look at this! Wow! Who are they all from?

> JO
> *(laughing)*
> I haven't the slightest idea.

Dinah sits on the bed.

> DINAH
>
> You feeling all right now?

> JO
>
> Mmmm. Marvellous.

> DINAH
>
> It was a sort of . . . womb thing, I suppose, was it?

JO

Yes . . . something like that.

DINAH

Does it happen to everyone?

JO

No, of course not.

DINAH

Just happens to some women, does it?

JO

Mmmmmm.

A silence.

Look, come on, help me make this list, we're going to make a clean sweep.

Jo gives Dinah pencil and paper.

DINAH

What list?

JO

There's going to be some changes made.

DINAH

Good. What?

JO

We're going to do things. First, sack that Nanny.

DINAH

Good!

JO

Sack Nanny, put it down.

DINAH

I am. When?

JO

Immediately.

DINAH

Right. Next.

JO

Start moving things to the new house.

DINAH

Wonderful. What things?

JO

Anything.

DINAH

All that junk in the attic?

JO

Yes, all that junk.

DINAH

It isn't all junk.

JO

Just put it down.

DINAH

How?

JO

Move junk to new house. Send everything to cleaners.

DINAH

We haven't phoned the removal people.

JO

Phone removal people.

DINAH

Get your hair cut.

JO

Sack the Nanny.

DINAH

We've got that.

JO

Throw away junk.

DINAH

But we're going to move the junk.

JO

No, we're not going to move the junk, we're going to move the things we want.

DINAH

Sort out the things we want.

JO

Make a clean sweep.

Another angle to include door.

Jake comes in.

JAKE

Hullo, what's all this?

Jo hides the list.

JO

Nothing.

JAKE

Let's have a look.

DINAH

You can't.

Jake slips list out from under pillow, reads it.

Jake writes.

179

JAKE

Here you are.

DINAH

What have you put?

She grabs it.

'Love Jake.'

A short laugh between Jo and Jake.

He goes to flowers and looks at them.

He goes to flowers and looks at them.

There's a pile of old sheets in the cupboard. We never use them.

JO

Throw them out.

JAKE

Beautiful flowers. Very nice of them all, isn't it?

Dinah looks at Jo.

JO

Yes.

JAKE

Have you . . . written to them, thanked them?

JO

Yes.

JAKE

Good. Good. Written to the Conways?

JO

Mmmm.

JAKE

Good.

THE PUMPKIN EATER

INT. MAIN BEDROOM. ST JOHN'S WOOD. HOUSE. DAY.

Jake putting suitcases down. Jo comes into the room. They look at each other. She flings herself into his arms. Onto bed.

INT. HALL. DAY.

Jo, Removal Men, Children. Jo crisp, decisive, authoritative. Children are playing games in the hall.

> JO
> (*to Man*)
> You will keep that upright, won't you?

> MAN
> Yes, Miss.

> JO
> (*to Child*)
> Come on now, let the man get through.

As Man starts out through door with his load:

> (*To Foreman.*)
> Is that it?

> FOREMAN
> That tallboy, Miss . . .

> JO
> No, no. That stays here.

> FOREMAN
> That's about it then.

The phone rings. Jo goes into sitting room.

> CHILD
> (*to Man*)
> I'll give you a hand.

MAN

I can manage, thanks.

INT. SITTING-ROOM.

Jo at phone.

JO

Hello . . .

CONWAY

This is Bob Conway.

JO

Who?

CONWAY

Conway, you know, Beth's husband.

JO

Oh, Mr Conway, how are you? I'm afraid Jake's at the studio.

CONWAY

Actually, I wanted to . . .

JO
(*interrupting*)

Could you hold on for just a minute . . .
(*To Removal Man.*)
Mrs Teff will be waiting for you at the house.

REMOVAL MAN

Mrs Teff. Right Madam. Thank you.

JO

Thank you.
(*To Conway.*)
Sorry . . .

CONWAY

I was wondering if you could have tea with me
tomorrow.

JO

What?

CONWAY

Something I wanted to talk to you about.

JO

Oh, I don't think I could really manage tomorrow. I'm
taking the children to the zoo.

CONWAY

Splendid! What could be nicer?

JO

What?

CONWAY

I mean, why don't I see you there?

JO

All right. Why don't you meet us all at that place by the
penguins – the tea place. Do you know it?

CONWAY

Perfect!

JO

Fine.

CONWAY

I shall look forward to it. Thank you.

JO

See you there about four o'clock.

CONWAY

Good-bye now.

JO

Bye-bye.

EXT. ZOO CAFÉ.

Jo, Conway, Fergus, Elizabeth and Nanny seated around tea table. Mark feeding penguins.

CONWAY
(*to Elizabeth*)
Don't you look pretty in that dress?
(*To Fergus.*)
What animals do you like best?

JO

Mark . . .

Mark moves forward.

CONWAY
(*to Mark*)

What about you?

MARK

Penguins.

Laughter.

CONWAY

Aren't they delicious!

ELIZABETH

May we see the bears now?

JO

All right. But don't run away from Nanny.

NANNY

Elizabeth!

They run down the steps, Nanny following Elizabeth.

184

CONWAY
(*warmly*)

Well, how are you?

JO

Fine.

CONWAY

So nice of you to come. I'm very pleased you could manage it, I must say. Was it very inconvenient?

JO

No, no, it's all right, don't quite know what . . .

CONWAY

No, it's a bit of a mystery, isn't it, never mind, let's have some tea.

Calls.

Miss!

Then.

Got a surprise did you, when I phoned?
Ha-ha. Still, I think secret meetings are rather gay, don't you?

JO

Well, it depends on what . . . they're all about.

CONWAY

Ah! Too true! What are you going to have, brown bread and jam, or marmalade, scones, toasted tea cakes, a lettuce sandwich, cucumber sandwich, cakes, gateaux, pastries, Welsh rarebits, anything you like.

A Waitress has come up to the table.

(*To Waitress.*)

Isn't that true?

WAITRESS

What?

CONWAY

That we can have anything we like.

WAITRESS

Anything that's on there.

CONWAY

Well, what'll it be?

JO

Just tea.

CONWAY

Really? That all? Ah well, right, tea for two, and . . .
(*looks at menu*)
. . . tea for two. Wait a minute, what about lemon tea?
Look, it's on the menu.

JO

All right, lemon tea.

CONWAY
(*to Waitress*)
Lemon tea – for two.

Waitress goes off.

I nearly missed it. I nearly missed it on the menu, didn't
see it, and then suddenly I looked and there it was –
lemon tea! How are you? You look marvellous.

JO

Yes, I am. You seem in pretty good trim yourself.

CONWAY

I always am, quite frankly. I'm always on top of the
world, as a matter of fact. Feel better after your stay in
the Nursing Home, do you?

JO

Yes. Oh, thank you for the flowers.

CONWAY

Don't mention it. Beth and I thought of you a lot. Yes, we did. We thought of you a great deal. Especially quite recently.

Waitress brings tea.

(*To Waitress.*)

Oh, thanks. Lovely.

Pause. Waitress goes off.

It's rather fun meeting you like this, isn't it? Just you and me. All alone. You're an intelligent woman. Why don't we make a habit of it, eh?
(*He takes her hand, continues.*)
What do you think?

She looks at his hand on hers – withdraws hers slowly.

JO

(*with a smile*)

I'd have to ask my husband.

CONWAY

Oh yes, of course, you're married aren't you. Yes. Yes, that reminds me of what I wanted to talk to you about. I'll tell you what it is. It's nothing much. It's just that a letter has come into my hands, you see. I won't bother to tell you how. But anyway, I've got this letter on me, you see. I mean, I've got it on me now, you see, in my pocket . . . can I read you . . . something of it . . . ?

Pause.

JO

Why?

CONWAY

It's from my wife.
>(*Takes out letter, opens it, reads.*)
'Jake baby, How are you, honey lamb, are you still managing without me? Poor darling . . .'

Another angle on Jo listening, Conway's Voice continues, very dim, indecipherable.

Another angle on Conway reading.

'. . . Don't let your eyes stray to those luscious bits hanging round the set, they're no good when it comes to it as well you know. I'm saving myself for you like you told me, although it's pretty difficult, you understand . . .'

Another angle on Jo listening.

Another angle on Conway reading.

'. . . waiting to soothe you, honey love. How brave, courageous, and tough you are to face it all alone . . .'

Conway and Jo at table.

I've been checking up. He rang her this morning. Did you know that? When they were in the studio, he sent her flowers every day, did you know *that*? He's crazy about her, duckie, he's mad about her. He can't keep off it. He had that other one before Beth, whats-her-name, it doesn't matter, until she got fed up with him. He's not much good in bed, I understand.

Jo stands up. He pulls her down. She holds her side.

JO

I'm ill.

CONWAY

You had an abortion, didn't you? Shall I tell you why?

Because Beth's a good girl at heart, she would have left him. He made you have it so that he could keep Beth. She told me, for Christ's sake! She's a lovely girl. She's going to starve for me. She's going to starve. I wouldn't touch her with a barge pole, not even if she came crawling . . .

JO

I want to go.

CONWAY

Listen, if he ever rings her or sees her again, I'll fry him. You understand? I'll boil him. You tell him that.

JO

No.

CONWAY

You'd better. He's not a grown man, your husband, he's a puking boy. He can't even lay a girl without the whole world knowing it. Beth says he makes her sick with his slop. I made her swear on the baby's head she was telling the truth. I brought the baby in and told her to swear on its head. Tell him to keep off, well off . . .

JO

You can tell him yourself.

CONWAY

If I hear his stinking voice I'll pull it out of his throat.

JO

Is that all? I want to go.

CONWAY

Listen. Tell me something. Is it true that when he's in bed he likes to . . .

Jo stands, runs out of the café.

EXT. TEASHOP.

Jo, clasping her side, running, past monkeys.

INT. SITTING-ROOM. NIGHT.

Jake and Jo.

> JO
>
> Did you sleep with Philpot?

> JAKE
>
> Oh, Christ, it's years ago, it's gone –

> JO
>
> Did you?

> JAKE
>
> Yes, of course I did.

> JO
>
> You told me you hadn't.

> JAKE
>
> I lied. So what? What else did you expect me to do?

> JO
>
> Here? In the house?

> JAKE
>
> I don't remember. Yes.

> JO
>
> Often?

> JAKE
>
> As often as we could. What's the point? What the hell does it matter?

> JO
>
> What about all the others?

JAKE

What others?

JO

The others.

JAKE

There weren't any others.

JO

How many?

JAKE

Half a dozen. A dozen. I don't know. What does the number matter?

JO

When you were away, or when you were here?

JAKE

When I was away! Is that what you want me to say?

JO

If it's true.

JAKE

Then it was while I was away.

Pause.

You live in a dream world, you know that?

Pause.

JO

Why did you marry me?

JAKE

You know why.

JO

What do you think of marriage?

JAKE

It doesn't exist, it doesn't exist, so what? What do you
mean? It doesn't matter what I think about it. It exists,
that's what I think about it.

JO

Why did you go to bed with Beth?

JAKE

Oh –

JO

Didn't you ever . . . try not to?

JAKE

Yes . . . Yes.

JO

When I was in the nursing home, didn't you mind?

JAKE

Mind? Of course I minded! I came to see you every
evening, didn't I?

JO

And you met her afterwards.

JAKE

That's ridiculous, for God's sake, it's –

JO

Where did you meet?

JAKE

It's not true!

JO

Near the nursing home?

JAKE

Not very far. I don't know where it was. Anyway, it

never happened. What are you doing? You haven't
exactly been a model of faithfulness yourself, have you?

JO

I was never unfaithful to anyone. To anyone. Ever.

JAKE

Christ, what a bloody hypocrite you are.

JO

Did you stay the night, or just a few hours?

JAKE

Why don't you shut up? Why don't you die?

JO

How should I die?

JAKE

I don't know. Leave me.

JO

I can die here . . . What shall we do?

JAKE

Nothing. I love you. I've always loved you.

JO

He says you love her. He says you make her sick with
your love.

JAKE

He's crazy, he's a madman.

JO

Was Philpot the first, or were there others before?

JAKE

Of course there weren't.

JO

How many? Who were they?

JAKE

What others?

JO

How often?

JAKE

There weren't any others.

JO

Did you bring them here?

JAKE

How could I bring them here?

JO

Where did you take them?

JAKE

It never happened.

EXT. GARDEN OF JO'S FATHER'S HOUSE, SHOOTING FROM
GARDEN THROUGH HOUSE TO FRONT. AFTERNOON.

*We can see right through the house to the front gate where the
Floride is parked. Jo and Mother are walking into house. Jo is
carrying an overnight bag. She walks uncertainly, nervously.
Mother is talking without pause.*

MOTHER

I don't know what to do. I wish I knew what to do. I've
been sitting here, thinking about it. And then you came. I
had a feeling you'd come. I don't know what to do, but I
think we ought to face it. You're shivering. Are you cold?

JO

No.

*The Mother continues talking and, as she does so, moves forward
into foreground, into the garden. Jo puts bag down, stands a
moment in doorway alone before following.*

MOTHER
(*as she comes into garden*)

Put your bag down. It's not cold. But we've got to face
it. George loved his garden. He wouldn't want strangers
in his garden with spades and things digging up his
garden. I'm not going to do it. I've made up my mind.
Don't you think I'm right.

JO
(*joining her*)

Yes.

*Another angle as they approach a table on the lawn where tea is
laid out. Deck chairs.*

MOTHER

When the boys get back we'll have tea.

JO

The boys?

MOTHER

Pete and Jack. They came to see me yesterday. They'll
always come, they said. George was so fond of them. He
was fond of Jake too. They'll be back in a minute, then
we'll have tea. I was so pleased you had such a sensible
operation. So sensible. It must be so wonderful for Jake,
not to have that awful worry over his head any more.
He's worked so hard for you.

*In the distance by the back gate, behind some bushes, we see the
boys, Pete and Jack, meandering haphazardly, kicking a ball
slowly between them. Jo watches them approach.*

George would never forgive me. He loved his garden,
but the boys will look after it.

The Boys appear on the lawn, approach slowly, kicking.

They're here. They came in the back gate.

The Boys reach them, with the ball. They smile faintly at Jo, who does the same.

Did you come in the back gate?

PETE

Mmmm.

MOTHER

Did you see who's here?

The Boys mutter 'hullo'. Jo does the same.

PETE
(*to Jo*)

You're looking very well.

JACK

Very well.

MOTHER

We'll have tea in a minute. Pete won the hundred yards. Did you tell your mother?

Jack giggles.

JO
(*to Pete*)

Did you?

PETE

Yeh. The two-twenty, too.

JO

Oh good.

Silence.

PETE

I like your car.

JACK

It's a Floride.

JO

Yes.

PETE

Good car. Fast.

Pete kicks the ball to Jack. The Boys sit on the grass.

Did you have lots of traffic?

JO

Traffic?

PETE

On the way down.

JO

Oh. No.

Silence. Jack turns on his front, whispers something to Pete. They giggle. Mother closes her eyes, murmurs:

MOTHER
(*murmuring*)

I often think . . .

The Boys whisper and giggle.

. . . the birds wake me up now . . .

Pete balances the ball on his head.

. . . every morning . . .

Jo sits in deckchair, clutching her arms.

INT. SITTING-ROOM. DAY.

Jo at window.

She goes to table, looks in an address book, puts it down. Goes to mantelpiece. One bottle on it. She pours a drink, looks at bottle. It is almost empty. Knock at door.

197

JO

Come in.

Door opens. Smallest Child comes in, on reins, held from outside. Young Nanny can just be seen in hall.

NANNY

Say 'Good-bye Mummy'.

Jo and Child look at each other. Silence. Jo looks at Child. Child totters, smiles, is doubtful.

Say 'Good-bye Mummy'.

Jo stands still.

The reins tighten. The Nanny remains outside. Child scratches its head.

JO

Have a nice walk.

Child is pulled back, looks round for Nanny.

Child disappears. Hear bells on reins tinkling.

INT. HALL. NIGHT.

Empty. Doorbell rings.

Another angle.

Jo opens door, drink in hand. A Jamaican in camelhair coat, beard.

MAN

Good evening.

JO

Good evening.

MAN

I hope you are not alarmed by my call.

JO

No.

MAN

May I introduce myself to you?

JO

Yes. Do.

MAN

I am the new King of Israel, appointed by Yahweh, the
Eternal Lord God. I have come to give you my blessing.

Pause.

I have been anointed. I am the King of Judah.

JO

I see.

MAN

In the Emphasized Bible, the name of Yahweh appears
over seven thousand times. I have been appointed to
fulfil the prophecy of Ezekiel. The prophecy appears
seventy-two times in the Book of Ezekiel.

Bows his head.

I bless you.

JO

Would you . . . come inside a second . . .

INT. HALL. ANOTHER ANGLE

The Man stands.

JO

Just a minute.

INT. SITTING-ROOM.

Jo goes to desk, looking for purse. The Man can be seen in the hall.

> MAN
>
> The people are unhappy because they give the gift of their love to unworthy men and unworthy women.

Jo finds purse on mantelpiece, takes out five shillings. When she returns the Man is in the room.

> Continents are no obstruction, mountains are no obstruction, oceans are no impediment. The Word is the work.

She gives him the money.

> JO
>
> Here, please.

> MAN
>
> This will help me. My aim is to build a radio station in Jerusalem.

The phone rings. Jo half turns, uncertain.

> The music of the Word can emanate and issue out through the miracle of the medium of the modern channels of communication . . .

> JO
>
> Excuse me.

She picks up phone.

> CONWAY'S VOICE
> (*over phone*)
>
> Mrs Armitage – ?

> JO
>
> She's not in.

Pause.

> CONWAY'S VOICE
> That's you, isn't it?

> JO
> I don't know what you mean.

> CONWAY'S VOICE
> All right. Give her a message. Tell her Beth Conway's pregnant.

Another angle on Jo.

Silence.

> It's not mine. I thought she might be interested.

> JO
> I'll tell her.

> CONWAY'S VOICE
> Tell her my wife's going to have this kid in a public ward, and if there's any way of stopping her getting a whiff of gas I'll find it.

> JO
> She can't have it.

> CONWAY'S VOICE
> She's going to have it all right. She's going to wipe its bottom and stare at its ugly mug for the rest of her life. No more gay life for my little Beth. This kid's going to make her curse Jake Armitage until she's dead . . . I'm going to grind the slime out of her. I'm going to see her oozing in her own slime. Until she's dead. She's going to hate that kid almost as much as I will. I'm going to see that she bleeds to death in Jake Armitage's dirt.

Another angle to include Man.

Jo puts the phone down. She turns, looks at the Man. He smiles.

MAN

You will be blessed for this.

INT. MAIN BEDROOM.

Close on Jo's fist crashing into Jake's face. A violent clash of wrists, gasps, sobs, broken sounds.

Jo's feet kicking.

Jake's arm and elbow thrusting her away.

Her nails.

His hand striking her.

His shirt torn.

Her nails on his neck.

His hands at her throat.

Her body falling spread-eagled on the floor.

A bedroom stool hurtling across the room.

Dressing-table mirror as stool smashes into it. It shatters.

Silence. Moans. Breathing.

Long shot. Main bedroom. Jo and Jake.

They remain still, staring at each other, panting.

INT. BEDROOM IN GILES'S FLAT. EVENING.

Jo and Giles in bed. Jo is half dressed. They are smoking and drinking tea.

JO
(*murmuring*)
You always were the sexiest of my husbands.

GILES

Was I?

JO

Hmmm.

Pause.

Why did I leave you?

GILES

I was too sexy.

JO

Yes, perhaps that was it. Perhaps I should try each of my old husbands in turn, see what it's like.

GILES

You could. One of them's dead, that's the trouble.

JO

Which one?

GILES

The one I took over from. Remember? You were a widow at the time.

JO

Oh yes, of course. He was in the army or something, wasn't he?

GILES

That's right. Killed in action.

JO

Well, I couldn't try him again then.

GILES

Old husbands are only good for a night. Dead husbands are only good for a night.

JO

Are they?

GILES

Yes.

JO

But you cried when I left you.

GILES

Did I?

JO

You were heartbroken.

GILES

Yes, I cried. I remember.

JO

That means you must still be mad about me.

GILES

I'm not.

JO

Why not?

GILES

You've changed. You go to bed with your clothes on.

JO

That's only because I have scars I don't want you to see.

GILES

You always had scars.

JO

I have a very new scar.

GILES

What about your husband? Does he mind?

JO

Oh, he doesn't mind. He did it himself, with a monkey wrench.

INT. BAR OF LONDON CLUB. EVENING.

Jake sitting alone at the end of the long bar. A group of Men are in foreground. Conway is one of them, although we don't immediately see him. The Men are laughing. Barman moves down the bar towards Jake with a drink, as:

FIRST MAN

Cyril? Now wait a minute, I haven't seen Cyril –

SECOND MAN

I haven't seen him since –

FIRST MAN

Just a minute, let me think –

SECOND MAN

Cyril?

Laughs.

My goodness!

FIRST MAN

Wait a minute, let me . . . Just a minute, let me think . . .

Jake is given his drink and looks up. Conway raises his glass.

CONWAY
(*calling*)

Cheers! How's the wife?
(*To the two Men.*)
Will you excuse me a moment. Friend of mine.

FIRST MAN

Yes, of course.

(*to Second Man.*)
I'll tell you the last time I saw Cyril . . .

Jake and Conway together on bar stools.

CONWAY

You don't mind my coming up to speak to you, do you?
I mean, I know that script writers after a hard day's
work at the studio like a little drink in peace. But when I
saw you I said to myself, my goodness, there's Jake
Armitage, I've been to his house, we've met, I wonder if
he'd mind if I had a word with him.

JAKE

What makes you think script writers mind being spoken
to?

CONWAY

Don't they?

JAKE

Script writers love being spoken to.

CONWAY

Really?

JAKE

Anyway, it isn't often I get a night out with the boys.

CONWAY

Oh, where's your little wife tonight then?

JAKE

She's opening the Chelsea Flower Show.

CONWAY

Go on!

Pause.

JAKE

By the way, do you play snooker?

206

CONWAY

I do, as a matter of fact.

JAKE

What a shame I don't.

CONWAY

What games do you play?

JAKE

What games? Do you know, honestly, I can't remember.
What games do you play?

CONWAY

Snooker for one.

JAKE

I bet you're pretty good.

CONWAY

Not as good as you.

JAKE

But I don't play.

CONWAY

I don't believe a word of it.

JAKE

Cheers.

A Man passes.

MAN

Hello, Jake.

Jake raises his head and smiles.

CONWAY

Oh, you haven't heard the glad tidings, have you?

JAKE

What's that?

CONWAY

My wife's going to have a baby.

JAKE

Is that so? I say!

CONWAY

Yes, you and your wife must come round to see it. I
understand she's very fond of children.

JAKE

Yes, we'd adore to. How is your wife, by the way?

CONWAY

Tip top. She's at a reception tonight for the Duchess of
Dubrovnik.

JAKE

I thought she *was* the Duchess of Dubrovnik.

CONWAY

My wife? No, no, not at all. Not at all. Not at all.

JAKE
(*laughing*)
Well, you're not the bloody Duke anyway.

*Jake's glass slips from his hand, falls on Conway's lap and then to
the floor. Whisky stains Conway's trousers.*

CONWAY

You've made me wet.

*They stare at each other, their faces close together, bending
forward on their bar stools.*

INT. BEDROOM IN GILES'S FLAT. EVENING.

Giles sits on bed. Jo strokes his arm.

JO

Shall I stay?

Giles smiles, ruffles her hair.

> GILES
> *(gently)*
>
> No, you can't. Killer.

She stiffens.

> JO
>
> What do you mean? Killer? It's him. He's responsible.
> He is.

> GILES
>
> He phoned this morning.

> JO
>
> Did he? Why? Is his bed cold? He doesn't suffer. What
> has he suffered? It's happened to me. It's me. Look at
> me. Look at me.

> GILES
>
> I am.

*They stare at each other for a moment. She slowly closes her eyes.
Silence. She suddenly whispers.*

> JO
>
> What should I have done? It was the only thing I ever
> really . . . that I ever really . . . I've lost it. There was
> something we had . . . It's gone.

Slight pause.

> I don't know . . . how to keep things . . . whole.

Slight pause.

> GILES
>
> He phoned to say his father's dead.

EXT. CEMETERY. DAY.

It is very windy and dull. A coffin is being lowered into a grave. There is a spare group of elderly men, obviously friends of Jake's father, around the grave. Jake stands alone.

As the Parson speaks a short prayer, which we can hardly hear through the wind, we see that Jo has joined the group on the other side of the grave from Jake.

Jake steps forward and throws earth into the grave, then steps back to where he was.

Jo moves round towards Jake. As she does so, we see the old men begin to throw earth into the grave.

Jo stands beside Jake, takes his hand, looks at him. He glances at her and then away. His hand slips from hers. She looks at him. His gaze is fixed on the grave. Jake turns and walks out of the cemetery.

The gravediggers begin to fill in the grave.

Jo is left standing.

EXT. HILLSIDE LEADING TO NEW HOUSE. LATE AFTERNOON.

Jo walking up towards new house.

INT. MAIN ROOM OF NEW HOUSE.

Jo enters. Enormous windows high up, looking down at the silent stillness of the fields. The sky a mist. Mist hanging in the valleys. Noise of birds.

The rooms are empty except for isolated pieces of furniture. Jo pauses for a moment, then locks all the doors.

INT. KITCHEN OF NEW HOUSE.

Jo wanders in. No food. No sign of life. Empty. Unused. Bare.

INT. MAIN ROOM.

Jo takes telephone off hook, sits down by window.

The window.

Sun through mist.

INT. MAIN ROOM. CATS.

Snaking, on bare floorboards.

INT. BEDROOM. NEW HOUSE. NIGHT.

Jo lying awake. The moon through the uncurtained windows.

Cats asleep on bed.

INT. MAIN ROOM. NIGHT. JO.

At window, smoking.

The window. Daylight.

INT. STAIRCASE.

Jo climbs stairs.

INT. ROOM AT TOP OF NEW HOUSE.

Jo enters, opens window, looks down towards barn.

Jo's face.

Another angle: Jo at window.

She opens window wider. Stops.

Jo's face.

Another angle: Jo at window.

In the distance, through the window, see numbers of Children fanning out like trappers, converging on house, Jake bringing up the rear.

Close-up on children's legs.

Sticks whipping grass.

Long shot. Jake and Children.

Jo at window motionless. She shuts window. Calls from Children as they reach house. Bangs on the locked doors. Glass breaking. Door opening. Sudden flood of voices.

> CHILD'S VOICE

Where is she?

> SECOND CHILD'S VOICE

Upstairs.

> THIRD CHILD'S VOICE

Probably still in bed.

> FOURTH CHILD'S VOICE

I'm going to feed the cats.

> JAKE'S VOICE

Jo –

Jo's face calms, becomes still.

High angle shooting down staircase.

Jo walks down the stairs towards them, stops midway.

Jake stands at foot of stairs, arms full of parcels, surrounded by Children. The Children look at Jo curiously, but do not go to her.

> JAKE

We thought we might join you for a while.

He goes towards the kitchen with some of the Children, also carrying parcels. Other Children rush past Jo up the stairs. She remains standing on the stairs.

INT. KITCHEN. NEW HOUSE.

Jake and Children undoing parcels. Jo can be seen on the stairs in background.

                    JAKE
Where's that coffee pot?

                    CHILD
                (shouting to Jo)
We didn't know where you were.

                    JAKE
Let's give it a wash. Get the cups out, Dinah.

                    DINAH
Where are they?

                    CHILD
I know.

More Children rush in with cats. During the ensuing dialogue Jo slowly descends the stairs and enters the kitchen. The Children speak to her from a distance, tentatively.

                    JAKE
Did we bring any milk?

                    CHILD ONE
Where's the big red ball?

                    JAKE
Later. Who's got the milk? Where are all those bags?

                    DINAH
Let me do it.

CHILD THREE
(*to Jo*)

I've got a bandage. Look!

CHILD TWO

I want some orange squash.

JAKE
(*pulling cans of beer from bag*)

Where's the opener?

CHILD ONE

I won't play with it. I just want to put it on the grass.

DINAH

Put all that paper in the bin.

JAKE

The opener . . .

CHILD THREE
(*to Jo*)

Can I tell you a story?

CHILD TWO
(*to Jo*)

I've got ten stars for reading.

Dinah hands opener to Jake.

DINAH

Here you are. Do you want cabbage or carrots?

Jake opens beer can. It spurts. Children react noisily.

I'll wipe it.

CHILD FOUR

I'll do it.

DINAH

Where's the tea-cloth?

214

Jake offers can of beer to Jo.

                        JAKE
    Want one?

                        JO
    Yes, I'll have one.

She takes it, starts drinking from the can.

The Quiller Memorandum

The Quiller Memorandum was first presented by The Rank
Organization on 10th November 1966 with the following cast:

KENNETH LINDSAY JONES Herbert Stass
RUSHINGTON Robert Flemyng
GIBBS George Sanders
QUILLER George Segal
POL Alec Guinness
HENGEL Peter Carsten
BARMAN Hans Schwarz
DORFMANN Victor Beaumont
HASSLER Gunter Meisner
WENG Robert Helpmann
SCHOOL PORTER Konrad Thoms
FRAU SCHROEDER Edith Schneider
INGE Senta Berger
MAN, A John Rees
MAN, B Philip Madoc
MAN, C Harry Brooks
GRAUBER Ernst Walder
MAN, F Bernard Egan
OKTOBER Max von Sydow
DOCTOR Paul Hansard
MAN, H Sean Arnold
MAN, I Janos Kurucz
BARMAN Carl Duering
NIGHTPORTER Philo Hauser
ASSISTANT Brigitte Laufer
MAN, J Nikolaus Dutsch
NAGEL Ves Delahunt
MAN, K Peter Lang
MAN, L Herbert Fux
MAN, M Peter Goldmann
MAN, N Malte Petzel
MAN, O Axel Anderson
MAN, P Wolfgang Priewe
HUGHES Claus Tinney

Directed by Michael Anderson

EXT. BERLIN TIERGARTEN. SUMMER NIGHT.

A long road. Derelict buildings at either side.

It is late at night.

In the distance, Kenneth Lindsay Jones is walking towards the camera.

Silence.

The camera moves sideways to disclose a brightly lit telephone box. It is the one hard source of light.

His face, as he stops by a lamp post. He lights one cigarette from another, flips the first one away and glances up at the buildings and along the road behind him.

There is no one in sight.

He continues to walk towards the telephone box. From the telephone box see him approach. His footsteps echo. He walks slowly past the telephone box and stops. He glances up the street again. No one. He drops his cigarette.

He moves suddenly and enters the telephone box.

INT. TELEPHONE BOX. NIGHT.

Jones inserts a coin, lifts receiver. He begins to dial. He dials one figure and a second figure.

A sudden report. Window smashes. Glass falls in.

Jones hits interior of box with great force. He falls in a heap, his head cracking against telephone.

EXT. ROAD. NIGHT.

The telephone box, brightly lit. A shape on the floor. No movement or sound along the road.

INT. LONDON CLUB. DAY.

A Waiter is serving potatoes to two gentlemen.

> RUSHINGTON
> Thanks. That's . . . quite sufficient, thank you.

The Waiter nods and goes.

> GIBBS
> Salt?

> RUSHINGTON
> Oh, thanks.

They salt their food and begin to eat.

> GIBBS
> What exactly is he doing now?

> RUSHINGTON
> He's on leave, actually. On vacation.

> GIBBS
> Ah.

They eat.

> Well, perhaps someone might get in touch with him.

> RUSHINGTON
> Oh yes, certainly. No difficulty about that.

> GIBBS
> Ask him if he'd mind popping over to Berlin.

> RUSHINGTON
> Mmmm. I think so.

GIBBS

Good.

They eat.

Shame about K.L.J.

RUSHINGTON

Mmmm.

GIBBS

How was he killed?

RUSHINGTON

Shot.

GIBBS

What gun?

RUSHINGTON

Long shot in spine, actually. Nine point three. Same as Metzler.

GIBBS

Oh, really?

They eat.

How's your lunch?

RUSHINGTON

Rather good.

GIBBS

What is it?

RUSHINGTON

Pheasant.

GIBBS

Ah. Yes, that should be rather good. Is it?

RUSHINGTON
It is rather, yes.

EXT. OLYMPIC STADIUM. BERLIN. DAY.

Quiller is walking towards the entrance, away from the camera.
He passes through the gates.

INT. OLYMPIC STADIUM. DAY.

A group of people pass in foreground.

As their voices recede, the camera remains on Pol who is sitting on
the edge of one of the tiers below. He is eating sandwiches.

Quiller comes into the foreground and stands for a moment
looking down at Pol, his back still to the camera.

Quiller descends the steps and stops by the side of Pol.

Pol does not look up. He continues eating.

QUILLER
Excuse me. Do you have a light?

Pol looks up.

POL
Certainly.

Pol takes out a lighter and lights Quiller's cigarette.

As Quiller bends to the light his face is seen for the first time.

Quiller takes a packet of Chesterfields from his pocket.

QUILLER
Do you smoke this brand?

POL
No I don't think I know that brand.

QUILLER

Perhaps I might introduce it to you.

POL

Thank you.

Pol takes a cigarette from the packet and puts it in his top pocket. He moves his legs and indicates the seat beside him. Quiller crosses him and sits down. Pol bites into his sandwich and grins at Quiller.

Ever been here before?

QUILLER

No.

POL

Impressive isn't it? Built by Werner in 1936. For the Olympics. It holds one hundred thousand people.
(*He points.*)
Certain well-known personalities used to stand right up there. Must have been quite noisy. One hundred thousand people – all cheering. Wouldn't you say? Yes, quite noisy.

He offers the sandwiches to Quiller.

Some leberwurst?

QUILLER

No thanks.

POL

Or some schinken?
(*He examines the sandwich.*)
No, wait a moment, what am I talking about, this isn't schinken, it's knackwurst. What about some knackwurst?

QUILLER

I'm not hungry.

POL

Aren't you? I am.

He bites into the sandwich, chews a moment and then stands.

You don't mind if I eat while we walk?

He walks up to the circular covered passageway which runs round the perimeter of the Stadium.

Quiller remains seated for a second. He then stands abruptly and walks up to join Pol.

QUILLER

What do you want?

POL

You've been on holiday, I understand.

QUILLER

I *am* on holiday.

POL

By the sea?

QUILLER

What do you want?

POL

Oh, my name's Pol, by the way.

QUILLER

What?

POL

Pol.

QUILLER

Mine's Quiller.

POL

I know that.

(*Pause.*)

I understand you've been working in the Middle East
for some time.

QUILLER

Yes, I've been working there.

POL

We've been engaged in some rather tough work here. I
think we're coping moderately well with the situation in
other parts of the country, but it's getting a little out of
hand in Berlin. They're quite a tough bunch. Nazi from
top to toe. In the classic tradition. But not just the
remains of the old lot. Oh no. There's quite a bit of new
blood. Youth. Firm believers. Very dangerous. It won't
do to underestimate them.

They walk.

Quite complex, of course, the over-all issue. Difficult to
pinpoint. Nobody wears a brown shirt now, you see. No
banners. Consequently, they're difficult to recognize –
they look like everybody else. They move in various
walks of life all over the country but they're very careful
and quite clever and they look like everybody else.
Intriguing. Don't you think? However, I agree with you
– that's all politics. Not our job. I'll tell you what our job
is. Our job is to get to the hard core – the extreme
element – the ones you *can* recognize – if you get close
enough to see them. The hard core. They have a base
here. But we don't know where it is. We need, rather
urgently, to find it.

QUILLER

I've read the files.

POL

The files till when?

QUILLER

Till June.

POL

Oh yes, of course, you've been on holiday. You read them while you were in London, did you?

QUILLER

That's right.

POL

Who was our leading operator here, in the last file you saw?

QUILLER

Metzler.

POL

He's dead. Another colleague of yours took over from him. Kenneth Lindsay Jones.

QUILLER

Uh-huh.

POL

He's dead too. He was killed two days ago. Long range nine point three, in the spine.

Quiller's face.

We'd like you to take over.

Pol takes the cigarette from his top pocket and lights it.

He was obstinate. He refused cover. If he'd allowed us to give him cover he might not be dead and we might have a little more idea of where he'd got to.

QUILLER

He was justified in using any method he thought fit.

POL

Not a very efficient method – in his case.

QUILLER

What do you know about it? You only talk to people.

They stare at each other.

POL

This is a very strong operation. Fully urgent. They have killed two of our men. We want you to take over from Jones.

Pause.

I've been asked to say that this is not an order but a request. Consider it, will you? At your leisure. I'll give you five minutes. Perhaps you would join me for coffee in Section E at –

(*Looks at watch.*)

– 11.26.

Pol strolls away.

Quiller looks after him.

EXT. HOTEL. BERLIN. DAY.

People passing. Taxis drawing up. Lights. Traffic.

Quiller walks down steps of hotel. He stops, lights a cigarette. He glances lightly across the street. His eyes run quickly along the windows opposite. Smoking, he looks along the street. Among all the people moving there is one person stationary. He is standing under a lamp post by a newspaper stand, reading a paper.

Quiller walks up the street, past the man, buys a paper at the paper stand and walks back past the man.

EXT. BERLIN. DAY.

Quiller walking. Crowds of people. Quiller looks behind him, casually. The Man is standing some way along the pavement, reading a theatre bill.

Quiller walks quickly towards a bookshop and goes in.

The Man follows at a distance.

EXT. SIDE EXIT. BOOKSHOP.

Quiller walks through the bookshop and out by the side exit.

From the same point of view see the Man approach the main entrance.

He peers through the window into the shop and enters. He looks about, observes the side exit and walks quickly out by it.

He stands on the pavement and looks about.

There is no sign of Quiller.

The man walks quickly down the street.

Quiller enters the shop and follows him.

EXT. BERLIN. DAY.

Quiller walking. He watches, from a distance, between moving figures. The Man's head twisting, looking about him. The Man goes to the edge of the road and looks across it. He stands, looks at newspaper in his hand and throws it into the gutter.

He goes into a small bar.

INT. BAR.

The man, Hengel, is sitting at a table with a glass of beer. He is alone in the bar.

Quiller enters, crosses to Hengel's table and sits.

Hengel stares at him. Quiller smiles.

Silence.

The Barman moves towards the table.

QUILLER
I'd like a double Jack Daniels on the rocks. Do you have it?

BARMAN
Yes, sir.

The Barman goes back to bar.

Quiller smiles at Hengel.

QUILLER
Would you like to see the evening paper?

He passes his newspaper across to Hengel.

Hengel does not pick it up.

They look at each other.

The Barman brings the whisky. Quiller drinks. Hengel takes out a packet of Chesterfields.

HENGEL
Do you smoke this brand?

QUILLER
No, I don't think I know that brand.

HENGEL
Perhaps I might introduce it to you.

QUILLER
Would you say they're milder than other brands?

HENGEL
They're milder than some other brands.

QUILLER

Okay, I'll try one.

They light their cigarettes.

HENGEL

I lost you.

QUILLER

Why? Were you following me?

HENGEL

You were playing a game with me. I didn't appreciate it.

QUILLER

Now come on, don't be silly, you might have been one
of the adverse party.

HENGEL

They don't know you're here. Yet.

QUILLER

You don't think so?

HENGEL

No. I'm one of your cover, by the way.

QUILLER

Hi.

Pause.

HENGEL

I'd like to ask what method you intend to employ.

QUILLER

Well . . .

He clicks fingers at Barman, gesturing to man and self.

Same again.

He turns to Hengel.

Well, I'll tell you. If you say they don't know I'm here, I think I'd better let them know I'm here. Otherwise how are we ever going to get together?

HENGEL

I see. That's your business. The fact is, I've been asked to give you certain fragments of information, to do with some of KLJ's movements. We've no idea whether it's of any value.

The Barman brings the drinks, takes empties and goes.

Quiller looks at Hengel.

QUILLER

What's your name?

HENGEL

Hengel.

QUILLER

Why are you so tense, Hengel?

HENGEL

Are you being funny?

QUILLER

Look at your hand. It's so tight. And look at your skin. Your skin's terrible.

Pause.

HENGEL

I have a feeling, Mr Quiller, that you won't find life here so funny for very long.

QUILLER

Why don't you drink your beer?

HENGEL

I don't want it.

QUILLER

I bought it for you.

HENGEL

You can't make me want it, Mr Quiller.

Quiller takes Hengel's beer.

QUILLER

Well, I need a chaser.

He drinks.

HENGEL

I worked with KLJ. I knew him.

QUILLER

Oh, really?

HENGEL

I was one of his cover until he insisted that all his cover was called off. I consider that to have been a very stupid decision, if I may say so, on his part. Once he was alone, of course, he was killed. I knew he would die. Did you know him?

Pause.

QUILLER

Yes, I did.

HENGEL

If he'd allowed me to stay with him I could have saved his life.

Quiller looks at him and finishes his drink.

QUILLER

Give me the information.

HENGEL

What?

QUILLER

You said you had information. Give it to me.

Hengel glances at Barman, takes an envelope out of his pocket and puts it on the table.

Quiller slits the envelope and takes out various pieces of paper.

There are two torn tickets, one from a bowling alley and one from a swimming pool, and a German newspaper cutting, the headline of which is glimpsed: School Teacher Arrested – War Crimes.

Quiller puts these items in his pocket, stands and walks to the door.

Quiller goes out, leaving Hengel at table.

INT. BOWLING ALLEY.

Lines of men bowling. Some lanes empty. Quiller walking with manager (Dorfmann).

QUILLER

Yes, I'm thinking of starting a big chain of these places in the States.

DORFMANN

Don't they have quite a few there already?

QUILLER

Yes. Oh quite a few. Quite a few. Thousands. But there's always room for a few more.

DORFMANN

Always.

They reach a lane and stop to watch about half a dozen men bowling.

QUILLER

What kind of business do you do?

233

DORFMANN

Quite good. We have . . . many regulars.

They watch the game.

QUILLER

Yes, a friend of mine was telling me about this place. He
was in here a couple of nights ago. Don't know if you
met him. Fellow by the name of Jones – Kenneth
Lindsay Jones.

DORFMANN

Jones? No. I don't think so. No. I think I would
remember the name.

QUILLER

Yes.

Pause.

DORFMANN

Would you like to bowl?

Quiller looks at his watch.

QUILLER

No. Not now thanks. But maybe I'll come back another
night.

DORFMANN

Please come back. Show me how to bowl.

They laugh.

QUILLER

Right. Bye Mr Weiss.

DORFMANN

Auf wiedersehen.

Quiller goes.

The last pin is knocked over.

INT. INDOOR SWIMMING BATH. DAY.

A young man dives from the diving board into the pool. Young men are diving, swimming, sitting at the pool edge. There is a continual echo.

From pool level see Quiller appear on the changing room gallery. He is fully dressed. He stands, looking down.

INT. SWIMMING BATH GALLERY.

Quiller's view of the pool. Shining water and bodies. Two men leave the pool and walk up the steps. They look at Quiller curiously and pass him, brushing close. Quiller brushes water from his arm. An Attendant approaches him.

> ATTENDANT
> (*in German*)

You are not swimming?

> QUILLER

Sorry. I don't understand.

> ATTENDANT
> (*in English*)

You are not swimming?

> QUILLER

No.

> ATTENDANT

This is for swimming, this place.

> QUILLER

I'm a coach, back in the States. I teach swimming at Williamsburg, Virginia. I heard some of the best swimmers in Berlin come here. A friend of mine was telling me. An Englishman. Name of Jones.

ATTENDANT

This place is for swimming. You cannot watch. It is not
allowed to have onlookers.

QUILLER

Oh, what a pity. I'd hoped I'd have been able to watch.

ATTENDANT

No.

Quiller looks again at the swimmers.

They are diving and swimming with great grace.

QUILLER

Pity. Well . . . danke.

He walks along the gallery and out of the exit.

The Attendant watches him go.

EXT. SWIMMING BATH. DAY.

*Quiller comes out of swimming bath into the street. Across the
street a man, Weng, leans against a wall. Quiller walks to the
corner, to a taxi rank, followed by Weng.*

He gets into a taxi. It drives off.

Weng gets into a taxi. His taxi follows Quiller's.

EXT. HOTEL. DAY.

Two taxis draw up at hotel.

Quiller gets out of one, goes up steps into hotel.

Weng gets out of other, looks up at hotel.

Quiller, at top of hotel steps, glances round at Weng.

Weng walks slowly along.

Quiller goes through swing doors.

INT. HOTEL LOBBY.

Quiller comes through swing doors. He looks out to the front of the hotel. There is no sign of Weng.

Quiller turns.

In the corner of the lobby Hengel is sitting. Hengel starts to get up. Quiller goes towards him. Hengel sits.

Quiller sits by him. Hengel is drinking coffee.

> QUILLER
>
> What do you want?

> HENGEL
>
> I have been asked to inquire if you carry anything useful.

> QUILLER
>
> I don't carry anything.

> HENGEL
>
> I think they'll be disturbed to hear that.

> QUILLER
>
> Let them be disturbed.

> HENGEL
>
> Certain objects can be valuable to a man in your position.

> QUILLER
>
> I decide that. You don't.

Pause.

> QUILLER
>
> I'm going somewhere. Have another cup of coffee.

> HENGEL
>
> It's my job to accompany you.

QUILLER

I don't need you today.

HENGEL

I am your cover. I must keep with you.

QUILLER

Go and see a good movie. Take the day off.

HENGEL

You want a bullet in your spine, too?

QUILLER

There's a spy film on at the Palace.

Hengel leans forward.

HENGEL

I shall report this.

Quiller stands and clicks his fingers at the waiter.

QUILLER

A cognac for the gentleman.

Quiller walks out of the hotel.

EXT. HOTEL. DAY.

Quiller standing on steps a moment. No sign of Weng.

EXT. HERTZ GARAGE. DAY.

Sign saying 'CAR HIRE' in a number of languages. Quiller, seen from street, walking from office with car keys. He gets into an Auto-Union and drives into the street.

EXT. SCHOOL. OUTSKIRTS BERLIN. DAY.

Children playing in the front playground.

Quiller walks into the shot, stands a moment looking at the school and then walks towards it.

EXT. SCHOOL. DAY.

Quiller enters the school. He can be seen speaking to a Porter. The Porter lifts a telephone, speaks into it and then points up the stairs.

Children are changing classes. Quiller walks up the stairs.

INT. HEADMISTRESS'S STUDY.

QUILLER

My name's Cooper. I'm a journalist.

HEADMISTRESS
(FRAU SCHROEDER)

I speak English, I am afraid, not so very well . . .

QUILLER

Don't speak German at all.

They both laugh, and sit.

HEADMISTRESS

How can I . . . help you?

QUILLER
(briskly)

I'm writing an article for the *Philadelphia World Review*.

HEADMISTRESS

Uh . . . huh?

QUILLER

You haven't heard of it?

HEADMISTRESS

Oh . . . no.

QUILLER

That's because it hasn't started yet. This is going to be the first number.

HEADMISTRESS

Ah.

QUILLER

We in Philadelphia are convinced that current affairs in
Europe have a great deal of bearing on the lives of the
citizens of Philadelphia – you know, the people back
home in Philly.

HEADMISTRESS

Uuh . . . I don't understand . . . exactly . . . what . . .

QUILLER
(*speaking very deliberately*)
I'm collating material for an article about the Nazi
situation in Germany.

HEADMISTRESS

Nazi?

Quiller takes out newspaper cutting.

QUILLER

That's right. We understand that you had a school
teacher here recently, name of Steiner, who was
discovered to have been a war criminal. Is that right?

HEADMISTRESS

That is . . . so.

QUILLER

Well – we'd like a little more information for our Philly
readers.

Pause.

HEADMISTRESS

It was all reported.

QUILLER

I didn't think it was reported in any great detail. The
man hanged himself, I believe.

HEADMISTRESS

Hanged?

QUILLER

Yes, you know . . .

Quiller mimes a rope round the neck, and jerks it.

HEADMISTRESS

Oh, hanged . . . yes but I am so sorry, my English . . . I
have a teacher here, who has . . . replaced . . . this man.
She knows English. Perhaps . . . you would like to speak
to her?

QUILLER

Sure. Thanks.

HEADMISTRESS

If you will come with me. I will see if she's still here.

They stand.

INT. SCHOOL. CORRIDOR AND CLASSROOM.

*The Headmistress leads Quiller down a corridor. Children pass
them. They reach the open door of a classroom. Inge is within,
talking to a little girl.*

INT. CLASSROOM.

Inge looks up. Headmistress and Quiller at the door.

Headmistress speaks German.

HEADMISTRESS

Have you a moment?

INGE
(*in German*)
Yes, of course. All right, Hilde.

The little girl bobs to them all and goes.

241

HEADMISTRESS

Inge – this is Herr Cooper – Fräulein Lindt.

They nod to each other and smile.

Herr Cooper is a journalist. He is writing an article about Herr Steiner. Perhaps you might be able to help him – in English.

INGE

(in German)

Yes, of course.

HEADMISTRESS

Good.

(To Quiller.)

Good-bye.

QUILLER

Thank you.

She leaves the room.

Inge and Quiller look at each other for a moment.

INGE

So – you are writing an article about Herr Steiner?

QUILLER

No, no . . . he's just an item. The article is about the present day Nazi question in Germany. I don't know much about it myself, I've been a sports writer all my life.

INGE

Oh.

QUILLER

But you know what boxing is these days.

INGE

No? What?

242

QUILLER

The golden days are over. You're not a boxing fan?

INGE

No, I'm not.

QUILLER

Ah.

Pause.

Well listen, this man Steiner, can you tell me anything
about him?

INGE

Not very much, I'm afraid.

QUILLER

I mean, what was he like?

INGE

He was a very good teacher.

QUILLER

Was he?

INGE

Oh yes. We were . . . so surprised . . . when we heard
about his past. We couldn't believe it. I mean he was so
wonderful with the children.

QUILLER

Is that a fact?

INGE

Yes, he seemed to feel . . . I don't know . . . a great
responsibility towards them. It's funny, how little you
know about people, however closely you work with
them. But I . . .

Pause.

243

QUILLER

What?

INGE

Oh, I think it is true to say that, at heart, he was part of the old Germany.

Quiller takes out a notebook.

QUILLER

That's quite an interesting angle. The old Germany and the new Germany.
(*Writing.*)
Yes . . . that's quite an interesting angle.

He looks at her.

What would you say were the aims of the new Germany?

INGE

Oh, that's a very big question.

QUILLER

What are your aims?

INGE

Mine?

QUILLER

As a school teacher.

INGE

Oh . . . I think, perhaps . . . to try to teach the children a broader attitude towards Europe, a broader attitude towards the world.

QUILLER

Uh-huh.
(*Lifts pencil.*)
Mind if I quote that?

INGE
(*laughing*)

I'm not an important person, really. I'm just a school teacher.

QUILLER

But you're a young German woman. That's what's going to interest the readers back home. The feminine point of view.

INGE

You seem to approach your work with a lot of enthusiasm.

QUILLER

Well, listen, that's the kind of man I am. It's all or nothing with me.

They smile.

She puts a few books into her bag and goes for her coat.

He watches her.

You've been most helpful.

He helps her with her coat.

Do you live near the school?

INGE

No, I live in Bundesallee.

QUILLER

Why don't I give you a lift?

She looks at him.

INGE

That's very kind of you.

EXT. BLOCK OF FLATS. AFTERNOON.

The Auto-Union draws up. Inge and Quiller get out and stand on the pavement.

                                INGE
Thank you.

                              QUILLER
Thank *you*.

                                INGE
Good luck . . . with your article.

                              QUILLER
Yes . . . umm . . .

They stand a moment.

I might like to . . . reach you again . . . about the article.
Can I call you?

                                INGE
I'm at school every day.

She puts out her hand. He shakes it.

Good-bye.

She walks to the door of the block.

He stands, uncertain, suddenly calls to her.

                              QUILLER
Hey, wait a minute.

He joins her at the door.

That bag looks heavy.

He tests it for weight.

Very heavy.

He looks at her.

Why don't I help you carry it?

Inge laughs.

INGE

All right.

INT. INGE'S FLAT. AFTERNOON.

Quiller is sitting with a drink, stretched out.

QUILLER

The point about Louis was Louis's co-ordination. Louis
had wonderful co-ordination. He was really –
(*puts fists into a boxing posture*)
– you know – he was really of a piece, that guy. And he
had a killer insider him. I mean look what he did to
Schmeling.

INGE

Who?

QUILLER

Schmeling. German fighter. Louis killed him.

INGE

I thought Schmeling beat him.

QUILLER

He beat him the first time. But Louis killed him the
second time.

INGE

Ah.

QUILLER

He massacred him. Yes, I don't know what it is, but the
Germans have been a great disappointment – I mean
from the boxing point of view. I mean, you know, you'd
think, that the way the German mind goes – I mean the
old German mind, not the new German mind – you'd

247

have thought they'd have done well in the fight game.
But it ain't worked out like that. We got them beat.

Inge looks at him with a half smile.

INGE

So it seems.

QUILLER

But that's the way it goes.

Pause.

INGE

A little more?

QUILLER

Oh, thanks.

Inge rises, takes his glass, fills it, adds ice.

He watches her.

She brings glass back to him.

He watches her.

She smiles at him.

INGE

Here you are.

He takes glass.

She turns, fills her own glass.

He watches her.

She sits.

QUILLER

Cheers.

They drink.

248

What kind of men do you know?

INGE

I don't know many.

QUILLER

Why not?

INGE

Oh, I'm . . . busy.

Pause.

QUILLER

You know, someone was telling me that there are some
people who don't think like, for instance, you do.

INGE

How do you mean?

QUILLER

Well, someone was telling me that there are some
people here who wouldn't agree with your attitude –
about Europe, about education – you know, about
things like that.

INGE

That's true, I suppose.

QUILLER

That's what this man was telling me.

INGE

Yes.

Pause.

QUILLER

You mean there are certain people here who believe that
this country should be . . . very strong, that it should be
dominant?

INGE

That's right.

QUILLER

They still believe that?

INGE

Oh yes. Still.

Quiller drinks.

QUILLER

Well listen, I don't think there's anything basically
wrong with that, is there? I mean we believe the same in
the States. We believe our country should be strong. I
wouldn't say dominant – I mean we don't want to
dominate anybody – but I would say strong. Yes, I'd say
that.

Silence.

But listen . . . what kind of people are they exactly?
Nazis?

INGE

Well, they are . . . I would say. But of course they don't
call themselves that any more.

QUILLER

They don't?

INGE

No.

QUILLER

You know, this fits in with what this man was telling
me. He was saying that these boys don't show
themselves, they keep themselves pretty much under
cover.

INGE

Yes. So I believe.

QUILLER

Yes . . . he was saying they've got a kind of long-term policy, that they want to infiltrate themselves into the mind of the country, over a period of years. But they're not in any kind of hurry, this time . . . you know . . .

He laughs.

INGE

Yes.

QUILLER

But that they're very convinced men. Very convinced.

INGE

I would say that, yes.

QUILLER

Yes, that's exactly what this man was telling me.

Pause.

INGE

Who is this man?

He looks up from his drink.

QUILLER

What man?

INGE

The man . . . who was talking to you.

QUILLER

Oh, just a guy I met in a bar.

INGE

Oh.

Pause.

Are you going to write about this . . . question . . . in your article?

QUILLER

No, no, it's outside my range. I'm not political. I haven't got a political brain.

INGE

Ah.

They drink.

QUILLER

It's very pleasant here.

INGE

Yes, I like it.

QUILLER

You like living alone?

INGE

I've been alone for a long time. My family was killed in the war.

Pause.

I live for my work now.

Pause.

How long are you staying in Berlin?

QUILLER

Until I've finished my assignment.

Pause.

Why don't we go out one night?

INGE

That would be very nice.

EXT. BLOCK OF FLATS. AFTERNOON.

Quiller emerges from the building. He stops in the porch and arranges his tie. He then walks in the direction of his car, parked at the side of the road. For no apparent reason he walks past his car, without looking at it, and continues round the corner.

EXT. OTHER SIDE OF BLOCK.

Quiller suddenly turns on his heel and walks straight back in the direction he has come.

A man is walking slowly along by the shops.

Quiller walks up to him and stands in front of him. The man stops, looks at Quiller with surprise.

> QUILLER
>
> Are you following me?

Silence.

Then in fluent German.

> I said are you following me?

> MAN (A)
> (*in German*)
>
> I am not.

The rest of the scene is played in German.

> QUILLER
>
> Why are you following me?

> MAN
>
> I am not. You are mistaken.

The Man attempts to move. Quiller blocks his path.

> MAN
>
> Excuse me.

                    QUILLER
Where are you going?

                      MAN
To meet a friend.

                    QUILLER
Where?

                      MAN
Here.

Quiller turns. Another man stands behind him. First Man speaks to the Second Man (B).

                  FIRST MAN
This man has accused me of following him.

                 SECOND MAN
Following? Why?

                  FIRST MAN
I do not know.

                 SECOND MAN
                  (*to Quiller*)
Why do you say such a thing?

A Third Man (C) joins the group.

                  THIRD MAN
What is the matter?

                  FIRST MAN
This man is being offensive.

                  THIRD MAN
Offensive?

Third Man moves closer to Quiller.

                  THIRD MAN
Are you being offensive?

                     254

Quiller is closed in by the three men by the shop window.

He smiles, and speaks to the Third Man.

QUILLER

Don't come any nearer, will you?

Silence. The Third Man is still.

Quiller smiles at the First Man.

Well, perhaps I was mistaken.

Pause.

Perhaps you weren't following me.

The men are silent.

He looks at each of them in turn.

He points at Third Man.

You're in my way.

Third Man moves back. Quiller walks through them and back down the street. The three remain at the window.

EXT. BLOCK OF FLATS.

Quiller gets into his Auto-Union and drives off.

EXT. HOTEL. EARLY EVENING.

Quiller running up steps of hotel.

A porter is collecting cases from a taxi and arranging them on the pavement.

INT. HOTEL LOBBY.

Quiller walking through lobby. He stops, grimaces. He has seen Hengel sitting in the corner.

He walks over and sits by Hengel, who has a glass of beer in front of him.

QUILLER

How was the movie? Instructive?

HENGEL

There are two things to tell you. Firstly they do not understand why you carry no kind of instrument.

QUILLER

What's the second thing?

HENGEL

I am still your cover. I will tag you. I am to keep with you.

Quiller looks at him.

QUILLER

You carry instruments, I suppose?

HENGEL

I do.

QUILLER

Yes. Then I'll probably feel more secure with you around.

HENGEL

You should.

QUILLER

You'll see I don't come to any harm.

HENGEL

That's my job.

QUILLER

Well thanks, Hengel. Thanks a lot.

Hengel looks at him suspiciously.

> HENGEL

We see that you've hired a car.

> QUILLER

That's right.

> HENGEL

How is your operation proceeding? We'd all like to know.

> QUILLER

It's difficult to say, Hengel.

Pause.

Well, I'm just going for a little ride about the town, to see the sights.

> HENGEL

I'll tag you.

> QUILLER

Okay.

Quiller stands.

Don't lose me now.

EXT. HOTEL. EARLY EVENING.

Quiller on steps. He lights a cigarette.

INT. A WINDOW OPPOSITE.

A hand on a curtain. Curtain slightly shifts.

Quiller can be seen standing. A Porter ascends hotel steps, with suitcases.

EXT. HOTEL.

Quiller begins to descend the steps.

The Porter is going up. As they pass, the Porter hoists a suitcase up in his arm. The edge of the case hits Quiller on the thigh. Quiller grimaces, holds his thigh.

> QUILLER

What the hell –

> PORTER

Oh, I am sorry, sir.

Quiller rubs his thigh.

I do apologize, sir.

Hengel comes out of hotel.

> QUILLER

What's your name?

> PORTER

Grauber, sir.

Quiller moves down the steps and gets into his car. Hengel moves down steps and gets into a Volkswagen.

They drive off.

INT. WINDOW OPPOSITE.

The hand drops the curtain.

EXT. BERLIN STREETS. DUSK.

Quiller's Auto-Union turns sharp left, quickly.

Hengel's Volkswagen follows.

Auto-Union turns sharp right.

Volkswagen follows.

Auto-Union crosses crossroads at speed.

Volkswagen just makes lights, following.

INT. AUTO-UNION.

Quiller looking in rear mirror. The Volkswagen just in sight.

Quiller grins.

EXT. STREETS. DUSK.

Auto-Union turns left, right and right again and comes out into a wide avenue. The Volkswagen is no longer in sight.

INT. AUTO-UNION.

Quiller chuckling to himself, as he drives.

He glances in the rear mirror. No sign of the Volkswagen.

He glances in his wing mirror. A Mercedes 300 is approaching.

Quiller lessens his speed and looks out casually at the tree-lined avenue.

EXT. AVENUE.

The Auto-Union and the Mercedes 300 proceeding sedately along the avenue.

INT. AUTO-UNION.

Quiller glances back from the window.

His eyes blink. He shakes his head, grunts.

He pulls up at traffic lights.

He moans lightly. The red traffic light winks foggily.

EXT. AVENUE. TRAFFIC LIGHTS.

The Auto-Union at the traffic lights. The Mercedes beside it.

Three other cars behind the Auto-Union. The lights go to green.

Auto-Union remains still. Cars begin to hoot. One car pulls round and goes past.

The Mercedes remains. The Auto-Union remains.

The other cars pull away and go past, hooting.

INT. AUTO-UNION.

Quiller grunting, blinking.

The green light winks.

Quiller's hand is on the gear lever. He presses but is unable to put the car into gear. His hand falls to his thigh, clutches it.

The driving door opens. A man steps in.

> MAN (D)
> I'll drive. Move over.

Quiller tries to resist, is too weak. The Man shifts Quiller into the passenger seat. Quiller slumps. The Man drives off.

EXT. AVENUE. DUSK.

The Auto-Union and the Mercedes proceeding sedately along the avenue.

INT. A LARGE RECEPTION ROOM.

Quiller's point of view.

A large brilliantly lit chandelier.

Camera descends to see an oil painting of a nude blonde, leaning across a chair, on the far wall.

Below the painting a pair of white and golden double doors.

A man, F, in a dark suit stands by them.

The room is large, high-ceilinged, well-furnished.

Quiller in a silk brocade chair.

Quiller sits, a cushion behind his head.

He clenches his eyes, looks at his watch.

His point of view.

A carpet stretches from his chair to the doors.

A man, Grauber, walks across from the curtained window to join the other at the doors.

A third man, Oktober, stands by an enormous fireplace.

A fourth, in a white surgeon's gown, walks towards Quiller.

Quiller's eyes close.

The Doctor raises one of Quiller's eyelids.

The Doctor steps back. Quiller's eyes open.

The Doctor turns his head towards the fireplace.

Oktober leaves the fireplace and walks slowly to Quiller.

Quiller looks up at him and shivers.

OKTOBER

Are you cold?

Quiller looks at him.

QUILLER

What is it? Day or night?

Oktober studies him.

OKTOBER

My name's Oktober. What's yours?

Silence.

QUILLER

What's the time?

261

OKTOBER

You've just looked at your watch.

QUILLER

It may be slow. Or fast. What time do you make it?

OKTOBER

Oh, time isn't really very important.

QUILLER

It is to me. I have an appointment.

He points at painting.

She looks something like that, too. So . . .

OKTOBER

She'll wait.

Pause.

QUILLER

Listen, can I make a suggestion?

OKTOBER

Surely. But we would like to know your name first.

QUILLER

Let me make this suggestion first.

OKTOBER

No. Tell us your name first.

Pause.

QUILLER

They call me Spike.

OKTOBER

Not your nickname. Your surname.

QUILLER

Canetti.

Pause.

OKTOBER

What is your suggestion?

QUILLER

I think this is a case of mistaken identity. I work for Doubledays in New York. I came to Berlin looking for rare books.

OKTOBER

Have you found them?

QUILLER

Well no, not quite yet. I haven't found them yet.

Oktober smiles.

OKTOBER

What is your real name?

QUILLER

My mother's maiden name was O'Reilly.

OKTOBER

What is your real name, please, Mr Quiller?

QUILLER

Well, originally I had to walk around with a double-barrelled name. O'Reilly Canetti. But I found it a bit heavy.
(*Turns to Doctor.*)
Wouldn't you find it heavy? So I dropped the O'Reilly and kept the Canetti.

OKTOBER

What does your father do, Mr Quiller?

QUILLER

He's dead.

> **OKTOBER**
>
> And your mother?

> **QUILLER**
>
> She's dead too.

> **OKTOBER**
>
> And your sister?

> **QUILLER**
>
> She's dead too. What I mean is I never had one. I was an only child.

> **OKTOBER**
>
> You must be lonely.

> **QUILLER**
>
> No, no . . . no.

> **OKTOBER**
>
> You must feel lonely now, sitting here amongst strangers.

> **QUILLER**
>
> No, I like meeting people. You know . . . new faces . . .

Pause.

> **OKTOBER**
>
> How's your leg?

> **QUILLER**
>
> My leg? Oh yes. Someone scratched it – with a suitcase.

Oktober clicks his fingers to Grauber at the door. Grauber comes forward, down the carpet.

> **OKTOBER**
>
> He did it.

Quiller looks at Grauber and waves, vaguely.

QUILLER

Oh, hi. Hullo.

Grauber goes back to the door.

OKTOBER

We know . . . a little about you.

QUILLER

Me?

OKTOBER

A little. But we would like to know a little more. I shall tell you quite simply. We would like to know the exact location of your local Control in Berlin. We would like to know a little more about your current code systems. We would like to be able to appreciate the extent of your knowledge about us, and also what information, if any, your predecessor managed to pass to your Control. We would like to know the exact nature of your present mission in Berlin.

Pause.

You are a sensible man, and you know perfectly well you must give us this information since you have no alternative.

Pause.

QUILLER

Have you got a telephone here?

He looks inquiringly about.

I think I should call my lawyer in New York. Guy called Cuspensky. I'll make it collect. So don't worry about that.

OKTOBER

You don't work in New York, Mr Quiller. You work in Europe and the Middle East.

Oktober turns and moves a few paces away.

The Two Guards, Grauber and F, move from the doors and approach Quiller's chair.

They stand with their hands in their jacket pockets.

A Third Man, C, comes into view from behind his chair, hand in pocket.

The Doctor wheels a small table towards chair. On it is a hypodermic kit. The Doctor selects equipment.

Silence.

Doctor fills a syringe. A colourless fluid.

Take off your coat.

QUILLER

Sure.

All the men watch him begin to take off his coat.

Quiller takes his coat off.

Very fast, he whips it into Oktober's face and kicks him in groin, and in a continuing move swings the small table at the head of C at his right. It hits him. The man's gun, out, falls. The hypodermic kit scatters. Oktober has fallen. C clutches his head.

Quiller swivels. A gun descends on his shoulder as he ducks.

Quiller seizes Grauber's leg, his shoulder on his knee, his left hand behind his ankle, and breaks Grauber's leg. Grauber screams.

F kicks at Quiller's head. Quiller grasps his foot and twists. F is thrown off balance.

Quiller begins his run to the door.

He is tackled and brought down by F.

They sprawl.

266

F grips Quiller's leg.

Quiller kicks him in the face with his free leg.

F continues to grip and twist leg.

Quiller, writhing, kicks him again in the face.

C's arm locks round his throat.

Quiller's head jerks back as the pressure tightens.

F's face, bloodied, comes into picture.

He hits Quiller in the face.

All this has taken place in silence.

A sharp word from Oktober.

Sound of doors shutting.

Shoes move by Quiller's locked head. A shoe kicks his head. The arm loosens on his neck.

Quiller, nose bleeding, looks up at bloodied face of F. The arm is taken from his neck. F and C stand.

Legs stand above him. Oktober's voice:

OKTOBER
You may get up.

Quiller stands, tucks his shirt in and looks about. Four men, A, B, H and I, stand by the door, guns out. F stands, breathing heavily.

C stands still, a cut on his forehead.

Grauber lies on the floor, still, his leg at an odd angle.

Oktober stands stiffly, slightly sweating.

OKTOBER
(*to Quiller*)

Sit down.

Quiller looks at the faces of the men surrounding him.

He walks down the carpet to the chair and sits.

Quiller's point of view.

A, B, C and F walk down the room towards him, guns out. They stop.

The Doctor rolls up his sleeve, cleanses the skin and picks up the syringe.

Quiller glances at the Doctor.

His face twists.

EXT. TERRACE. FROM ROOM. NIGHT.

Cigar smoke rising on the terrace. The long windows are ajar.

Oktober stands on terrace, looking down into the dark garden.

A man, B, comes through the curtain and stands.

Oktober turns and walks back into the room.

Quiller's point of view. His eyes flicker, open.

Four Men, A, B, C and F, stand by the doors, indistinct, blurred, in soft focus.

Oktober stands in the middle of the room, looking at him.

Behind him, Two Other Men, H and I, by the windows. No guns in sight.

The Doctor straps a constrictor on Quiller's arm, for blood-pressure. He feels Quiller's pulse.

Oktober walks forward.

He smiles.

> OKTOBER
>
> My name's Oktober. What's yours?

> QUILLER
>
> Quiller.

> OKTOBER
>
> And your first name?

> QUILLER
>
> Inge.

> OKTOBER
>
> Your name is Inge? Really?

Quiller breathes heavily, hisses through his teeth.

> That's a girl's name. It's the name of a girl. She must be
> a very beautiful girl. Tell us about her.

Pause.

> You're not worried, are you? There's nothing to be
> worried about. Is there?

> QUILLER
>
> No.

> OKTOBER
>
> You can talk to me quite easily, can't you?

> QUILLER
>
> No.

> OKTOBER
>
> Of course you can. You need to relax. They work you
> too hard. That boss of yours, what's his name?

Pause.

> What's his name?

QUILLER

Inge.

OKTOBER

No, she's a girl. She's not your boss.

Quiller's eyes close, his head droops.

Open your eyes.

The eyes remain closed.

Open your eyes.

The eyes open.

Sit up. You seem to be sleepy. Don't fall asleep. Not yet. Jones hated your boss. They betrayed him and killed him. What was his name?

QUILLER

She has long legs.

OKTOBER

Really? I'm so glad to hear that. You're very lucky. After you leave us you can go to her. She's waiting for you.

QUILLER

White . . .

OKTOBER

She adores you.

QUILLER

No.

OKTOBER

Oh yes. Adores you. She wants you only. She longs for you only.

QUILLER

Longs . . . adores me . . .

Pause.

> Wants me . . . only . . .

> **OKTOBER**
> Don't sleep. It's too early.

Quiller's head drops onto his chest. He is asleep.

Oktober looks at the Doctor.

> **DOCTOR**
> He forced himself . . . to sleep.

> **OKTOBER**
> Wake him up.

The Doctor fills another syringe and injects Quiller's sleeping body. He signals to a Guard (A). A moves to the chair, holding some leather straps. He bends at the chair.

Quiller's point of view.

The chandelier, abnormally ablaze, swimming on ceiling.

The room seems larger than it is.

Everything is in sharp focus, to infinity.

Quiller's eyes are open, bright, very alive.

From his point of view figures, furniture, etc. are etched with an abnormal distinction.

The Doctor stands close to him.

A basin of water stands on the side table. Lights shine brilliantly in the water.

The ripple of the water is deep. The tick of the watch is sharp.

He looks up. The chandelier jolts, dazzles.

He takes his eyes from it.

Oktober stands in front of him.

> **OKTOBER**
> That was a good sleep you had. How do you feel?

> **QUILLER**
> (*loudly*)

Great.

Quiller speaks involuntarily, compulsively, on every cue.

He is sweating.

He jerks forward, is stopped. He looks down.

His ankles and wrists are strapped to the chair.

He jerks forward again and falls with the chair.

Two Guards, B and C, from behind, set the chair upright and remain holding it.

> **OKTOBER**

Talk to me.

> **QUILLER**

Nothing to talk.

> **OKTOBER**

Oh come on, Quiller, we don't want to keep you here all night. Your Control will be worried about you. You haven't reported for a long time.

> **QUILLER**

Don't report. I'm my . . .

> **OKTOBER**

What?

> **QUILLER**

My own master.

OKTOBER

But you mustn't lose touch with them. Why don't you phone them? Or we can take a message for you? What's the address?

QUILLER

Not waiting.

OKTOBER

Of course they're waiting, and Inge's waiting. Who is Inge?

QUILLER

Who?

OKTOBER

What's her second name? Inge what?

QUILLER

Who?

OKTOBER

Inge who?

QUILLER

What?

OKTOBER

Inge what?

QUILLER

Lin – link – link –

OKTOBER

Is she your link?

QUILLER

No link.

OKTOBER

Of course you have a link. You have colleagues. She's with your colleagues now.

QUILLER

No colleagues.

OKTOBER

You have a cover man. What's his name?

QUILLER

Heng – Hang – hang him –

OKTOBER

That's unkind. He's your friend. What's his name?

QUILLER

Jones.

OKTOBER

Jones knows Inge. He's with Inge now.

QUILLER

Dead.

OKTOBER

With her now. He's in bed with her now. He's enjoying her now. You must tell your base.

QUILLER

He's dead.

OKTOBER

You mustn't let her touch him, he's a corpse. Where's your base? Tell us your base. She's your colleague, how does she get signals from local Control?

QUILLER

She's not –

OKTOBER

Where's your base?

QUILLER

Secret! It's secret! Pol doesn't –

OKTOBER

Who is Pol?

QUILLER

Pop it in the box.

OKTOBER

Who is Pol?

QUILLER

Polly, pol, good polly –

OKTOBER

A pet shop? Which pet shop? Is that where your Control is now? Which pet shop?

QUILLER

In the Zoo.

OKTOBER

Who is your cover?

QUILLER

Getting in my way, never out of my way, do you smoke this brand?

OKTOBER

What brand?

QUILLER

Don't know it – too strong –

OKTOBER

Would you like a cigarette?

QUILLER

Not right brand.

OKTOBER

Which is your favourite brand?

QUILLER

No smoking. Call the guard.

OKTOBER

The next station is Kurfurstendam. What number do you want?

QUILLER

No number.

OKTOBER

Don't be silly. Your Control is in Kurfurstendam. We know that. You must get a message to your chief. But we've lost the number. What is it?

QUILLER

Too late –

OKTOBER

It's never too late. They're waiting for you. They're worried. They want to know where you are. What is the number?

Quiller, for the first time, does not answer.

He breathes, is silent. From this moment his replies become gradually slower, more controlled.

The number.

QUILLER

What?

OKTOBER

The church. The churches. Where are we?

QUILLER

In your base.

OKTOBER

Don't be stupid, Quiller, you're not a baby. Inge what?

QUILLER

Lin – lie – lying low –

OKTOBER

What is the number of your base? Three? Five? Eight?

QUILLER

Nine. Ten. Out.

Quiller lets out a long breath, draws in his shoulders, relaxes back in the chair.

OKTOBER

We've just had a call from your Control. You are ordered to make an immediate report.

Quiller is silent.

Begin your report, Quiller.

Quller's eyes turn to Doctor's watch. It is one o'clock.

Can you hear me? Begin.

Quiller looks at him, speaks slowly.

QUILLER

Do anything.

Pause.

It won't matter.

OKTOBER

No. You've wasted my time.
                    (*To the Doctor.*)
Inject him.
                    (*To Guards B and C.*)
When he's unconscious kill him.

INT. LONDON CLUB. EVENING.

Gibbs walks down a long room towards the bar. He is dressed in full evening attire, with medals. Rushington is at the bar. He looks round. Gibbs sits on stool.

RUSHINGTON
Hullo. Where are you off to tonight?

GIBBS
Midsummer Banquet.

RUSHINGTON
Oh yes? Who's giving that?

GIBBS
The Lord Mayor, old boy.

RUSHINGTON
Oh yes, of course.

GIBBS
(*to Barman*)
Vodka, please.

Pause.

RUSHINGTON
You've been before, have you?

GIBBS
Where?

RUSHINGTON
The Lord Mayor's Midsummer Banquet.

GIBBS
Oh yes.

The Barman gives Gibbs his drink.

RUSHINGTON
I've never been asked.

GIBBS
Haven't you?

278

Gibbs drinks.

Any news from Berlin?

RUSHINGTON

No. Not really.

GIBBS

Chase them up in the morning, will you? Find out what's going on.

RUSHINGTON

Yes. I will.

Pause.

GIBBS

I always enjoy the Banquet. It's a very splendid occasion.

RUSHINGTON

Yes, I'm sure it is.

The camera withdraws, leaving them at the bar.

EXT. RIVER NIGHT.

Quiller's face. His body lies on the river's edge. The water laps along it. Very gradually, his face lifts up.

The lights of the bridge.

There is no one on the towpath.

Quiller's body in the mud.

He raises himself up. He touches his neck, looks down at his body and touches it, with a certain surprise.

He slowly climbs the steps to the road.

He walks, soaked and dripping, along the road.

INT. SMALL BLEAK BAR. NIGHT.

A Barman is sitting with coffee reading a paper.

The chairs are up on the tables.

The door opens. Quiller walks in.

> BARMAN
> (*in German*)

We're shut.

> QUILLER

Give me a drink.

> BARMAN
> (*in English*)

We're shut.

> QUILLER

Rum.

Quiller sits on a bar stool.

The Barman goes behind the bar and slowly pours a rum.

Quiller looks at it.

> QUILLER

A double.

Barman pours another into glass.

> BARMAN

Four marks.

Quiller takes out wallet and waves some notes.

> QUILLER

Just a little wet.

He throws notes on bar, drinks.

Barman watches him.

I'd like a taxi.

BARMAN

Get one.

QUILLER

What?

BARMAN

There's a phone. Get one.

QUILLER

You get one.

BARMAN

This place is shut.

Quiller looks at him quietly.

QUILLER

You get one.

BARMAN

Drunk Americans. I will call the police.

Quiller stands and goes round the other side of the bar.

The Barman reaches under the counter.

Quiller points to his hand.

QUILLER

Don't do that.

They stare at each other.

Call a taxi.

Barman picks up telephone on bar and dials.

They listen to the line buzz. A voice.

BARMAN

Taxi. Friedhof Bar.

He puts phone down. Quiller goes back to stool, drinks.

Barman slowly begins to wipe a glass.

A clock ticks.

INT. ZENTRAL HOTEL. NIGHT.

Quiller enters.

The lobby. it is very shabby, dusty. A Nightporter walks towards Quiller. He looks at him without interest.

> PORTER

Bitte?

> QUILLER

I'd like a room.

INT. HOTEL ROOM. NIGHT.

Clothes drying in front of electric fire.

Quiller in hotel bathrobe at door. He locks it.

He lies on bed, looks at ceiling, then at telephone.

He picks it up.

Pause.

A voice answers.

> QUILLER

346897.

Pause.

Ringing tone. Inge's voice.

> INGE
> (*in German*)

Yes?

QUILLER

I'm sorry – it's very late.

INGE

Who is this?

QUILLER

Me. Cooper.

Pause.

INGE

I was in bed.

QUILLER

Did you . . . get out of bed?

INGE

No, I'm still there. What is it? What's the time? It's so late.

QUILLER

Are you alone?

INGE

I'm asleep.

Pause.

Are you all right?

QUILLER

I want to see you.

INGE

Not now, I'm afraid.

QUILLER

When then?

INGE

Tomorrow, if you like. After school. Come and have a drink.

Pause.

QUILLER

All right. I'll be there. Good night.

INGE

Good night.

INT. INGE'S BEDROOM. NIGHT.

Inge, in bed, in a nightdress, replaces the telephone receiver on its hook, and draws the bedclothes about her.

The light goes out.

EXT. HERTZ GARAGE. DAY.

A car roars up the ramp and out into the street.

Quiller stands in fumes from the exhaust, looks up and down street, sees no one, goes into garage and walks towards glass fronted office. One woman can be seen in the office.

Quiller enters.

Camera shifts to reveal a telephone box in the wall near to the entrance. A man is speaking into the phone. He replaces receiver.

Quiller leaves the office and walks into the depth of the garage.

The back of the man leaves the phone box.

INT. HERTZ GARAGE. TOP LANDING.

Lines of cars.

Quiller seen in the distance, sitting in a Mercedes-Benz 230 SL.

A Man's back moves towards the car.

INT. MERCEDES-BENZ.

Quiller watches torso of man passing from bonnet to passenger window.

The Man opens door. Quiller looks at him. The Man holds a packet of Chesterfields in his hand. He is Weng. He sits next to Quiller.

                    WENG
   Do you smoke this brand?

                    QUILLER
                    (*wearily*)
   Oh Christ. No, I don't think I know that brand.

                    WENG
   Perhaps I might introduce it to you.

                    QUILLER
   All right, all right. What do you want?

Pause.

                    WENG
   They're milder than some other brands.

                    QUILLER
   I know they are. What do you want?

                    WENG
   Would you like to try one?

                    QUILLER
   God, you boys are tough, Yes, I'd love to try one. May
   I? Please?

                    WENG
   Certainly.

Quiller takes a cigarette.

                    QUILLER
   Won't you join me?

                    WENG
   I don't smoke.

Weng watches Quiller as he lights his cigarette.

You don't look too well.

> QUILLER

Listen, don't try to be an intellectual. What do you want?

> WENG

I've been waiting for you here. Your car was found abandoned. I was posted here in case you turned up for a new one. Hengel is very annoyed, by the way. You led him a dance and lost him. We really don't know what you're up to.

> QUILLER

Uh-huh. I see.

> WENG

I have to take you to meet someone.

> QUILLER

You do, eh?

> WENG

Yes. I do.

INT. TOY DEPARTMENT. LARGE STORE.

Hengel looking intently at something.

It is a toy mountain train set. He is absorbed.

Quiller's voice:

> QUILLER

Why don't you blow the track up? Go on. You're a spy.

Hengel turns. Quiller and Weng stand by him. The crowds move about them. The three speak very quietly, almost in whispers.

WENG

That's a very odd kind of remark to make.

QUILLER

What's odd about it?

HENGEL

I have to take you somewhere.

QUILLER
(*to Weng*)

What exactly do you find odd?

WENG

You.

QUILLER
(*to Hengel*)

What do you mean, take me somewhere?

HENGEL

I have to take you to meet someone.

QUILLER

I was brought here to meet you.

HENGEL

You were brought here to meet me in order for me to take you to meet someone else.

QUILLER

Now who would that be?

HENGEL

I have not been told to tell you.

QUILLER

I'm ordering you to tell me.

HENGEL

You can't order me.

QUILLER

Of course I can. You're just a cover man. I'm the leading operator.

Pause. A lady assistant approaches.

ASSISTANT

Can I help you?

They look at her.

WENG

I don't think so, thank you. We're just looking.

She smiles – goes.

HENGEL

It's Pol.

QUILLER

Yes.
(*Pointing to Weng.*)
Well, he can come too.

HENGEL

He has not been invited.

QUILLER

But I'm ordering you to bring him along.

Pause.

HENGEL

Come on, Weng.

They all move to the door.

QUILLER
(*to Weng*)
What are you, Chinese?

WENG
In a way.

INT. CAFÉ. DAY.

Pol is sitting at a corner table, with coffee and a selection of cream cakes.

Quiller, Hengel and Weng walk to his table. He looks up.

They all sit.

Pol looks at each in turn.

POL
I'm sure the adverse party would be thrilled to see us all together.
> (*To Hengel.*)

Surely you can find Mr Weng some coffee somewhere else?

HENGEL
Mr Quiller ordered us to join you.

Pol looks at Quiller.

POL
Hullo, Quiller. How are you?

QUILLER
Great. I want to make a public announcement. I don't want any more cover.

Pause.

POL
You don't want any more cover?

QUILLER
No.

POL

You can't be said to have *had* very much cover, really, can you? You've made your cover's work rather hard.

QUILLER

That was just play. It's over.

Quiller looks at them.

No more cover.

POL

Will you have coffee?

QUILLER

I'd like you to call them off. please.

POL

I'm glad you said please . . . Quiller.

Pol sips his coffee. He looks at them all.

Silence.

Pol puts his cup down. He speaks quietly to Hengel and Weng.

All cover called off until further notice.

A pause.

QUILLER

I would like my car to be taken to the Hotel Zentral lock-up garage and left there.

POL

Could you see to that, Hengel?

HENGEL

Certainly I'll see to it.

Silence.

QUILLER

I would be glad if I could talk to you privately.

Pol cuts into his cake. Eats a piece and nods to Hengel and Weng.

Hengel and Weng stand and go out.

Silence.

POL

I'm sorry. Did you say something?

QUILLER

I would like some black coffee.

Pol looks at him.

Please.

Pol signals to waiter.

POL
(*in German*)

One black coffee, please.

Pol slices another piece of cake and eats.

QUILLER

I've been to their base.

POL

Oh yes?

QUILLER

But I don't know where it is.

POL

You were sleepwalking.

QUILLER

I was taken there.

POL

Ah.

Pause.

QUILLER

Met a man called Oktober.

POL

Oh yes.

QUILLER

Know him?

POL

We've never actually met.

QUILLER

At the end of our conversation he ordered them to kill me.

POL

And did they?

Pause.

QUILLER

No.

POL

Odd.

Pause.

Do you think they disobeyed him?

QUILLER

I wouldn't think so.

The waiter brings coffee, sets it down, goes.

They didn't take me through the full course, either.

POL

Didn't want to hurt you unduly, I'm sure.

QUILLER

They hurt KLJ.

POL

He got too close.

QUILLER

I was close.

POL

You were helpless.

Pause.

QUILLER

I'm alive, anyway.

POL

I'm so glad.

Pol takes out a small cigar.

QUILLER

They wanted to know where our base was.

POL

Did you tell them?

Quiller chuckles, looking at Pol.

Pol lights cigar.

QUILLER

They obviously think –

Pol coughs as he inhales.

POL

I'm so sorry. What did you say?

QUILLER

You're smoking the wrong brand.

Pol looks at him.

POL

No I'm not.

QUILLER

They obviously think they can find our base – through
another method.

POL

Do you know I think you're right? But what other
method?

QUILLER

I can find *their* base – by another method.

POL

Can you really? Good. How? Would you like to tell me?

QUILLER

No.

POL

Oh.

Pol puffs his cigar. Quiller drinks coffee, lights cigarette.

QUILLER

Mind if I smoke?

POL

I've agreed to withdraw cover – for twelve hours. But I
shall want a full report from you – very shortly. In the
meantime, of course – without cover – you may die. I
would like to emphasize that you're not on a routine
mission.

QUILLER

Go ahead. Emphasize.

POL

I'll want my report shortly.

QUILLER

You'll get it.

> POL

Why don't you carry weapons?

> QUILLER

You'll get your report.

> POL

You haven't answered my question.

> QUILLER

I don't have to. I use my own judgement. If you don't like it, call me off. That's all you can do.

Pause.

> You'll get your report.

> POL

You're on a delicate mission, Quiller. Perhaps you're beginning to appreciate that. Let me put it this way.

He takes two large cream cakes and arranges them on the table.

> There are two opposing armies drawn up on the field. But there's a heavy fog. They can't see each other. They want to, of course, very much.

He takes a currant from a cake and sets it between the cakes.

> You're in the gap between them. You can just see us, you can just see them. Your mission is to get near enough to see them and signal their position to us, so giving us the advantage. But if in signalling their position to us you inadvertently signal our position to them, then it will be they who will gain a very considerable advantage.

He points to the currant.

> That's where you are, Quiller. In the gap.

He pops the currant in his mouth and eats it.

INT. INGE'S FLAT. EARLY EVENING.

Quiller is with Inge. He is pouring drinks. He takes Inge's glass over to her but does not give it to her.

He stands looking at her.

> QUILLER
>
> Did you get to sleep?

> INGE
>
> What?

> QUILLER
>
> Did you get to sleep again, after I phoned?

> INGE
>
> Yes.

Quiller gives her her glass.

> Not immediately. Did you?

> QUILLER
>
> Not immediately.

Pause.

> INGE
>
> It was a strange time to call.

Pause.

> You seem different.

> QUILLER
>
> Do I?

> INGE
>
> Quieter.

> QUILLER
>
> I've been thinking about you.

Pause.

> #### INGE
> How's your article? The one you were going to write?

> #### QUILLER
> I haven't written it.

Pause.

> Actually . . . that wasn't exactly true. There's no such
> thing as the Philadelphia World Review.

> #### INGE
> Then who are you writing for?

> #### QUILLER
> No one. I'm not a writer.

Inge stares at him and laughs.

> #### INGE
> What are you?

> #### QUILLER
> I'm a kind of investigator.

> #### INGE
> What do you mean?

> #### QUILLER
> I'm investigating those people we were talking about last
> time.

Pause.

> #### INGE
> Those people? What do you mean?

> #### QUILLER
> Those people.

INGE

But you said you were a journalist.

QUILLER

I'm not.

Inge moves away from him to the window, stands with her back to him, eventually turns, looks at him.

INGE

Why are you telling me?

QUILLER

I thought you ought to know.

Pause.

INGE

But do you realize . . . what kind of people they are? They're quite ruthless . . . they're . . . ruthless. Everyone here knows about them. They've killed people.

Quiller goes to her.

QUILLER

You don't have to worry about me. I just thought you ought to know, that's all.

He holds her shoulders.

INGE

Do you . . . have a gun?

QUILLER

No, no.

INGE

Why not? Shouldn't you?

QUILLER

If you don't carry one you're less likely to get yourself killed. Believe me.

He draws her towards him.

I've missed you.

He touches her mouth.

Ssshh.

He kisses her.

I've missed you, all the time.

He draws her onto the sofa and caresses her face.

INGE

No. Please.

QUILLER

I've been wanting to touch you.

He kisses her throat.

You're so white.

He kisses her deeply.

She does not resist.

He murmurs, very close to her.

Have you been waiting for me?

INGE

Yes.

QUILLER

Yes.

Pause.

I know you have.

They look at each other.

INT. INGE'S FLAT. LATER. EVENING.

Inge and Quiller lying on the carpet, with cushions, smoking.
Evening light through the window.

Silence.

Inge at length turns on her elbows and looks down at him.

She kisses him, tenderly.

INGE
I am worried about you, you know.

QUILLER
No need.

INGE
Oh yes there is. A friend of my father's . . . he's told me
about them.

QUILLER
About who?

INGE
Those people . . . He was with them.

QUILLER
A friend of your father's?

INGE
Yes. I know what they're like. He's told me what they're
like.

Pause.

QUILLER
He knew them, eh?

INGE
Oh, he knew them. Yes.

Pause.

300

QUILLER

Where is he . . . this man?

INGE

What?

QUILLER

Do you know where he is? Can you reach him?

INGE

Yes, I . . . I think so. Why?

QUILLER

I think I'd like to speak to him.

INGE

But why?

QUILLER

Just a word.

INGE

But I've told you, he's not with them any more.

QUILLER

He might be able to help.

INGE

He might not want to.

QUILLER

Listen. I want to know where their base is, you see.

INGE

But he wouldn't know.

QUILLER

If he was with them he might know.

Pause.

Can I see him?

Inge is silent. She looks at him.

> INGE

You . . . really want to?

> QUILLER

Yes.

She turns away from him.

> INGE
> (*quietly*)

All right.

INT. SWIMMING BATH. NIGHT.

Inge and Quiller enter by a side door, into a passage.

The passage is dark.

They walk up it. Their steps echo.

INT. SWIMMING BATH. THE POOL.

The pool bathed in soft night light from a large skylight.

There is no water in the pool.

Silence.

Quiller and Inge enter by door onto the changing room gallery.

> INGE

He must be here. The door was open.

Quiller walks down the stairs to the side of the pool. He looks about, and gives a cheerful whistle of call. The whistle echoes. There is no other response.

Inge joins him at the side of the pool.

> QUILLER

Well . . . let's wait.

He walks down into the empty pool.

She follows. Their steps echo.

Want to dance?

INGE

No, thank you.

Pause. She moves a few steps.

QUILLER

Let's go down to the deep end.

They walk down the slope and stand in the deepest corner of the pool. He puts his arm around her.

We could do an underwater ballet.

He kisses her.

Ever done that?

She looks up at the diving board, looming above them. A changing room door creaks. She looks at Quiller.

Draught. What's his name?

INGE

Hassler.

Long shot of pool.

Their figures in the far corner.

Quiller shouts.

QUILLER

Hassler!

INGE

Don't!

The shouts of 'Hassler' and 'Don't' echo round the bath and die.

Quiller walks into the middle of the pool.

He feints a few football moves, stops.

QUILLER

Maybe the bar's open.

A door bangs. They hear steps.

Hassler (the swimming bath attendant) appears on the gallery, hurries down the stairs to the pool side and down into the pool.

They all meet in the middle of the pool.

HASSLER

I had to be late.

INGE
(*to Hassler*)

This is the man.

QUILLER

We've met.

HASSLER

I had to be late. I had to make some inquiries. I wanted to give you this information. I am glad you are someone to do something.

QUILLER

Uh-huh.

HASSLER

I was checking. But I have to tell you . . . they have moved . . . some months . . . from the old house. I do not know the new house. I keep away from things, you see.

QUILLER

Ah.

HASSLER

But I think . . . I know someone who does.

Quiller looks at him.

QUILLER

Who?

HASSLER

The name is Schroeder.

QUILLER

What does he know?

HASSLER

I don't know. I think . . . I think . . . perhaps . . . where they are.

Pause.

QUILLER

Can I see him?

HASSLER

I can try. I can ask. There is a telephone.

Hassler looks at them both.

Shall I ask?

QUILLER

Where's the telephone?

HASSLER

In the back.

Quiller walks towards the steps.

Silence.

A changing room door creaks. Inge looks up.

It's only a draught.

QUILLER

We'd better get you home.

INGE

No. I want to stay with you.

Quiller looks at her a moment. They then all move up the steps, and disappear along the gallery.

The diving board looms above the pool.

EXT. ROAD BY CANAL. NIGHT.

Hassler's car draws into the side of the road, by the trees.

The engine cuts off.

Silence.

Suddenly another car draws up.

A Woman gets out of it and walks towards Hassler's car.

INT. HASSLER'S CAR.

The Woman gets into Hassler's car. Quiller looks at her.

It is Frau Schroeder.

SCHROEDER
(*to Inge*)

You are surprised to see me?

INGE

Yes, I am.

SCHROEDER

I told the police about Steiner.
(*to Quiller*)
I am glad to see you again. I am glad to be of help. I tried to help your friend, but . . .

QUILLER

You know the house?

SCHROEDER

Yes.

QUILLER

Where is it?

SCHROEDER
(*pointing*)

That's it.

Quiller looks.

QUILLER

Is anyone in there?

SCHROEDER

I don't know. I just know that's the house.

Silence in the car.

HASSLER

We must all go now. Come on. You can tell your
people.

QUILLER

Oh no. I have to check whether she's right.

INGE

How?

QUILLER

I've got to go over there, to check whether's she's right.

SCHROEDER

I am right.

INGE

Others can check. Why do you have to do that?

307

QUILLER

Well . . . it's part of my job, you see.

SCHROEDER

I'm going. I've shown you the house. That's all I can
do.

HASSLER

It's stupid to stay here. We must get out.

QUILLER
(*to Inge*)

You go with them.

Pause.

INGE

No. I'll wait for you.

HASSLER
(*to Inge*)

You're stupid.

(*To Frau Schroeder.*)

I'll go with you.

(*To Inge.*)

You keep the car.

Hassler gets out. Frau Schroeder opens his door.

QUILLER
(*to Frau Schroeder*)

Thank you.

SCHROEDER

Don't mention it.

Frau Schroeder gets out.

Quiller and Inge look at each other.

QUILLER

Don't worry. I'm just going to check, that's all. Now

listen, I want you to remember a telephone number. All right?

                              INGE
Yes.

                            QUILLER
Now. Fix it. 21.89.62. Got it?

                              INGE
21.89.62.

                            QUILLER
If I'm not back in twenty minutes ring that number. Tell them you've run out of Chesterfields. Tell them where you are. Okay?

                              INGE
Yes.

                            QUILLER
What's the number?

                              INGE
21.89.62.

                            QUILLER
Stay here. Twenty minutes.

Quiller opens the car door, gets out.

                              INGE
    Listen –

He bends in.

    I love you.

Quiller looks at her and smiles faintly.

He walks across the road.

She watches him, sitting still in the car.

EXT. HOUSE. NIGHT.

Quiller walks towards it. He comes to a garden gate.

He opens it and goes through.

INT. GARDEN. NIGHT.

Quiller is in a large dark garden. Many overgrown shrubs.

Ahead of him, a dark, dim house.

He walks softly through the garden towards the back of the house.

He reaches it and stops.

Silence.

He tries a window. It is locked.

He examines other windows. One window is slightly ajar.

He squeezes his arm through the gap and unhooks the window from the inside.

INT. HOUSE. SCULLERY. NIGHT.

Quiller, with difficulty, climbs through the small window into the scullery.

He looks about. The scullery is bare, dirty, damp, bleak.

Quiller opens the inner door.

INT. HOUSE. HALL.

Quiller walks into the hall.

The floorboards are cracked, broken. Plaster is broken on the walls.

The house appears to be derelict.

INT. HOUSE. STAIRCASE.

Quiller ascends the stairs.

Silence.

Sudden shot, with Quiller's eyeline.

A Man, J, standing by a wall in shadow.

Quiller looks sharply to his right.

Another Man, B.

Another Man, C.

Quiller looks up to the first landing.

Another Man, A, is standing on the landing.

All the Men are still, but stand in quite relaxed postures.

Quiller looks about him.

There is no way out.

The Man on the landing speaks.

MAN (A)

Come up, please.

Slowly, Quiller begins to walk upstairs.

INT. FIRST LANDING. NIGHT.

Quiller reaches the landing and looks back.

B and C are following him up the stairs.

A walks to a door and opens it.

A burst of light.

MAN (A)

This way, please.

311

Quiller walks into the room.

INT. HOUSE. RECEPTION ROOM.

Quiller enters.

It is the room he has been in before.

B and C follow him into the room and stand.

Oktober is alone in the large room.

He turns.

> OKTOBER
>
> Hullo, Quiller. Do come in.

He waves to chair.

> Sit down. What a surprise. What will you have to drink?

> QUILLER
>
> A double Jack Daniels on the rocks.

> OKTOBER
> *(to a Man, B)*
>
> A double Jack Daniels on the rocks.

> MAN
>
> We have no Jack Daniels, Reichsführer.

> OKTOBER
>
> No Jack Daniels? Tch, tch, tch.
> *(To Quiller.)*

> What would you say to some old Kentucky Grandad?

> QUILLER
>
> Make it Scotch Malt.

> OKTOBER
>
> Ah. I wish we could help you there but unfortunately I
> know we can't.

QUILLER

What kind of a bar is this, for Christ's sake?

OKTOBER

I am not a barman Mr Quiller.

He walks to the door.

I am a German gentleman.

He opens the door and gestures to Quiller.

Please.

Quiller remains still.

QUILLER

Where are we going?

OKTOBER

Downstairs.

Quiller does not move. Oktober stands by the door.

B and C move a few steps towards Quiller. They stop, close to him.

Quiller goes to the door.

INT. HOUSE. LANDING.

Oktober, Quiller and B and C walk along landing to back stairs.

They stop by an old service lift.

One of the men opens the doors. They all get in.

INT. LIFT.

The lift goes down.

It has an open top.

The four stand in silence.

Oktober speaks sharply in German to the two men.

OKTOBER

Would you mind not standing so close.

B and C move away.

INT. HOUSE. BASEMENT.

The lift arrives. They get out.

There is a long corridor of whitewashed stone. There are a number of doors at either side, closed.

They begin to walk down the corridor.

A door opens suddenly and a Man in a boiler suit comes out, wheeling a trolley. On the trolley is a large filing cabinet.

He wheels the trolley down the corridor, round a corner and out of sight.

QUILLER

He's working late.

OKTOBER

We're moving tomorrow.

QUILLER

Oh?

OKTOBER

Yes, we have a busy night ahead of us. We're moving all our equipment. We're changing our base.

QUILLER

Oh.

They continue walking.

Quiller pauses in his step and stops.

He glances at the two men behind him.

314

They all stop.

Where are we going?

OKTOBER

In here.

He goes towards a door.

Oh, I hear you've called off your cover by the way. That was an odd thing to do.

He opens the door and goes in.

Quiller follows, flanked by the two men.

INT. CELLAR.

The cellar is a long low-ceilinged room. A long metal-framed, hooded strip light shines from the ceiling.

The rest of the room is in shadow.

Inge is sitting in a chair under the light.

Two men, Dorfmann and Nagel, well dressed, sit at a distance from her in half shadow, in easy chairs.

The room appears to have been stripped.

There are two or three closed crates, a rolled carpet and two chairs piled on top of each other.

Inge looks at Oktober, not at Quiller.

Oktober gestures to the two men.

OKTOBER

Herr Dorfmann. Herr Nagel. Mr Quiller.

Neither Quiller, Dorfmann or Nagel respond to this introduction.

Oktober looks at Inge.

And this is Fräulein Lindt.

Turns to Quiller.

We have just found her sitting in a car, quite near here. Her first name is Inge.

Pause.

QUILLER

So what?

OKTOBER

She's your friend.

QUILLER

I've never seen her before.

OKTOBER

Yes, yes. She's your close friend. Inge.

Pause.

I remember the name well.
          (*To a Man.*)
You. Do you remember the name?

MAN (C)

Yes, Reichsführer.

The recorded voices of Quiller and Oktober are suddenly heard in the room. They listen, still. So does Inge.

Oktober looks at Quiller and then, gradually, his gaze rests upon Inge.

Inge glances at him.

Quiller is aware that Oktober and Inge are looking at each other throughout the recording.

The recorded voices:

OKTOBER

That boss of yours, what's his name?

316

QUILLER

Inge.

OKTOBER

No, she's a girl. She's not your boss. What was his
name?

QUILLER

She has long legs.

OKTOBER

After you leave us you can go to her. She's waiting for
you.

QUILLER

White . . .

OKTOBER

She adores you.

QUILLER

No.

OKTOBER

Oh yes. Adores you. She wants you only. She longs for
you only.

QUILLER

Longs . . . adores me . . .

Pause.

Wants me . . . only . . .

The tape recorder is switched off.

Silence. Quiller and Inge still do not look at each other.

OKTOBER
(*gaily*)

And here she is.

QUILLER

No, no. Not at all. The Inge I was talking about was fat.
Very fat. Gigantic.

He looks at Inge.

I don't know this girl.

OKTOBER
(to Inge)
For a nice innocent German girl you pick very bizarre
friends. Do you understand English?
(Sharply, in German.)
Do you understand English?

INGE

Nein.

Oktober laughs.

OKTOBER
You must find him very attractive. What's it like to be so
sexually attractive, Quiller?

Pause.

Mmmnnn?

Pause.

Anyway, I'm glad you were able to drop in tonight.
You're quite free to go now.

Silence.

Really. You can go – now.

Quiller remains still.

But there is just one thing. We're still very interested in
the location of your base. We feel . . . that there might
be some information there which could be of
importance to us.

Pause.

> So let me make a proposal to you. If you would like to tell us where your base is you can take . . . her . . . with you. Truly. You will be quite safe, quite free.

Pause.

> If not, she will stay here, with us.

Pause.

> But do go, if you like, and consider the matter. Take a walk. Think about it. But please don't forget you have complete freedom to return here at any time, give us the information we require and leave . . . with this lady.

Pause.

> We'll give you till dawn.

He looks at Inge, then back at Quiller.

> If you're still undecided by dawn – we'll kill you both.

Pause.

> How's that? Fair?

QUILLER

Sure.

OKTOBER

Good.

Pause.

QUILLER

Right. I'll get some air.

OKTOBER

Yes, why don't you? I hope to see you a little later tonight. In fact I'm sure I will.

319

Oktober turns to B and C.

Take Mr Quiller up in the lift will you? He knows the way out.

Quiller without looking at Inge leaves the room.

INT. CORRIDOR.

B, C and Quiller walk towards the lift.

INT. LIFT.

Quiller, B and C enter the lift.

The doors close.

The lift goes up, very slowly.

Silence in the lift.

The lift stops.

INT. HALL.

The lift doors open. Quiller, B and C walk into the hall.

The two men stand. Quiller looks at them.

They remain still.

INT. HOUSE. STAIRS AND HALL.

Quiller walks to the door.

A is standing by the door. He opens it.

Quiller goes out.

EXT. HOUSE. FRONT. NIGHT.

Quiller walks down the steps of the house, along the front gate, and out on to the road.

EXT. BERLIN TIERGARTEN. NIGHT.

A long road. Derelict buildings at either side.

It is late at night.

In the distance, Quiller is walking towards the camera.

Silence.

The camera moves sideways to disclose a brightly lit telephone box. It is the one hard source of light.

His face, as he stops by a lamp post. He lights a cigarette and glances up at the buildings and along the road behind him.

There is no one in sight.

He continues to walk towards the telephone box.

From the telephone box see him approach.

He walks straight past it and up the road.

As he passes it a Man, K, emerges from the shadow of trees on the opposite side of the road and walks slowly along, in the same direction.

EXT. CORNER OF ROAD. TIERGARTEN AREA. NIGHT.

Quiller approaches street corner.

There is a Man, L, at the opposite corner, standing.

Quiller looks up at the moon and glances back.

Two men, M and N, are walking slowly down the road, on opposite sides of it.

A fourth Man, K, is standing by a dark café.

EXT. CITY. NIGHT.

Quiller walking.

Three men, L, M and N, one in front and two behind, also strolling.

Their steps resound on the road.

Apart from them, the street is empty, silent.

Quiller pauses a moment by a telephone box.

The others halt.

Silence.

Quiller walks on. So do the others.

INT. ALL NIGHT CAFÉ.

Steam. Lorry drivers talking loudly.

Quiller walks in, walks to bar, asks for coffee.

He looks at telephone behind the bar.

In the mirror he sees the door open and K walk in.

K sits down.

Quiller receives his coffee, sips.

EXT. ALL NIGHT CAFÉ. NIGHT.

Quiller comes out of the café.

He strolls casually towards an overhead railway station.

L, M and N saunter, at a distance, behind him.

Quiller stands a moment by the entrance. A signal is heard from the platform.

Suddenly Quiller dashes into the station and up the stairs.

EXT. PLATFORM. NIGHT.

The train is pulling out.

The camera moves to see, in the street below, L, M and N jumping into a car. The car pulls away with great speed and follows the direction of the train.

EXT. PLATFORM.

Quiller comes into shot.

He steps carefully across the tracks and disappears down the opposite stairway.

EXT. OTHER SIDE OF STATION. NIGHT.

Quiller comes out of the station and stops.

A Man, O, is standing by a lamp post.

Another Man, P, is standing at the corner.

Quiller looks at O and walks slowly towards him. O stares at him.

QUILLER

Do you have a light?

Another man walks into Quiller's vision.

He is K. Quiller glances at him.

MAN (O)

No.

QUILLER

Non-smoker, eh?

The three men stand looking at him.

Quiller walks past them, down the street.

The three men walk slowly after him.

EXT. TREE-LINED AVENUE. NIGHT.

Shot through foliage onto street of Quiller walking along very slowly, a very small figure.

The three men, at intervals, are glimpsed through the trees, walking in the same direction.

EXT. BRANDENBURGERSTRASSE. NIGHT.

Quiller walking slowly down the long deserted avenue, followed by the three men.

EXT. HOTEL ZENTRAL. NIGHT.

Quiller comes down street, followed by men.

He walks up the steps, into the hotel.

The men stay, singly, at the other side of the road.

INT. HOTEL LOBBY.

In the lobby the nightporter is brushing shoes.

He goes to the desk.

> PORTER
>
> What number?

> QUILLER
>
> Twenty-one.

Porter gives him key.

Quiller moves up the stairs.

Porter calls after him.

> PORTER
> Do you want a morning paper?

Quiller turns and looks at him. At length he speaks.

No.

INT. HOTEL. QUILLER'S ROOM.

Quiller shuts the door and looks at the room.

It has been ransacked.

He locks the door, goes to the phone, lifts it, listens.

A regular sound of tapping.

He holds it a moment, replaces it.

He looks at his watch. It is five o'clock.

He goes into the bathroom.

INT. BATHROOM.

Quiller looking at his face in the mirror.

His face is streaked, creased, grimy, strained. He throws water on his face.

Reaching for a towel, he suddenly finds himself looking out of the small bathroom window.

The window overlooks the garages, garage yard and gates to street at the back of the hotel.

GARAGE YARD. QUILLER'S POINT OF VIEW.

It is dawn.

Light filters gently over the yard.

Camera concentrates on the garage.

INT. ROOM.

Quiller walks into room, wiping his face.

He throws towel on the bed, bends and takes off his shoes.

He switches the light off and goes to the door.

Very slowly, he turns handle and pulls door softly towards him.

INT. HOTEL CORRIDOR.

The corridor is dimly lit.

Quiller emerges from room. He turns the door-handle soundlessly and closes door. He carries his shoes.

Sound of a shoebrush from below.

Quiller walks down the corridor to a back flight of stairs.

He walks in time to the sound of the shoebrush, freezing when the brushing pauses.

INT. SIDE DOOR. HOTEL.

He approaches door. There is a key on the inside.

He unlocks the door and steps out into the yard.

EXT. GARAGE YARD.

The dawn light is growing.

He puts on his shoes.

He stands in the yard, facing the lock-up garages.

In front of him the yard gates leading to a narrow back street.

There is one lamp on the street, by the gate.

Silence.

Quiller walks to garage. He unlocks garage door quietly and pulls it.

A stone jammed under the door screeches. The door jars.

He looks quickly behind him and up at the dark hotel.

No movement of any kind.

He frowns and, still looking towards the hotel and the gates, pulls the door again, harshly. It scrapes.

No movement. No sound.

Quiller listens to the silence and feels the stillness.

His eye begins to twitch.

He walks to the gate.

EXT. BACK GATE. STREET.

Quiller stands in the light of the lamp, on the street. There is no one in sight.

He opens the gate. It swings back with a slight clang. The street is empty.

A car is parked in the street, empty.

All doors and windows are empty, silent.

The roofs are bare.

There is no figure in any shadow.

Quiller stands frozen in the lamplight.

Far away the throb of a Diesel truck.

EXT. GARAGE YARD.

Quiller goes back into yard, and looks about him. An oil drum, timber, dustbins. Nothing more.

He goes into garage.

INT. GARAGE.

Quiller takes out a pencil torch and flicks it over the garage. He then goes to his car, the Mercedes 230 SL. He looks at his watch.

It is 5.24.

He examines the doors. No marks.

He opens the boot and examines it. Nothing.

He gets into the car.

INT. CAR.

He examines the interior of the car quickly but meticulously.

He releases bonnet and gets out.

INT. GARAGE.

His torch probes the engine. He finds nothing.

He stands upright and still, sweating.

He presses his hand against his forehead.

His torch points down to the cement floor.

He glances down. A chip of stone, some splinters.

He suddenly squats, gets on to his back and pulls himself under the car.

UNDERNEATH OF CAR.

Quiller shines his torch up.

A small bomb, six inches by three, is attached to the underside of the car.

He wipes the sweat from his hands, takes bomb from its perch, holds it to his chest and slides out from under car.

INT. GARAGE.

Quiller stands with bomb.

He looks at the partitions in the garage. They are six feet high. There is a back door at the far end.

He leans into car, checks the gears for neutral and starts the engine.

He goes to the bonnet, looks at it.

He rests the bomb about a third of the distance from the front edge. The engine throbs.

He looks at his watch, flicking torch to catch the second hand.

He shines torch on the bomb.

The bomb is still. Then it begins to slide.

He catches it. Looks at his watch.

He places the bomb some inches higher on the bonnet. It rests there.

Quiller climbs first partition and drops.

He climbs second partition and drops.

He kicks over an oil tin, nearly falls.

Climbs third partition and drops. Runs to back door of garage. Pulls it. It is stuck. He pulls it violently. It still will not open.

He looks down and sees bolt, unbolts it, goes out.

EXT. GARAGE. HIGH WALL. TREES OVERHANGING.

It is now light. Sound of birds.

Sounds of distant traffic.

Quiller crouches by the wall, tense.

The engine of car can be heard throbbing faintly.

He looks at his watch. It is 5.55.

He waits. The car still throbs.

His eyelid twitches. He claps his hand over it.

He grits his teeth.

Starts to cough, stops.

The car still throbs. Quiller is hunched. He suddenly stands upright, moves to the corner of the garage.

The ground shakes. The wall shudders.

Quiller swings back and throws himself flat on the ground.

The roof bursts open. Doors break off and crash across the yard.

Silence. Quiller remains down.

Another explosion. A sheet of hot air and flame.

Silence.

EXT. THE GARAGE YARD. DAWN.

The yard in chaos. Hotel windows broken.

Shouts.

Quiller is out of sight behind the garage.

K runs in from the gate to the wide open garage.

The Mercedes is consumed with flame and smoke.

K peers.

K turns away and walks back to the gate.

O and P join him. K nods to them.

They walk out into the street.

It is daylight.

EXT. CITY CENTRE. BERLIN. EARLY MORNING.

Two churches, one ruined, one new. A solitary taxi passes them.

The taxi draws up at an office building.

Quiller gets out, pays the driver.

The taxi drives off.

Quiller enters the building.

INT. ROOM. LOCAL CONTROL.

The lift arrives. Quiller gets out.

Hengel, Weng, Hughes and two others are in the room.

They are in shirtsleeves, unshaven, bleary-eyed.

Cigarette ends in trays. Numbers of coffee cups.

Hengel picks up the phone and presses button.

> HENGEL
> (*into phone*)
> He's here. Yes. Right.

He puts phone down.

They all look at Quiller.

He too is unshaven, his face creased with dirt.

> QUILLER
> Any coffee?

> WENG
> I think so.

Weng looks into a jug and pours.

QUILLER

Where's Pol?

HENGEL

He's been on all night. He's just gone to bed. He's
coming.

Weng gives Quiller coffee.

WENG

Sugar?

QUILLER

No thanks.

Silence.

HENGEL

We've been up all night too.

QUILLER

Have you?

Quiller drinks his coffee, clasps the cup.

He shivers.

HENGEL

Do you want the fire on?

QUILLER

No. That's all right.

They all sit in silence.

Pol comes through an inner door, in a dressing gown.

POL

Hullo, Quiller.

QUILLER

Tiergarten. Number six. That's their base. Big house by
the canal. Looks derelict.

POL

Will they be there?

QUILLER

Yes. They're not worried. They think I'm dead. They think I was blown up in a car.

POL
(*to Hughes*)

Get Ziegler.

Hughes dials.

Silence.

A voice.

HUGHES
(*into phone*)

Just a second, please. This is Local Control, Berlin.

Pol takes the phone.

POL

Hullo Ziegler. Our man's back. Tiergarten. Number six. By the canal. You can go in now.
(*He listens.*)
Right.

He puts the phone down.

I'd like a full report as soon as possible, Quiller.

Quiller looks at him.

QUILLER

You'll get it.

POL

Have a little rest first, of course.

QUILLER

Oh, thanks.

POL

I'm going to change.

Pol goes out.

Quiller sits looking at his cup.

INT. ROOM. LOCAL CONTROL. FORTY MINUTES LATER.

Quiller is standing by the window, looking down into the street below.

The street is crowded with people going to work.

There is a great deal of traffic.

It is a beautiful morning.

Quiller turns into the room.

Hengel is sitting with his feet up.

Hughes is sitting by the telephone.

Quiller walks across the room, sits down.

Pol comes through the inner door, shaved and dressed.

POL

Any word?

HUGHES

No.

The telephone rings. Hughes picks it up.

LCB.

Hughes listens a moment.

Hold on, please.

Hughes nods at Pol. Pol takes phone.

POL
(*to Hughes*)

Take it.

Hughes lifts extension and takes shorthand transcript of the conversation.

There is a clatter of a voice at the other end of the line.

Pol grunts occasionally. The voice stops.

POL

Thank you. Good-bye.

Pol puts the phone down.

Quiller looks at him through slit eyes.

Pol stands.

They've got them all. Good.

He waves to the door.

Where's my breakfast?

As Pol reaches the door Quiller speaks.

QUILLER

Where's mine?

Pol turns to him.

POL

Oh. Are you hungry?

They regard each other.

Why don't we have breakfast together? Upstairs. In about . . . eight minutes?

QUILLER

I'm too tired to go upstairs.

POL

We'll have it sent to you, Quiller. Don't put yourself out. Will you join me, Hengel?

HENGEL

With pleasure.

Pol and Hengel go out.

Quiller and Hughes are left alone.

Pause.

HUGHES

Well . . . that's that . . . for the time being.

Quiller lights a cigarette.

QUILLER

What are the details?

HUGHES

Not many. They got them all. Got Oktober.

Pause.

QUILLER

Did they find a girl there?

HUGHES

No. No mention of a girl. They got Dorfmann and Nagel.

Pause.

QUILLER

Are you sure they didn't find a girl?

Hughes examines his transcript. He looks up.

HUGHES

Yes. Quite sure. No girl.

Quiller lifts his cigarette to his mouth and draws on it.

336

EXT. PLAYGROUND. SCHOOL. DAY.

Children playing in the playground.

In background, the school.

Quiller comes into shot.

He walks towards school. A few children look at him.

INT. SCHOOL. DAY.

Quiller walking down corridor. Children pass.

He reaches Inge's classroom. He stands at the door and looks in.

Inge is there, talking to a boy. She looks up, sees Quiller.

She speaks to the boy, who leaves the room.

Quiller goes in.

INT. CLASSROOM. SCHOOL.

Quiller shuts the door. He stands. They are alone. Silence.

                    INGE
    Hullo.

                    QUILLER
    Hullo.

Pause.

Quiller walks down the classroom, flips a book on the desk.

    How are you?

                    INGE
    I'm – all right –

Quiller flips open another exercise book and reads it.

    I was very lucky.

337

QUILLER
(*shutting book*)

What? Sorry?

INGE

I said I was very lucky.

QUILLER

Oh! How?

INGE

They let me go.

Pause.

QUILLER

Did they?

INGE

Yes.

Pause.

Yes, they suddenly . . . told me to go.

QUILLER

Well . . . you must have felt pretty relieved.

INGE

I did.

Pause.

QUILLER

We got all of them.

INGE

Oh, really?

Pause.

Oh, good.

338

QUILLER

Well . . . not all of them, perhaps. Most of them.

Pause.

INGE

You seem tired.

QUILLER

I had a heavy night.

Pause.

INGE

Oh, I tried to phone that number, by the way. After I got out. You remember? The number you gave me.

QUILLER

Oh yes.

INGE

Yes, I tried. But it didn't exist.

QUILLER

Oh, really? I must have made a mistake.

Pause.

Anyway . . . I'm glad to see that you're all right.

INGE

And you.

He walks up the classroom.

QUILLER

Well, I'm leaving Berlin.

INGE

Are you?

QUILLER

I'm a little tired.

INGE

You work too hard.

QUILLER

Well, you too. I'm sure you could take things a little
easier, you know.

INGE

Oh, no. I have my work to do. I must do it. I want to do
it.

Pause.

QUILLER

Uh-huh. Well, if I ever get back to Berlin I'll look you
up.

INGE

Yes. Please.

They look at each other.

That would be nice.

He puts out his hand. They shake hands.

Pause.

QUILLER

By the way, did you ever meet a man called Jones?

INGE

No. No, I don't think so.

QUILLER

Good-bye.

INGE

Good-bye.

*He goes to the door. As he closes door, he sees her placing books
into her bag.*

340

EXT. SCHOOL. PLAYGROUND.

Quiller walks away through playing children.

Inge comes to the top of the school steps.

She calls to the children.

They collect around her.

They talk eagerly to her. She listens to them, smiling.

She glances up.

Quiller, in the distance, walks through the school gates.

Accident

Accident was first presented by London Independent Producers (Distribution) Ltd on 9th February 1967 with the following cast:

STEPHEN Dirk Bogarde
WILLIAM Michael York
ANNA Jacqueline Sassard
POLICEMAN Brian Phelan
SECOND POLICEMAN Terence Rigby
CLARISSA Carole Caplin
ROSALIND Vivien Merchant
TED Maxwell Findlater
CHARLEY Stanley Baker
PROVOST Alexander Knox
HEDGES Nicholas Mosley
RECEPTIONIST Jane Hillary
SECRETARY Jill Johnson
BELL Harold Pinter
MAN IN BELL'S OFFICE Freddie Jones
FRANCESCA Delphine Seyrig
LAURA Ann Firbank

Directed by Joseph Losey

EXT. THE HOUSE. NIGHT. SUMMER.

Long shot.

The camera is still, looking at the house from outside the gate, up the short curved drive, across the circular gravel court.

In a meadow behind the house, dim shapes of animals. The camera moves slowly forward to a position inside the gate. It comes to rest.

The house is silent, dark. One lower front window is curtained. Light filters through it on to the gravel. Gradually, over picture, the hum of a car, in the distance.

The hum grows.

Closer but still distant, a sudden screech, grind, smash and splintering.

Silence.

Light goes on in the hall of the house.

The front door opens.

Stephen is silhouetted in the light.

EXT. LANE. NIGHT.

Camera jolting down the lane.

Sound of footsteps running.

Dark lane winding.

Tree shapes crossing, retreating, advancing.

Glimpsed fields through hedge. Shapes of cows.

A horse moving, head up.

Camera to sky. Stars.

EXT. FOOT OF LANE. NIGHT.

Stephen halting.

Moonlight hits his face, sharply and briefly.

EXT. THE CAR.

Close shot from underside of car.

The smashed mass of the car, shooting at passenger seat front-section, lying on camera.

Broken metalwork, jagged shapes of glass.

Two bodies heaped together, still, forming one shape.

Silence but for the ticking of ignition.

EXT. LANE.

Long shot from corner of the lane, which forms part of a road junction.

The car seen clearly lying on its side in the middle of the road. Mounds of earth rise at either side of the road, by the hedges.

Trees stand sharply against the sky.

Moonlight passes gently over glass of the car.

Camera moves slowly towards car, until it is quite close to it.

Long shot across top of car (which has its driving seat uppermost) to corner of lane. Stephen seen standing.

Stephen walks towards car. Camera closes in.

He is lost behind it.

His hands appear, grasping the car top.

His face.

EXT. LANE. MOONLIGHT.

Long shot of Stephen climbing on to the top of the car.

EXT. CAR.

Stephen looking down through driving window.

Bodies heaped within.

Ticking of ignition.

Long shot across bonnet from hedge of Stephen trying to wrench car door open.

He does, with great effort.

The door crashes back against bonnet.

He almost falls off car.

INT. CAR.

The car jolts. The bodies jolt. A bottle of whisky rolls.

Looking up.

Stephen at open door, above him the sky, looking down.

Foreground of skirt, legs, shoes.

Stephen shifts his body, the car sways, his legs and feet descend into car.

Legs descending slowly. Ignition ticking.

From above. Close.

William's face. Blood and glass.

Stephen's feet placing themselves carefully by it.

Ignition key is heard to be switched off. Silence.

The car jolts. William's head shifts.

EXT. CAR.

Top shot.

Stephen's hand clutching door frame, moving along it.

EXT. CAR.

From underside.

Jagged glass. Back of William's head.

Camera moves through broken glass to William's temple.

STEPHEN'S VOICE
William?

Stephen's feet searching for surer support, avoiding bodies.

Moonlight sharp and splintered through smashed windscreen.

Anna's legs move. She groans.

STEPHEN'S VOICE
Anna?

Anna's voice whimpering.

Camera moves up her body. Her face is clenched. She whimpers, yelps. Her eyes open. She begins to push herself up. She mutters, her teeth chatter. She pushes herself up. Stephen's hands seize and help her.

EXT. LANE.

The car, rocking, in the middle of the road.

INT. CAR.

Anna's shoes on William's chest.

EXT. LANE.

Long shot of Anna rising slowly from car.

Her head and shoulders rise against a background of stars.

She tosses her head.

A sudden scream from Stephen over picture:

STEPHEN
Don't! You're standing on his face!

EXT. CAR.

Close shot:

Stephen.

Medium shot of Stephen and Anna. They are standing by the side of the car. He is holding her under her shoulders, staring at her.

His face.

Her face, still, eyes closed.

EXT. LANE.

Stephen walking through moonlight with Anna in his arms.

He carries her to a grass bank at side of lane and lowers her on to it.

Anna alone, lying on bank.

Her legs.

INT. CAR.

William's face. Shining glass splinters on it and around it.

ACCIDENT

Stephen's head, listening, at William's neck.

The car shakes. He looks up.

Anna above him, at open door, reaching into car.

His face large, hair falling.

Stephen's and William's faces, close, both staring.

Anna, supporting herself on steering wheel, reaching down into car to pick up her handbag.

EXT. LANE.

Anna walks to bank with handbag and sits.

She takes handkerchief and mirror from bag and wipes her face.

Stephen standing, looking down at her.

Anna tracing smudges with her finger.

STEPHEN'S VOICE

You can walk.

Anna does not look at him.

I'm going to telephone.

Anna takes out a comb and combs her hair.

STEPHEN
(looking down at her)

Can you walk?

Anna quietly completes her combing, puts comb, mirror, handkerchief into bag, closes bag.

She sits still.

He puts his hands under her elbows and lifts her up.

They stand, apart.

Behind them in background the car.

He puts his hand on her elbow. She withdraws her elbow, not sharply.

She begins to walk alone up the lane. He follows.

Long shot.

They walk slowly up the lane towards the house.

Stephen is no longer following. He is equal with her, but Anna keeps a distance between them.

They walk slowly at opposite sides of the lane, which slopes gently uphill, in the bright moonlight, the trees black above them, the sky large.

INT. HOUSE. THE HALL.

(The interior of the house is untidy and rambling, comfortable. Some of the walls are rough plastered. There is a careless mixture of contemporary and antique furnishing, none of it expensive. The air of the house is casual, relaxed.)

The camera rests in the rear section of the hall, by the open door of the sitting room.

The staircase rises up.

Under the staircase, half in half out of an open cupboard, broken toys, a child's wheel barrow, a large hoop.

The ting of a telephone receiver replaced.

INT. SITTING-ROOM. NIGHT.

Anna sitting still in an armchair.

Her handbag lies on a coffee table close to her chair.

An old dog pokes his head in the sitting-room door.

INT. THE HALL.

The dog turns from sitting-room door, walks up the hall, sits, looks up at Stephen.

Stephen sitting, by telephone, at hall table, looks down at the dog.

INT. SITTING-ROOM.

Stephen comes in. He walks slowly to Anna, puts his hand on her forehead.

Large close-up.

His hand on her forehead. Her eyes.

STEPHEN
(standing over Anna)

You were lying on top of him.

Pause.

Were you driving?

Anna leans back in armchair.

He touches her hair.

Don't worry.

INT. HOUSE. KITCHEN.

Stephen walking to kitchen table with teapot. He pours tea into cup.

INT. SITTING-ROOM.

Stephen bending over Anna with cup.

STEPHEN

Drink it.

He places cup by handbag on side table.

ACCIDENT

Anna remains still in armchair.

Stephen sitting, watching her.

Silence.

Sound of a car drawing up.

He turns to window.

EXT. HOUSE. FRONT GATE. NIGHT.

Police car driving slowly down drive towards house.

Stephen comes out of front door. The door swings half shut behind him.

The car stops. Two policemen get out.

Stephen and the Policemen stand a moment, talking.

INT. SITTING-ROOM.

Stephen enters the sitting-room, the Policemen following.

He stops, blinks, turns his head to the Policemen.

Policeman settling himself in the armchair in which Anna sat. He places his helmet on his lap, takes out notebook.

Stephen, standing, turns to other Policeman.

STEPHEN

Sit down.

SECOND POLICEMAN

No, it's all right.

Stephen sitting, with cigarette.

POLICEMAN'S VOICE

Yours is the only house for some distance. so he must have been coming to see you.

STEPHEN

He was.

POLICEMAN

You were expecting him?

STEPHEN

Yes.

Stephen glances at Second Policeman.

Second Policeman, standing, expressionless.

Policeman in chair, writing in notebook, suddenly coughs violently. He takes out handkerchief, wipes his mouth.

POLICEMAN

Sorry.

He places his helmet on the table where Anna's handbag and the teacup had been.

The coffee table.

The helmet is placed on the coffee table.

Stephen's face.

The policeman opening his notebook.

Second Policeman looks out of french windows into the black rear garden.

Did you know him well?

Second Policeman turns from window.

STEPHEN

He was my pupil.

Second policeman strolls back to his place in the room.

POLICEMAN

He was your pupil at the university?

STEPHEN

Yes.

Stephen's face.

He wanted to talk to me about something.

The room.

Silence.

POLICEMAN

You found –

A sound, from no specific place, from somewhere in the house. It is very brief. The Policeman continues.

POLICEMAN

You found the car at one forty-five?

STEPHEN

He was going to a party, then coming on to me.

SECOND POLICEMAN

It looks as though he was pretty drunk. There was whisky all over the car.

Stephen's face.

STEPHEN

I don't know what it was all about.
      (*Pause.*)
I mean I don't know what he wanted to talk to me about.

The room.

The Two Policemen. One sitting, the other standing.

Silence.

Stephen's face.

STEPHEN

He probably wanted my advice about something.

INT. SITTING-ROOM.

Empty. No sound.

INT. KITCHEN.

Stephen at long bare kitchen table.

STEPHEN

Anna?

INT. LANDING. BEDROOM DOOR.

Stephen rushes up stairs and enters bedroom.

INT. BEDROOM.

It is Stephen and Rosalind's bedroom. It is attractive, with clear feminine characteristics.

The bed is a fourposter.

Anna lies on the fourposter bed.

Her legs are curled. Her skirt is above her knees.

She is asleep.

Her handbag and the teacup are on a bedside table.

Stillness.

The camera, with Stephen, moves slowly towards Anna on the bed.

Anna on the bed.

Stephen standing by window, looking at bed.

Anna asleep. Her body curved.

Stephen at foot of bed.

Anna's feet.

One shoe is on.

The other lying on bedcover.

INT. CAR.

Anna's shoe, standing, digging into William's face.

Stephen's hands on her legs.

STEPHEN'S VOICE

Don't!

Close-up. William's face. Dead.

INT. STEPHEN'S STUDY, COLLEGE. MORNING.

William's face, smiling.

William and Stephen are sitting by the open window. The window looks down to a quadrangle. On the grass a white goat is tethered. The scene is framed between them, below.

STEPHEN

You haven't spoken to her?

WILLIAM

No.

STEPHEN

You've just seen her.

WILLIAM

I've just seen her. Walking about. A little.

STEPHEN

And you like the look of her?

357

STEPHEN

Yes. I do.

Pause.

STEPHEN

And what am I supposed to do about it?

WILLIAM

Nothing at all.

STEPHEN

Oh. Good.

WILLIAM

I'd just like to know what you think of her, that's all.

STEPHEN

You realize I'm her tutor?

WILLIAM

Naturally. I also realize you're my tutor.

STEPHEN

And that being her tutor, her moral welfare must be my first consideration.

WILLIAM

Ah. You mean besides being her tutor you are also her protector.

STEPHEN

I mean that I refuse to countenance or encourage male lust as directed against any of my woman students.

WILLIAM

Well said.

STEPHEN

Thank you.

WILLIAM

Anyway, what's her name, for God's sake?

STEPHEN

Her name? Her name. Ah yes, I remember her name.
Her name is Anna von Graz und Leoben.

Pause.

WILLIAM

German.

STEPHEN

Austrian.

Pause.

WILLIAM

Well, come on! What do you think of her?

STEPHEN

I don't think.

WILLIAM

I thought thinking was your job!

STEPHEN

Not about *that*.

WILLIAM

You're not past it, are you? Already?

From the same viewpoint, Anna appears in the quadrangle. She stops and talks to the goat.

William stands.

It's her.

STEPHEN

She's coming for her second tutorial.

359

WILLIAM

You didn't tell me.

STEPHEN

Wait. I'll introduce you.

WILLIAM

She's talking to the goat.

STEPHEN

They speak German.

Anna stroking the goat. The men at window.

William at door.

WILLIAM

No, not now. Really.

STEPHEN

You intend to go it alone, eh? Without introduction?

WILLIAM

That's right.

Stephen alone in middle of study.

He turns to window and looks down.

Stephen's head at window.

He watches Anna walk across lawn towards college.

William crosses lawn, at a distance from her.

Anna disappears under window.

William stops by the goat and bends his head to it.

INT. STUDY.

Anna sitting, knees together, with notebook.

Her face, listening.

STEPHEN'S VOICE

Philosophy is a process of enquiry only. It does not attempt to find specific answers to specific questions.

Close-up. His face, looking at her.

INT. HOUSE. SITTING-ROOM. AFTERNOON.

Large close-up of Clarissa's face (three years old).

She turns from camera, runs, jumps on her mother's lap, looks over her mother's shoulder at camera.

Stephen standing at door. Rosalind sitting, Clarissa on her lap. Ted (seven years old) lying on floor with book, looking up. The dog, asleep on floor.

STEPHEN

She loves her Dad.

ROSALIND

She hasn't eaten anything today.

Rosalind is pregnant. She is sewing. On the floor are paintboxes, papers in strips, scissors, children's books, a doll, cars.

Stephen looks at the floor and then walks across the room. He kicks Ted as he passes.

STEPHEN

Hullo.

TED

Hullo, Dad.

Stephen sits.

STEPHEN

What has she eaten?

ROSALIND

Some milk pudding at lunch.

STEPHEN

Well, that's all right.

Stephen calls 'Hoy!' to Clarissa and claps his hands.

Clarissa runs to him, clasps his legs.

Hullo.

TED

How many moons has Jupiter got?

STEPHEN

I don't know.

TED

Twelve.

STEPHEN

Twelve moons?

TED

Yes.

CLARISSA

Twelve moons.

STEPHEN
(*to Ted*)

Do you want to get that book about the elephant?

TED

Yes!

Ted rushes to far end of room, to pile of books, and starts to rummage.

Rosalind, sewing.

Stephen, with Clarissa on his lap.

STEPHEN

I've got a new pupil.

ROSALIND

Uh?

STEPHEN

She's an Austrian princess.

ROSALIND

Is she?

CLARISSA

A princess?

STEPHEN
(*whispering to Clarissa*)

I think so.

TED'S VOICE

I can't find the book!

ROSALIND

How do you know she's a princess?

STEPHEN

She's got a very long name.

ROSALIND

Has she got golden hair?

STEPHEN

Uuuh . . . No.

ROSALIND

Then she's a fake.

Ted at pile of books, looking at book.

TED

I've found it!
(*Frowns.*)

I think.

Stephen cuddling Clarissa.

363

STEPHEN

She's very sunburnt.

ROSALIND

Then she's definitely not a princess.

STEPHEN

Why not?

CLARISSA

She is!

ROSALIND

Princesses keep their skin . . . quite white.

STEPHEN

Your skin is quite white.

ROSALIND

I know it is.

Ted runs down the room, with book, sits on Stephen's lap.

TED

I knew I'd found it.

Stephen holds both children.

STEPHEN

Where do you want to start?

TED

You start.

STEPHEN

Where?

TED

Here.

ROSALIND

Has she made advances to you?

STEPHEN

Oh no. I'm too old.

ROSALIND

You're not too old for me.

STEPHEN

I know that.

(*To children.*)

Now come on. Who's going to start?

Rosalind stands and moves across to them.

CLARISSA

I'll start.

TED

She can't read!

Rosalind bends over him.

ROSALIND

And I'm not too old for you.

INT. STUDY. COLLEGE. DAY.

Anna sitting with notebook. She is writing in it. Camera spreads to find Stephen. He is lying back in his chair, feet on desk.

Silence.

STEPHEN

Write me an essay on what the problem is . . . or rather . . . on what the problem seems to you to be.

He lifts his head, looks at her.

Will you?

Anna smiles.

ANNA

I'll try.

365

ACCIDENT

INT. DON'S COMMON ROOM. COLLEGE.

Stephen, Charley, the Provost and Hedges, a scientist, sit in armchairs, reading. Charley reads a newspaper; the rest, books.

Silence.

CHARLEY

A statistical analysis of sexual intercourse among students at Colenso University, Milwaukee, showed that 70 per cent did it in the evening, 29.9 per cent between two and four in the afternoon and 0.1 per cent during a lecture on Aristotle.

Pause.

PROVOST

I'm surprised to hear Aristotle is on the syllabus in the state of Wisconsin.

Silence.

CHARLEY
(*still reading from paper*)
Bus driver found in student's bed.

Pause.

PROVOST

But was anyone found in the bus driver's bed?

Pause.

Did you ever hear the story of my predecessor, Provost Jones, and the step-ladder?

Pause.

It's a bizarre story. It'll amuse you. Provost Jones and his good lady decided one day to buy a step-ladder.

366

EXT. RIVERBANK. DAY.

Heat, punts, canoes on river.

Stephen walks along towpath.

Young girls and men call to each other from boats.

Stephen's head.

He walks quickly.

Flashes of light on water.

Girls turning in boats. Distant laughter.

A call: 'Stephen!'

Stephen stops, turns.

Under a willow in a punt are William and Anna.

Anna wears a white dress with large woven holes in it.

Stephen stares.

WILLIAM

Hullo.

Stephen bends to them, under the willow.

The punt rocks gently, surrounded by pinpoints of light. Anna smiles, lying back.

You can't wear a suit like that on a day like this. It's ridiculous.

STEPHEN

I didn't know you two had met.

WILLIAM

We have.
> (*To Anna.*)

Haven't we?

367

ANNA

Mmmnn.

WILLIAM

Jump in.

STEPHEN

Me?

WILLIAM

Come on. We're going up river.

Long shot of Stephen stepping into punt.

The punt rocks. William pushes off. Stephen squats by Anna.

The punt.

Stephen settles into a half leaning, crouching position by Anna's legs.

The punt.

William's legs.

Through them Anna sitting, Stephen reclining along punt, his head on the cushion by her hip.

Stephen's head at her hip.

Her legs are bare, crossed.

Vapour on her legs.

Left foreground Stephen's head. Above him Anna's back. Her hair glinting. Light in her hair.

Beyond them William standing, punting.

Her arm, still.

Her arm, moving.

Her armpit. Fuzzy hair.

Hole at the side of her dress.

Stephen's body, stretched.

Her hip. His head.

Her eyes closed.

The punt pole, dipping.

The back of Stephen's head. His ears.

William bending and straightening, with pole.

Long shot.

The punt draws towards an island.

Stephen standing, leaning from punt to grasp the branch of a tree.

EXT. QUADRANGLE. DAY.

Stephen and William appear from under arch into quadrangle.

Stephen walks straight-backed in a soaking suit.

William carries his gown.

> WILLIAM
>
> You look very dignified.

> STEPHEN
>
> I feel *wet.*

> WILLIAM
>
> You don't look wet.

Stephen stops, looks at him.

> STEPHEN
>
> I don't *look* wet?

> WILLIAM
>
> Nobody looked at you as though you were wet, did
> they? They thought you were quite normal.

369

ACCIDENT

They walk across lawn, Stephen pulling at his trousers.

It was all my fault. I stayed too far out.

INT. ARCHED DOOR OFF QUADRANGLE.

They enter out of sun.

Stephen snarls at William.

STEPHEN
I'm getting old! Don't you understand? Old. My
muscles. The muscles.

INT. STAIRWAY. COLLEGE.

They climb stairway.

STEPHEN
No judgement. No judgement of distance. It's all gone.
Vanished!

His voice echoes in the stone stairway.

INT. STEPHEN'S STUDY. COLLEGE. AFTERNOON.

Stephen is changing into sweater and light trousers.

William stands by window.

WILLIAM
I thought forty was the prime of life. I mean, I wouldn't
say you looked old. You've still got a pretty good figure.
But I tell you what, why don't you do an hour's squash
every morning? It'll do you the world of good.

Stephen hitches his trousers.

Do you want to borrow my belt?

STEPHEN
(*coolly*)

If you're going to be a farmer when you leave
University, why the hell are you taking philosophy?

WILLIAM

I've got to be able to talk to the cows properly, haven't
I?

INT. STEPHEN'S STUDY. EARLY EVENING.

*Stephen and William sit at the window, looking down, with
glasses of whisky.*

WILLIAM

It's nice knowing you really, you know. You're not a
bad fellow, for a teacher of philosophy.
(*Pause.*)
I haven't got many friends.

STEPHEN

That's because you're an aristocrat.

WILLIAM

Ah.

STEPHEN

Aristocrats were made to be . . .

He pauses.

WILLIAM

What?

STEPHEN

Slaughtered.

Pause.

WILLIAM

Oh.

He looks at Stephen's face, slightly shadowed in the evening light.

STEPHEN

Do you like her?

WILLIAM

Yes.

Pause.

STEPHEN

Why don't you bring her down for the day on Sunday?
To my house.

WILLIAM

Great.

STEPHEN

Come for lunch.

WILLIAM

Marvellous. Shall I ask her?

STEPHEN

No. No, I'll ask her.

INT. STEPHEN'S STUDY. COLLEGE. MORNING.

*Anna sitting on floor by bookshelves, examining books on the
bottom shelf.*

Stephen's legs stand by her.

Stephen looking down at her, book in hand.

STEPHEN

This might interest you.

She looks up.

It expresses another point of view . . . altogether. It's by
Charley Hall. Do you know him?

ANNA

Yes, I think . . .

STEPHEN

The zoologist.

ANNA

Yes. I have met him.

STEPHEN

But this is a novel. He writes novels as well, you see.
And appears on television.

ANNA

Does he?

STEPHEN
(*grinning*)

He's a versatile man. Read it. I don't think much of it,
but you might.

He stretches his hand down.

Here.

*He clasps her hand and draws her lightly to her feet. Anna takes
the book.*

ANNA

Thanks.

*She collects her notes from the desk, puts book and notes in her
bag. He watches her.*

STEPHEN

Would you like to come to my house for lunch on
Sunday?

ANNA

That would be lovely.

STEPHEN

You could meet my wife. And the children.

ANNA

Yes.

Pause.

Anna clears her throat.

STEPHEN

Perhaps William can bring you.

ANNA

Ah. Yes.

STEPHEN

I'll ask him.

INT. HOUSE. BEDROOM. LATE AFTERNOON.

Rosalind lying on fourposter bed.

The curtains are drawn.

Stephen, with camera, moves slowly towards the bed. He sits on the bed. She opens eyes, smiles.

ROSALIND

Hullo.

STEPHEN

How are you?

ROSALIND

All right.

She draws his head down, kisses him swiftly.

Children's voices raised from garden.

What are they up to?

STEPHEN

They're all right.

He kisses her fingers.

Sound of dog barking.

Have you been able to rest . . . with all this racket?

ROSALIND

Yes.

He continues kissing her fingers.

STEPHEN

Oh, I've asked some people over on Sunday.
                    (*He looks at her.*)
Is that all right?

                              (*Pause.*)

Mnn?

ROSALIND

What people?

STEPHEN

Well . . . William . . . you know . . .

ROSALIND

Mmn-hmmn?

STEPHEN

And this Anna von Graz.
                    (*Pause.*)
You know, that girl –

ROSALIND

The Princess.

STEPHEN

Yes. She's William's girl friend.

Pause.

What do you think?

ROSALIND

I'm not very good at mixing with royalty.

STEPHEN

She's not really a Princess. Don't be silly.

ROSALIND

I'm not silly.

Pause.

STEPHEN

Just for lunch, that's all. But I can easily put them off.

ROSALIND

Mmmn.

She gets out of bed.

STEPHEN

What are you doing?

ROSALIND

I'm going downstairs.

She takes a negligée from the back of the door. The negligée has frilled cuffs. She puts it on.

INT. HOUSE. STAIRS.

Rosalind walks down the stairs, followed by Stephen.

Silence.

INT. HOUSE. KITCHEN.

Rosalind goes to kettle, fills it with water.

Stephen stands inside the door, watching her.

She puts the kettle on the stove and lights the gas.

STEPHEN

Well, what do you think?

ROSALIND

About what?

STEPHEN

About Sunday? I can put them off.

ROSALIND

Why should you put them off?

Rosalind cuts bread on the breadboard.

STEPHEN

Well . . . the cooking and everything . . . if you don't feel up to it.

ROSALIND

I'm fine. Why do you keep going on about it? Let them come.

Pause.

STEPHEN

All right.

She goes to the back window and calls: 'Ted, Clarissa! Teatime!'

EXT. LANE. ROAD JUNCTION. MORNING.

Spot of accident.

Dog runs across road to earth mound.

Stephen's voice: 'Mike! Come on!'

Ted runs after dog.

TED

Come on!

Ted chases dog off the mound. They run on to grass bank.

Stephen comes into view, walks after them.

Long shot.

Heat.

Stephen, Ted and the dog walk slowly up the lane towards the house.

EXT. HOUSE. GARDEN GATE.

They pass through the gate and begin to walk up drive, flanked by bushes.

William's car can be seen parked in the gravel court.

The dog burrows in a bush. Ted stops with him, bends.

TED

What is it, Mike?

Stephen walks ahead.

He turns the corner of bushes, the house and court now in full view.

He stops still.

By the hedge to the left of the house a white sports car is parked.

Anna, in dark glasses, and Charley, stand by the car, talking quietly.

Light vibrates on the car. An intense shimmer and glint. The two figures and the car trapped, still, in light, heat.

Stephen's face, blinking in the sun, looking, his face creased.

EXT. THE COURT.

The scene, unmoving. The two figures by the car.

Stephen standing. Ted and dog rush past, run down side of house.

Charley and Anna turn, see Stephen.

Charley raises his hand in salutation.

Stephen walks across the gravel towards them. He reaches them. Charley is smiling.

> STEPHEN
> Hullo Anna. William here?

> ANNA
> Yes, he's inside. What a lovely day.

EXT. FRONT OF HOUSE.

Ted and dog round corner of house.

> ANNA
> Is that your son?

> STEPHEN
> Yes.

Anna walks over to Ted and dog.

Stephen and Charley remain by car.

Charley sits on bonnet, stretches his arms.

> ANNA'S VOICE
> What's your name?

> TED
> Ted. What's yours?

> ANNA
> Anna. What's his?

> TED
> Mike.

Stephen and Charley grin at each other.

STEPHEN
What are you doing here?

CHARLEY
I was just passing, so I thought I'd drop in.

STEPHEN
Passing?

CHARLEY
Yes, just passing. Just floating by.

Sounds of Ted and dog.

Charley chases Ted and dog round corner of house.

Hi! Hi! Hi!

Anna is no longer there.

Stephen stands by car.

INT. HOUSE. KITCHEN.

Rosalind and William peeling vegetables.

WILLIAM
Hullo.

STEPHEN
Hullo, William. Charley's here.

ROSALIND
(*laughing*)
We know.

STEPHEN
Is he staying for lunch?

ROSALIND
Of course.

Through the window into the back garden they watch Charley

380

throwing a large ball. Ted, Clarissa and dog run after it. Charley runs after them, crawls on his hands and knees among them.

Anna appears on the lawn. Charley kicks the ball to her. She bounces it.

STEPHEN
(*to Rosalind*)

Can I do anything?

EXT. LAWN. BACK GARDEN. AFTERNOON.

The camera moves slowly up a slight rise and along the lawn.

The garden is long, stretching down to trees. It is mainly grass, with a few flowerbeds.

It is after lunch. Coffee cups, brandy glasses on the grass, some lying on their side. Very hot.

William is lying, leaning on an elbow, picking at the grass, near Charley. Charley is lying on his back. Rosalind is lying in a garden chair, feet up. Anna sits, making a daisy chain with Clarissa. Ted and Stephen are doing some casual weeding at the verge.

Silence.

William and Charley.

WILLIAM

What are you writing now?

CHARLEY

A novel.

Pause.

The dog strolls, sniffing, between them, wanders towards Anna.

WILLIAM

I'd like to write a novel.

CHARLEY

You would, eh?

WILLIAM

But I can't.

CHARLEY

It's child's play. You just need a starting point, that's all.

WILLIAM

Oh.

Pause.

CHARLEY

Here, for instance.

WILLIAM

Where?

CHARLEY

Here on this lawn. What are we up to?

WILLIAM

I know what I'm up to.

CHARLEY

What?

WILLIAM

Anna and I were invited here for lunch. We've just had it.

CHARLEY

Ah.

Pause.

WILLIAM

What are you up to?

Anna and Clarissa.

CLARISSA

We're going to Granny's on Tuesday.

ANNA

Are you?

CLARISSA

Teddy and Mummy and me.

ANNA

Are you going for a long time?

CLARISSA

We're going for three weeks. Mummy's going to have a baby, you see. If you're going to have a baby you've got to have a rest.

ANNA

Of course.

William and Charley.

CHARLEY

Describe what we're all doing.

William looks about the garden.

WILLIAM

Rosalind's lying down. Stephen's weeding the garden. Anna's making a daisy chain. We're having this conversation.

CHARLEY

Good. But then you could go further. Rosalind is pregnant. Stephen's having an affair with a girl at Oxford. He's reached the age when he can't keep his hands off girls at Oxford.

WILLIAM

What?

CHARLEY

But he feels guilty, of course. So he makes up a story.

WILLIAM

What story?

CHARLEY

This story.

WILLIAM

What are you talking about?

Charley sits up, swats violently at flies.

CHARLEY

Oh, these flies are terrible.

WILLIAM

What flies? There aren't any flies.

CHARLEY

They're Sicilian horse flies, from Corsica.

Charley shouts across the lawn.

Have you heard our conversation?

Stephen weeding.

STEPHEN

Yes!

Rosalind lying, eyes closed.

ROSALIND

Yes.

Anna carefully places daisy chain around Clarissa's neck.

EXT. TENNIS COURT.

William whipping ball fiercely over net.

The tennis court is situated beyond the back garden. It is in a state of ruin. There are holes in the net. Weeds all over the ground.

Charley and Anna play against William and Stephen. Charley is in bare feet.

Rosalind sits in a chair by the side, watching.

The ball goes to and fro.

William drives, beating Charley.

Charley serving. Anna stands by the net. The ball hits Anna in the back. Charley laughs.

Stephen serving, into net.

Stephen rushing the net. Anna bobbing about on the other side.

Sun.

William drives between Charley and Anna.

Anna hits wildly, sends ball into bushes.

Stephen lobs ball over net. Charley heads it back.

Charley serves, hits Anna.

William serves powerfully, beats Charley, who falls flat on his back.

Long shot, across tennis court.

Rosalind's chair, empty.

INT. HOUSE. KITCHEN.

Rosalind cutting sandwiches. Stephen comes in.

STEPHEN
What are you doing?

ROSALIND
Making tea.

STEPHEN
I've just asked them to stay for dinner.

She looks at him.

ROSALIND

Dinner?

STEPHEN

No. Supper. Cold supper.

ROSALIND

Are they staying?

STEPHEN

I don't know. But I'll do it. I'll . . . do the supper.

The kettle boils.

ROSALIND

The kettle.

Stephen goes to it.

EXT. LAWN. BACK GARDEN. LATE AFTERNOON.

Shadows beginning. Tea trolley standing.

Anna and Stephen reclining on the grass, amidst cups and plates, leavings of sandwiches and cakes.

William standing near them, practising strokes with a boy's cricket bat.

STEPHEN

Do you have any . . . sisters or brothers?

ANNA

One sister.

STEPHEN

Is she beautiful?

ANNA

Very.

William bends down to Anna.

WILLIAM
(to Anna)

Come for a walk. Mmmn?

ANNA

Oh, I'm so comfortable.

William stands upright, is still a moment. He then picks up a tennis ball, bounces it, and slams it with bat down the side of the house. He strolls after the ball.

Anna looks at Stephen, smiles.

It's so lovely here.

STEPHEN

Yes . . . it is.

Pause.

I think I'll go for a walk.

ANNA

I'll come too.

Stephen stretches his hand down. She jumps up by herself. She giggles.

He leads her across the lawn towards the trees.

EXT. PATH THROUGH GRASS.

Stephen and Anna walking through long grass beyond the tennis court, going uphill.

Their legs swish through grass. Their voices:

STEPHEN

Are you fond of William?

ANNA

Why do you ask?

Silence. Their legs moving.

Anna's face.

Are there many dons like you?

STEPHEN

Certainly not.

EXT. A COPSE.

Long shot.

They appear, through fading light, through trees, into copse.
Shafts of dying sun still bounce off the wood. Silence.

Sound of their feet on the brush. Birds. Creaks in undergrowth.

Anna stops, holds the branch of a tree.

Silence. Sounds.

STEPHEN

Mind. There's a spider's web.

Anna looks at him.

ANNA

It won't hurt me.

She walks slowly away. He follows.

EXT. A STILE.

The stile looks down upon a valley.

They stand at the stile.

ANNA

What a beautiful view.

STEPHEN

I thought you'd like to see it.

Their hands, close but not touching, on the stile.

ANNA

It was so kind of you to ask me here.

Silence.

Stephen's hand grips the stile.

He looks at her.

STEPHEN

No, it wasn't. It's been lovely to see you.

They stand, silent. He looking at her. She gazing at the view. She turns, looks at him.

ANNA

Shall we go back now?

STEPHEN

Yes.

INT. KITCHEN.

Charley opening a bottle of beer. Rosalind comes in.

ROSALIND

Oh hello.

CHARLEY

Hello. How are you?

ROSALIND

Fine. How's Laura?

CHARLEY

Great. All right . . . you know . . . I don't know really
. . . I haven't seen her.

Pause.

> I've been pretty busy. You know . . . one thing and
> another.

ROSALIND

You look terrible.

CHARLEY

Me? I feel wonderful.

Rosalind pours beer into his glass.

ROSALIND

Well, this'll kill you.

CHARLEY

I know.

EXT. PATH THROUGH GRASS.

They are returning.

Long shot.

STEPHEN

Will you stay for supper?

ANNA

I'd love to, but I don't know about William.

STEPHEN

He'll stay.

INT. HOUSE. KITCHEN. EARLY EVENING.

Charley with beer. Stephen comes in.

STEPHEN

Have you seen William?

CHARLEY

No. How are you getting on?

STEPHEN

Fine. What do you mean?

Charley pours beer. Stephen opens a bottle.

CHARLEY

What does Rosalind think about it?

Stephen pours beer.

STEPHEN

What does Rosalind think about what?

William looks in at the door.

WILLIAM

Have you seen Anna?

CHARLEY AND STEPHEN

No.

They look at each other. Charley leaves the kitchen.

STEPHEN

You're staying for supper, aren't you?

WILLIAM

We ought to go.

STEPHEN

It's all arranged.

INT. HOUSE. DINING-ROOM. EVENING.

Stephen opening wine bottle at sideboard. He places salad bowl, containing salad, on table. He goes quickly to sideboard, takes out bottle of whisky, pours himself a large one and drinks it.

Voices from the front of the house.

He goes to window.

In the dusk, Rosalind and Anna are walking up the drive to the house, with dog, talking quietly.

Stephen leans out of the window.

STEPHEN

Where are the children?

The women stop.

ROSALIND

They're not back yet. They went out to tea.

STEPHEN
(*to himself*)

I didn't know that.

ROSALIND

How's the supper?

STEPHEN

Nearly there.

Stephen takes whisky bottle and goes out door.

INT. THE HALL.

Stephen crosses hall to sitting-room.

Rosalind and Anna come in front door.

ROSALIND

I think it's about ten years.

ANNA

You're a wonderful couple.

INT. HOUSE. SITTING-ROOM.

Charley and William are lying in chairs with beer. Stephen enters with bottle.

STEPHEN

Whisky.

INT. HOUSE. DINING-ROOM. NIGHT.

The men are at the table.

Anna and Rosalind clearing soup plates, setting ham plates.

One empty bottle of whisky on the sideboard. Two and a half empty bottles of red wine on table.

STEPHEN

Who made that soup? I didn't make any soup.

CHARLEY

Your wife! Your beautiful wife made the damn soup! It was beautiful soup. My wife's beautiful too, isn't she, Rosalind?

ROSALIND

Yes.

CHARLEY
(*to Anna*)

She's as beautiful as that soup.

William sways in his chair.

(*To Anna.*)

She's rich and intelligent and beautiful. And we've got three kids. Don't forget *that*. And she understands me. *And* . . .

STEPHEN

And.

CHARLEY

And . . . we're all very old friends. Him and his wife. And me and my wife. Don't forget that.

STEPHEN

But he's more successful than me because he appears on television.

393

ANNA
(*to Charley*)
Do you talk on television?

CHARLEY
What do you think I do, play the flute?

ANNA
What do you talk about?

CHARLEY
You name it I'll talk about it.

STEPHEN
He talks about history, zoology –

CHARLEY
Anthropology, sociolog . . . sociologigy –

STEPHEN
Sociology!

CHARLEY
Codology.

STEPHEN
And sex. In that order.

ROSALIND
He suits the medium.

STEPHEN
(*to Rosalind*)
Do you mean you don't think I would suit the medium?

CHARLEY
They wouldn't let you within ten miles of the medium!

Stephen points a long arm across the table at Charley.

STEPHEN
I have an appointment with *your* producer next week.

CHARLEY

With *my* producer?

STEPHEN

Your producer.

William slumps on to the table. Rosalind rises, goes to Anna. They whisper.

CHARLEY

What, with old Bill Smith?

STEPHEN

He's asked to see me.

CHARLEY

You're going to be on *my* television show?

STEPHEN

I'll run you out of town, kid.

ROSALIND

Stephen, he wants to drive back.

STEPHEN

Who does?

ROSALIND

William.

STEPHEN

Impossible. He's drunk.

ANNA

I'll drive.

CHARLEY

You haven't got a licence.

ANNA

William, can I drive?

ROSALIND

No. You'll have to stay.

WILLIAM

I'll drive.

ANNA

Oh, we'd better stay.

STEPHEN

I'll drive.

ROSALIND

No you won't.

STEPHEN

Charley can drive!

William stands. His chair falls.

WILLIAM

Oh, to hell . . .

Stephen stands, goes to him.

STEPHEN

Listen, old boy. You're slightly drunk. You can stay.

WILLIAM

Why the bloody hell do you want us to bloody well stay?

Rosalind takes William's arm.

ROSALIND

Oh, come on.

She leads him out. Anna follows.

Stephen leans on to the table. He stares across the table at Charley, who stares back at him.

Silence.

Stephen walks to the door.

ACCIDENT

STEPHEN

Will you excuse me?

CHARLEY

But of course, my dear fellow.

INT. KITCHEN. NIGHT.

Tap in sink turned full on.

Stephen's head bends underneath it.

He turns tap off, holds towel to his head, sits heavily in chair.

Charley comes in, sways slightly, leans on door frame.

CHARLEY

They're staying.

Silence.

Which room . . . is everyone in?

Pause.

STEPHEN

How the hell should I know?

Pause.

CHARLEY

Splendid day.

STEPHEN
(carefully)

It gives me great pleasure to know that you have enjoyed
your day with us. Good night.

CHARLEY

Good night.

Charley goes out of kitchen door.

ACCIDENT

INT. KITCHEN. LATER.

Dog, looking up.

Stephen, slumped in kitchen chair, wakes suddenly, looks at watch.

He stands, clenches eyes, goes to door.

INT. THE HALL.

Stephen switches out hall light.

He looks up the stairs.

In the faint light at the top of the stairs he sees a woman ascending in a negligée with frilled cuffs. He stares after her. She goes out of sight.

INT. BEDROOM.

He enters, closes door. Stops dead.

A woman lies in the fourposter.

He stares with disbelief and delight.

He mouths softly:

> STEPHEN

Anna.

He goes to bed, looks down. It is Rosalind.

INT. BEDROOM.

Stephen climbing onto the bed. He touches his wife.

> STEPHEN
> (*whispering*)

Rosalind.

> (*Pause.*)

Darling?

ACCIDENT

>   ROSALIND
>   (*blurred*)

What?

>   STEPHEN

I love you.

INT. TELEVISION BUILDING. DAY.

Stephen sitting by low table in third floor ante-room, glass-panelled.

A receptionist sits at a distance from him, at a desk.

Stephen flips through magazines.

He opens a trade magazine.

Photograph of Charley and others with cameras, entitled 'Conversation Piece'.

The phone rings. Receptionist lifts it.

>   RECEPTIONIST
>   Reception? . . . Yes . . . I see . . . Thank you.

She puts phone down.

>   (*To Stephen.*)
>   Mr Smith isn't here, I'm afraid. Will you see Mr Bell?

>   STEPHEN

Uuh . . . yes, all right.

>   RECEPTIONIST
>   (*pointing down corridor*)
>   It's the fifth door on the left.

INT. CORRIDOR.

Stephen walks down corridor.

Box cubicles on either side of wood and glass. Voices, as he passes, from offices.

399

ACCIDENT

A door marked: MR BELL. ASSISTANT. TALKS.

INT. BELL'S OFFICE.

Bell rising from desk. Secretary in corner, typing. Loud indecipherable voice from next office. Behind Bell, through small window, a building site. Cranes, bulldozers, etc. Bell wears a cardigan.

> BELL
> *(shaking hands)*
> Hullo . . . I'm Bell. Remember me? I'm Bell.

> STEPHEN
> Uuuhh . . .

> BELL
> I was at Oxford.

> STEPHEN
> Of course. How are you?

> BELL
> Bill Smith's ill. He's in hospital.

> STEPHEN
> Oh, I'm sorry.

> BELL
> I've got to go and see him. Sit down.
> *(To Secretary.)*
> Got that file?

Secretary goes to filing cabinet. Stephen sits.

> STEPHEN
> I don't . . . actually know him.

> BELL
> You don't *know* him?

Secretary gives Bell file. He flips through it.

400

What did he want you for, do you know?

STEPHEN

I think he . . . mmn . . .

BELL
(*flipping*)

Do you ever see Francesca?

STEPHEN

Who?

BELL

Francesca. The provost's daughter. The daughter of the provost.

STEPHEN

Ah . . . yes. No, I don't.

BELL
(*swift smile*)

You knew her well.

STEPHEN

I've been married some years.

BELL

Well done.
(*Finding letter.*)
Ah . . . yes. Bill was thinking of you for 'Conversation Piece'. I've got to go and see him in a minute. He's very ill.

A man enters the office hurriedly.

MAN

What's the matter with Bill?

BELL

He's very bad. He's in hospital.

MAN

What!

The Man sits heavily. The phone rings.

SECRETARY
(*on phone*)

Mr Bell's secretary.

STEPHEN

Yes . . .

SECRETARY
(*on phone*)

Who?

STEPHEN

I think he was thinking of me.

MAN

He was perfectly all right yesterday. I had a drink with him.

Secretary puts hand over receiver.

SECRETARY

Mr Dyce.

Bell waves hand irritably.

MAN

I can't believe it.

SECRETARY
(*to phone*)

No, I'm afraid he's not.

BELL

Listen, the point is I don't know what his plans were, you see.

MAN

What happened to him?

SECRETARY
(*on phone*)

Yes, I'll see he gets the message.

Bell stands.

BELL

Perhaps I could let you know.
                    (*To Man.*)
He collapsed last night. Look, why don't you come and
see him? I'm going over there now to see him.

MAN

What time you going?

BELL

I'm going now.
                    (*Shaking hands with Stephen.*)
Well, all right. Sorry about this. Give my love to
Francesca.

STEPHEN

I haven't seen her.

MAN

You're going straight away, are you?

BELL

I told you, I'm going right away. I'm going now.

INT. TELEPHONE BOOTH.

His tie in the square mirror.

He is dialling. The number buzzes. No answer.

His hand begins to replace receiver.

A sudden voice in receiver: 'Hullo'.

He holds the receiver still.

The voice: 'Hullo'.

He lifts the receiver and speaks.

> **STEPHEN**
> Francesca?

EXT. BLOCK OF FLATS. EVENING.

Stephen walks to door of flats. He stops, walks to edge of pavement. Walks past door, stops.

He turns and goes in.

The following sequence with Francesca is silent. The only sounds heard are the voices overlaid at stated points. The words are fragments of realistic conversation. They are not thoughts. Nor are they combined with any lip movement on the part of the actors. They are distributed over the sequence so as to act as a disembodied comment on the action.

INT. FRANCESCA'S FLAT. EVENING.

Sitting-room.

Francesca walking towards drinks table. She is smiling. She is no longer young.

> **HER VOICE (OVER)**
> You haven't changed at all!
> Not at all!

A silent record turns on the record player.

Stephen standing, looking after her, his eyes narrowed.

> **HIS VOICE (OVER)**
> *(gaily)*
> Wonderful to see you!

Francesca brings a glass to him, hands it to him. She smiles tenderly at him.

> HER VOICE (OVER)
> I was in my bath when you phoned!

She turns, goes back to drinks.

Stephen, with drink, sitting on sofa.

> HIS VOICE (OVER)
> Well, it must be ten years.

Francesca, at drinks table, concentrating, squirting soda into glass.

> HER VOICE (OVER)
> Ten years! It can't be!

Both sitting on sofa, slowly click glasses.

> HER VOICE (OVER)
> It can't be. It must be.

> HIS VOICE (OVER)
> It must be.

> HER VOICE (OVER)
> It is.

Francesca switching off silent record.

She walks towards bedroom. As she walks:

> HIS VOICE (OVER)
> You don't look a day older.

> HER VOICE (OVER)
> Oh really, I'm ten years older.

Francesca walking from bedroom with her coat.

Stephen walks towards her, helps her on with her coat. She leans back, puts her cheek to his, kisses his cheek.

HER VOICE (OVER)

How's your wife?

Flat door closing. Light goes out.

Sitting-room. Nightlight through window.

The room empty.

HIS VOICE (OVER)

That's a beautiful dress and a beautiful coat. You look marvellous.

INT. RESTAURANT. NIGHT.

Stephen and Francesca at a table.

Waiter pouring wine into glasses.

Stephen and Francesca looking at each other.

His face, looking.

Her face, looking.

HER VOICE (OVER)

I'm in consumer research. Did you know? It's fascinating.

Francesca refusing potatoes from Waiter, laughing.

Stephen beckoning the Waiter for potatoes, grinning.

HIS VOICE (OVER)
(*softly*)

Remember those times in the car? Do you? Do you?

Francesca eating.

HER VOICE (OVER)
(*softly*)

Of course I remember.

Both eating, talking.

> HER VOICE (OVER)
> (*softly*)

I remember.

Francesca accepting cigarette from Stephen.

She looks at him, cigarette in mouth, while he digs in pocket for lighter.

> HER VOICE (OVER)

I'm supposed to be on a diet. I'm too fat.

He lights her cigarette.

> HER VOICE (OVER)

So then you'll have three? Three children. Good gracious.

EXT. RESTAURANT. NIGHT.

Doorman opening taxi door for them. Stephen tips him.

> HIS VOICE (OVER)

You're not fat.

INT. FRANCESCA'S FLAT. SITTING-ROOM. NIGHT.

Dimly lit table lamp. Stephen sitting, leaning forward.

> HER VOICE (OVER)

I'm very happy.

Bathroom door opens. She comes out, walks across the room to him.

> HER VOICE (OVER)

My life is happy.

INT. BEDROOM. NIGHT.

Francesca and Stephen in bed, naked. His eyes are open. She lies in his arms, eyes closed.

HER VOICE (OVER)

Have I changed?

HIS VOICE (OVER)

You're the same.

HER VOICE (OVER)

The same as I was? The same as I was . . . then?

HIS VOICE (OVER)

The same.

INT. HOUSE. HALL.

Stephen switches light on in hall. He sits down heavily at the hall table, holding his head.

Pile of letters on table.

Silence.

Creaks from upstairs.

He looks up sharply.

Another creak.

He stands, tense, looks round for some kind of implement.

Footsteps along the landing. He stares up.

Charley looks over the banister. He comes down the stairs, sits on a step halfway down. He wears a dressing gown.

CHARLEY

Hullo.

Pause.

STEPHEN

Hullo. I've just come from London.

CHARLEY

I know.

Anna appears at the top of the stairs. She is dressed in sweater and trousers. Bare feet.

Stephen stares up at her.

Eventually his gaze drops to Charley.

                    STEPHEN
   To see the television people.

Anna remains still.

Silence.

                    CHARLEY
   Did you see them?

                    STEPHEN
   I'm hungry.

Stephen goes along passage to kitchen.

INT. KITCHEN.

One place is laid for breakfast on the kitchen table.

Stephen goes to the fridge.

Stephen's face at lighted fridge. He takes out eggs.

Stephen stands with eggs.

Anna and Charley at the kitchen door. Anna is whispering to Charley.

Stephen puts eggs in bowl, takes down frying pan.

                    STEPHEN
   I'm going to make an omelette.

                    CHARLEY
   We don't want anything.

Stephen puts butter in pan.

ANNA

Shall I cook?

CHARLEY

Can you?

Anna sits at table, takes crumpled cigarette packet and matches from trouser pocket, lights cigarette.

Can I have a cigarette?

She passes packet across table. He lights one.

Stephen heats frying pan and begins to beat the eggs.

I wrote to you. The letter's out in the hall. You didn't get it.

STEPHEN

I left early.

CHARLEY
(*to Anna*)

Get the letter.

She sits still. Charley grins, goes into hall.

Stephen empties eggs into pan. Anna smokes.

Charley returns with two letters, throws one on table.

Here it is.
(*Looks at other.*)
There's another one for you. From my wife. A personal letter from her to you. Open it.

Stephen holds pan handle. Charley opens letter and reads.

Silence.

Stephen twists pan.

(*Reading aloud.*)
De-da, de-da, de-da, de-da . . . Ah . . . So I just want to

beg you that while still being understanding, sympathetic, etc. you don't necessarily show to him you think it's the great thing of his life. You might even hint that sooner or later he'll be bored to death by her. I believe this of course, but naturally am in a wrong position even to hint. I always wondered what this would be like if and when it happened, but I must say it beats everything. Love. Laura. P.S. Don't say I wrote for heaven's sake.

Charley throws letter on table and grins at Anna and Stephen. Stephen flips omelette on to plate, puts it on table. Charley sits down, begins to eat it. Pause.

ANNA

I thought you didn't want any.

CHARLEY

I didn't.

ANNA

Then why are you eating it?

CHARLEY

Mind your own damn bloody business!

Charley shoves the plate away.

Stephen sits at other side of table and continues eating omelette.

The three sitting at the table.

Stephen pushes plate away and leaves the kitchen.

INT. LANDING.

Stephen on landing looks down passage into spare room.

The door is open.

He walks to it, goes in.

INT. SPARE BEDROOM.

Stephen looks about. The sheets and pillows on the bed are rumpled. The top sheet and blanket falling to the floor. Charley's clothes lie on a chair. Anna's shoes on floor. Handbag and tissues on dressing table. He leaves room, goes to bathroom.

INT. BATHROOM.

Stephen looks at his face in mirror, wipes his mouth briskly with towel, Looks at towel. He looks round at bathroom. A towel on the floor. Drops of water in bath.

Anna passes bathroom door.

INT. LANDING.

Stephen on landing looking down passage to spare room. Anna is straightening the bed.

Charley's voice from below, on telephone: 'Hullo. Hullo, yes. This is Palling 146 . . . Hullo.'

INT. SPARE ROOM.

Anna bending over bed. She looks up.

> STEPHEN
>
> What are you doing?

> ANNA
>
> Making the bed.

> STEPHEN
>
> No need to do that. A woman comes in every morning.

> ANNA
>
> I can do it.

> STEPHEN
>
> Leave it, please.

She stops, goes to handbag, puts tissues into it.

ANNA

We're going.

Charley's voice from below, raised: 'Yes. A taxi. Now. To go into Oxford.'

STEPHEN

You might as well stay. It's very late.

Anna and Stephen look at each other.

Charley's voice: 'Straight away. Okay. Right.'

Anna and Stephen remain looking at each other.

Charley's voice, ascending stairs: 'Anna! I've got a taxi.'

INT. LANDING.

Anna and Stephen seen standing in room.

Charley walks along passage to room.

INT. SPARE ROOM.

Charley at door of room.

CHARLEY

It's on its way.

ANNA

I'll wait downstairs.

Anna goes out.

CHARLEY

Shut the door, for God's sake.

Stephen shuts the door. Charley starts to dress quickly.

It was her idea, she knew Rosalind was away, she said you wouldn't mind.

413

STEPHEN

I don't mind. It's got nothing to do with me.

CHARLEY

It's your bloody house!

Charley struggles into his clothes.

Anyway, I wrote to you but you didn't get the damn
letter.

STEPHEN

When did it start?

CHARLEY

What? Oh, weeks ago. Weeks. We used to go to her
room in the afternoon. Didn't even have a lock on the
door. Anyone could have come in. Someone did come
in once. A girl. Can you imagine?

Charley pulls at his socks, sitting on the bed.

I'm sleeping at college most of the time now. I can't
take her there, can I? Where can I damn well take her?

STEPHEN

I thought she and William . . . were close friends.

CHARLEY

They are! They're just friends. It means nothing. She's
not a whore.

He puts on shoes.

I don't know what to do, you see. I can't have enough of
her.

Sound of taxi.

Stephen goes to window, draws curtains.

*Down below he sees taxi drawing up. Driver gets out, goes to front
door. A shaft of light from door onto the gravel.*

Charley's voice.

I don't know what to do.

The Driver gets back into taxi, sits.

Stephen turns from window.

STEPHEN

Where's your car?

CHARLEY

Laura's got it.

STEPHEN

I'm going to see Rosalind tomorrow. At her mother's.
Then I'm going to William's house. I've been invited
down there. You can bring her here for the weekend.

Pause.

CHARLEY

Thanks.

He puts on his jacket, combs his hair.

It's the children, you see. I'm never there. They're
missing me.

A call from Anna from below: 'The taxi's waiting.'

Charley shouts: 'Coming!'

Charley picks up dressing gown, hands it to Stephen.

This is your dressing gown.

STEPHEN
(*taking it*)
Can I ask you a question?

CHARLEY

What?

415

STEPHEN

How did you get in tonight?

CHARLEY

Through the lavatory window.

STEPHEN

You're a bit old for that.

CHARLEY

Yes, I am.

STEPHEN

Here's a key.

CHARLEY

Thanks.

Charley goes to door.

STEPHEN

One more question.

CHARLEY
(*with fatigue*)

What?

STEPHEN

Last Sunday night, when you all stayed, did you sleep
with her here?

Pause.

CHARLEY

Of course I did.

EXT. ROSALIND'S MOTHER'S SMALL HOUSE, IN THE
COUNTRY. THE GARDEN. DAY.

Stephen and Rosalind lie in deckchairs.

His eyes are closed. Sun.

ROSALIND
(*drowsily*)
Did you see anyone in London?

STEPHEN

No.

Pause.

ROSALIND
What happened with the television people?

STEPHEN
Nothing. Wasn't any good.
(*He looks at her.*)
You look wonderful.

ROSALIND
I feel it. I feel great.

Pause.

I wish you could stay.

STEPHEN

So do I.

ROSALIND
Still, you'll have a good time at William's house, won't you? With all the lords and ladies.

Stephen grunts, sits humped in the deckchair.

She looks at him.

What's the matter?

EXT. CHARLEY AND LAURA'S HOUSE IN COUNTRY. THE GARDEN. DAY.

A hose running off lawn into flower beds.

The water spouts.

Stephen from back door comes into garden.

He walks across it.

Laura comes into shot, stops. He waves, walking.

She watches his approach.

STEPHEN

Hullo, Laura.

LAURA

Hullo, Stephen.

STEPHEN

The door was open. How are you?

LAURA

Fine.

He looks at hose.

STEPHEN

What are you doing?

LAURA

Charley's not here.

STEPHEN

I got your letter.

Pause.

LAURA

I'm just doing the garden.

STEPHEN

What are you doing to it?

LAURA

Caring for it.

418

ACCIDENT

Stephen and Rosalind.

STEPHEN

I got home from London and found Charley and Anna there.

ROSALIND

Charley and Anna?

STEPHEN

Yes.

ROSALIND

Together? In the house?

STEPHEN

Yes. I got home late, a bit drunk. I was . . . astonished.

ROSALIND

Why were you drunk?

STEPHEN

Oh, I had dinner with Francesca. You remember. You remember Francesca?

ROSALIND

Yes.

STEPHEN

Just gave her a ring, you know. It was quite pleasant.

Pause.

ROSALIND

He's sleeping with her, is he?

STEPHEN

Who?

ROSALIND

Charley. With Anna.

419

STEPHEN

Of course.

ROSALIND

How pathetic.

STEPHEN

What do you mean?

ROSALIND

Poor stupid old man.

STEPHEN

He's not old.

ROSALIND

Stupid bastard.

Pause.

Does Laura know?

STEPHEN

Yes.

ROSALIND

What about the children? Has he told them?

EXT. GARDEN. LAURA'S HOUSE.

Laura re-setting hose on flowerbed. Stephen standing.

STEPHEN

It'll be all right . . . you know.

LAURA

What will?

She directs hose.

STEPHEN

I know it will.

420

> LAURA

Have you had lunch?

> STEPHEN

Yes.

Pause.

Didn't you want me to come?

> LAURA

Yes.

> STEPHEN

Well, I'm just trying to tell you . . .

> LAURA

Do you want some coffee?

> STEPHEN

No, I don't want coffee.

She walks along flowerbed. Hose spouting. He follows.

Listen . . . this thing . . . it's nothing. It'll all fall flat.

> LAURA

He says he's in love with her.

> STEPHEN

Love! Everyone thinks they're in love!

> LAURA

Do you?

EXT. ROSALIND'S MOTHER'S GARDEN.

> ROSALIND

I've never heard of anything so bloody puerile, so banal.

> STEPHEN

What's banal about it?

ACCIDENT

ROSALIND
That poor stupid bitch of a girl.

STEPHEN
You just keep calling everyone stupid, what's the use –?

ROSALIND
Well, they are. Except Laura. And she's stupid too.

Pause.

You chucked them out, I hope?

EXT. GARDEN. LAURA'S HOUSE.

Laura and Stephen standing middle of lawn.

LAURA
Well . . . don't worry about it.

STEPHEN
I'm not.

LAURA
Thanks for coming.

EXT. ROSALIND'S MOTHER'S GARDEN.

Stephen and Rosalind in the deckchairs, still.

Silence.

STEPHEN
I think I'll pop in and see Laura. It's on my way.

ROSALIND
Give her my love.

INT. LORD CODRINGTON'S COUNTRY HOUSE. EVENING.

*A large stone corridor. High windows. A green baize door at one
end. An archway to the main body of the house at the other.
Large family portraits on the walls.*

422

ACCIDENT

About a dozen Men are taking off their jackets and hanging them on a stand. They proceed to tuck their trousers into their socks.

Stephen is watching. William joins him.

They stand in archway.

WILLIAM

Anna was coming down, but she's got some of her family over, or something.

STEPHEN

Ah.

WILLIAM

Do you know, I've never thanked you for introducing us.

STEPHEN

I didn't.

A group of Ladies comes through archway.

William smiles at them, moves aside with Stephen.

WILLIAM

Haven't you ever played this game before?

STEPHEN

No.

WILLIAM

It's traditional. We all played it at school.

STEPHEN

Ah.

WILLIAM

You'll enjoy it. It's fun.

William goes to side table and picks up a long heavy stuffed shapeless cushion cover.

This is the ball, you see.

STEPHEN

Uh-huh.

William looks at him.

WILLIAM

I think you should go in goal.

STEPHEN

Where's that?

WILLIAM

Down there, by that door.

Stephen looks down corridor.

A few men are doing limbering up exercises.

Stephen turns to William.

STEPHEN

I've got a funny feeling this is a murderous game.

WILLIAM

Not at all.

STEPHEN

Isn't it true all aristocrats want to die?

WILLIAM
(*smiling*)

I don't.

STEPHEN

What do I do in goal?

WILLIAM

Defend it.

STEPHEN

How?

WILLIAM

Any way you like.

STEPHEN

Can't I just watch?

WILLIAM

No. You're a house guest. You must play. Only the old men watch. And the ladies.

Through the archway towards the corridor the Ladies walk, talking and laughing.

Stephen hangs his jacket on stand and walks uneasily down the corridor, between the men, to the door at the end. He stands by the door.

The Men collect at one wall, under the pictures.

Stephen watches them. He bends quickly and tucks his trousers into his socks.

The Men line up by the wall, leaving a space between them and the wall. One Man, at the far end of the row, holds the ball.

The corridor, which has echoed with voices and footsteps, becomes silent.

The row of Men by wall, tense, waiting.

The Man with ball in foreground.

The group of Ladies, with a few elderly Men, silent, watching, in the archway.

Stephen.

Long shot of corridor. Utter stillness.

The Man with ball dashes between Men and wall.

The Men fall on him. A scrum.

The Man attempts to break through, gripping the ball to him.

425

The others try to drag it from him. He shoves right and left with his elbows.

The struggling scrum inches along the wall.

It is silent but for grunts. Men, striving, become attached to the backs of others. A communal buggery. The Man with ball is lifted off his feet from behind.

William seizes the ball, dashes free towards goal.

Stephen standing. William dashing toward him.

William is tackled by four Men, is trapped at the waist from behind. The others attempt to pull the ball away. William kicks the Man behind him. He cracks his elbows sharply into the faces of two others and swiftly turning, butts the fourth Man with his head. William, free, runs. Others join to chase him.

He dodges, charges two Men down, still holding ball, and again dashes towards Stephen in goal.

Stephen's legs, moving out of goal, bracing, as William charges down upon him.

William charges him in the stomach.

Stephen is carried along a little way on William's back.

He swings off, pressing his fingers on the back of William's neck.

Stephen grappling with William, momentarily.

They are tackled and surrounded.

A Man jumps on Stephen's back. Stephen flings his head back, hitting Man in face. The Man falls, rolls away holding his face.

The scrum.

William, with ball, trying to force way out.

Stephen grappling with him, eyes staring.

426

Above them a canopy of arms flailing, bodies twisting.

The men fight with each other.

Elbows in stomachs. Feet kicking. Forearms cuffing.

Hands pulling at ball, which William clutches to him, as he kicks up. Stephen lashes out at Men above him.

Top shot of scrum.

It strives forward ponderously, brokenly; a bowel with a gut gone.

William's teeth bared.

The Ladies, watching.

Under canopy of bodies, William grapples with Stephen.

Stephen's face, teeth bared.

He savagely knees William in the face.

William's face, receiving knee.

Stephen felled from behind. He falls.

From above.

The scrum, squirming in a circle.

William, bloody, savaged by hands.

The ball torn from him.

EXT. CRICKET FIELD DAY.

William, batting, hitting ball savagely.

Vigorous applause.

William wipes his forehead.

William is immaculate in white.

The Provost, Charley and Stephen stand near the pavilion, watching the game.

ACCIDENT

PROVOST

He really is a magnificent athlete.

CHARLEY

Yes, he's a natural, that boy.

PROVOST

I was quite good myself. But not altogether in the same class. What about you, Stephen? Were you any good?

STEPHEN
(*smiling*)

No.

William hooks the ball through the field.

Provost applauds. Stephen looks at him.

I saw Francesca when I was in London.

The Provost looks at him, bewildered.

Your daughter.

PROVOST

Ah. How is she?

STEPHEN

Very well. She sent you her love.

PROVOST

Ah. Please give her mine when you see her again.

STEPHEN

Oh, I don't know when I'll be seeing her again.

William sends a ball high into the air.

A fielder, on the boundary, waits for it, catches it.

Applause, as William, bat raised, runs up steps of pavilion.

Stephen stands alone under a tree, applauding.

Stephen turns. Anna is beside him.

ANNA

Hullo.

STEPHEN

Hullo. Have a nice week-end?

ANNA

Yes. Thank you for your hospitality.

Pause.

I'm getting married.

STEPHEN

Oh. Who to?

ANNA

William.

Pause.

Stephen watches the game, which, in the background, continues.

STEPHEN

Ah. Have you told him?

Anna giggles.

Well, congratulations.

ANNA

I wonder if you could tell Charley for me.

Stephen looks at her.

Will you let me know what he says?

William runs up the side of the field to join them.

William puts his arm round Anna.

429

ACCIDENT

WILLIAM
(to Stephen)

Hullo.

STEPHEN

Well played.

WILLIAM

Thanks. Look, I want to come and see you, have a word with you. Can I come tonight, after this party? I'll be a bit late.

STEPHEN

Sure. What's the trouble?

WILLIAM

No trouble. No trouble at all.

STEPHEN
(to Anna)

You coming?

WILLIAM

No, I don't want her.

William punches Stephen on the chest, lightly, but Stephen staggers.

I want a man to man talk!

STEPHEN

We can talk when she's in bed. She can sleep in the spare room. Can't you?

ANNA

That would be nice.

WILLIAM

Okay. We'll see you later. Come on!

William, arms round Anna's waist, runs along the edge of the field with her.

Stephen walks along in their wake.

He looks down. Charley is sitting in a deckchair.

Charley looks up, winks.

Stephen looks after them.

William's face, Anna's face, together, as they run.

William's face dead at bottom of car.

Anna, head and shoulders rising out of overturned car. Moonlight.

Anna sitting on grass bank. Moonlight.

Anna lying on fourposter bed.

INT. HOUSE. BEDROOM. NIGHT.

Stephen sitting upright on chair by the window.

The bedroom.

Anna on bed. Stephen on chair.

Stillness.

Anna sighs in her sleep, rolls on to her side, half sits up, almost falls off bed.

He goes to her, holds her.

Stephen kneeling at the side of the bed, holding Anna's shoulders on the bed.

STEPHEN
It's all right.

She stares at him, lost, suddenly frowns, is still, tense, crouched at the edge of the bed.

He lifts his hand to touch her forehead.

She shies away, slides off bed, sits sharply on the floor.

She laughs, stops suddenly.

Stephen bends over her, squatting.

She looks swiftly up at his body, then down.

Did anyone know you were with him?

She does not look up.

He grips her jaw.

You can hear me.

She moves her jaw in his grip.

Can't you?

He tightens grip, twists her head to him.

Her eyes close, her head jerks back.

Her hands claw at him.

He seizes her hands. Her face jerks from side to side. She is whimpering.

He thrusts his body between her legs, fixes his elbows on her arms, and presses his thumbs on her cheeks.

Large close-up.

Her face, pulled out of shape by his thumbs. Her eyes slits.

His thumbs press her face back against bed.

Top shot.

The two bodies, hardly moving, battling, at the side of the bed.

The telephone rings from below.

His face, set. His eyes flicker towards sound of telephone. He concentrates on Anna.

Anna's face, stretched.

She suddenly becomes limp. The phone stops.

She looks at him. His grip relaxes on her face.

Did anyone know you were coming here with him?

She looks at him calmly. No response.

Was he supposed to have dropped you off at your room?

Her face, calm, non-committal.

His face.

Her ear. Long hair falling.

His mouth at her ear.

He's dead.

Her head turns to look at him.

Their faces very close.

You had an accident. You crashed.

Pause.

You *were* driving, weren't you?

The telephone rings below. He frowns, hesitates, stands. Anna remains still. He goes to door.

INT. HOUSE. LANDING.

He looks down stairs. Phone ringing.

INT. HOUSE. THE STAIRS.

He starts down the stairs. He is almost at the foot when the telephone stops ringing.

He stands, then turns back.

433

INT. BEDROOM.

Stephen at door.

Anna is not by the bed. He turns swiftly.

Anna is standing by the window, holding curtain, looking down into garden.

He walks quickly to window, pulls Anna away, pulls curtain into place, keeping hold of her arm.

STEPHEN
Someone might see you.

He still holds her arm. He looks at her, pulls her to him suddenly and kisses her.

The kiss is very brief. He draws back.

They stand, apart.

Their bodies standing. Waist level. Not touching. Their arms.

His hands touch her arms, move up.

He folds her in his arms and kisses her slowly.

She does not resist.

He withdraws from embrace, walks to bedside lamp, turns it off.

The bedroom door is still half open. Light from the landing comes into the room.

He stands by the lamp.

She remains by the window.

He is still by the lamp.

Slowly, she walks across the room towards him.

She passes through the channel of light from the door.

Her body, by the bed.

434

His body, by the bed.

Both of them, standing by the bed, in the dim light.

EXT. THE HOUSE. FRONT DOOR. MORNING.

The front door is open. Stephen stands by it, looking into hall.

Anna is sitting in chair in the hall.

> **STEPHEN**
>
> Right.

Anna stands, begins to walk to door.

> Your handbag.

She stops, turns, picks up her handbag, walks, to door, to him.

The telephone rings.

INT. HALL.

Anna and Stephen still, at door. Outside, morning light. The phone rings. He walks into hall and lifts it.

> **STEPHEN**
>
> Hullo? . . . Yes? . . . Oh, have you? . . . Sorry, I've been asleep, didn't hear it . . . Yes . . . Ah . . . I see . . . But she's all right? . . . Yes . . . I'll get dressed and . . . get there. Thank you . . . Thank you.
>> (*He lowers receiver, lifts it quickly.*)
>
> Oh, I'm sorry I didn't hear the –
>> (*He replaces receiver.*)

Stephen walks to the door. they go out. The door closes.

EXT. QUIET ROAD IN OXFORD. MORNING.

The road is silent. On one side of it is a tree-lined open space. On the other, a wall.

ACCIDENT

Stephen's car approaches at far end of road.

It approaches and slides quietly in to the kerb.

The car, stationary, in long shot.

Early sunshine. Silence.

INT. CAR.

Stephen and Anna sitting. He looks up the road and glances into the mirror.

STEPHEN
Can you get in . . . without anyone seeing you?

He looks at her.

ANNA
Mmnn.

STEPHEN
No one must see you.

Birds, seen through the windscreen, skim down across the road.

Anna gets out of the car.

Anna closes car door quietly and walks along by the wall. She stops and returns.

INT. CAR.

Stephen leans over and winds passenger window down.

She leans in at window.

STEPHEN
What?

ANNA
You'll have to help me up.

He grimaces.

436

I can't get over the wall by myself.

> STEPHEN
> (*muttering*)

Why didn't you say so –

EXT. CAR.

He gets out, closes door quietly.

EXT. ROAD. THE WALL.

Anna walking by wall, followed by Stephen.

She stops at a part of the wall where a large tree overhangs.

> ANNA

Here.

Stephen hoists her up.

EXT. WOMEN'S COLLEGE GROUNDS.

The other side of the wall. The tree.

Anna's head and shoulders rise above wall.

She clasps branch of the tree, sits on wall, throws handbag down on to grass.

EXT. ROAD. WALL.

Stephen looking up, his hands raised. Anna's left leg swings over. She disappears over wall.

His face, glancing sharply up the road.

INT. HOSPITAL.

Baby in gauze tent. Tubes lead into it.

The baby's mouth is moving. Its eyes are shut.

ACCIDENT

Camera moves up to see the back of Stephen's head going out of ward door.

INT. PRIVATE ROOM. HOSPITAL.

Rosalind in bed. Stephen sitting by bed.

Rosalind speaks very quietly.

> **ROSALIND**
> They phoned you. You weren't there.

> **STEPHEN**
> I was asleep. I didn't hear.

Pause.

> **ROSALIND**
> He can't breathe. It's difficult for him to breathe. Did you see that?

> **STEPHEN**
> But he is breathing. They're helping him.

> **ROSALIND**
> He isn't dead?

Pause.

> **STEPHEN**
> No.

INT. WOMEN'S COLLEGE. LIVING QUARTERS.

Stephen walking up stone stairway to Anna's room.

Below him, at foot of steps, sunlight frames in quadrangle arch. His steps echo.

Charley appears in arch, looks up, calls.

> **CHARLEY**
> Stephen.

*Stephen turns on step. Charley ascends, reaches him. Stephen is
calm, almost detached. Charley is panting.*

I've just heard. About William.

Pause.

You found him.

STEPHEN

Yes.

Pause.

CHARLEY

Does she know?

Pause.

STEPHEN

I don't know.

Charley looks up to her room.

CHARLEY

Have you just come to tell her?

STEPHEN

Yes.

Pause.

CHARLEY

It must have been terrible for you.

Pause.

Look, leave this to me, if you like.

STEPHEN

No, it's all right.

They turn up the stairs.

439

INT. ANNA'S ROOM.

There are two cases on the bed.

Anna is packing. There is a knock on the door and the door opens. Charley and Stephen enter.

She stops packing.

Charley walks forward, looks at cases.

CHARLEY

What are you doing?

She does not answer.

You've heard what's happened?

Pause.

ANNA

Yes.

Pause.

CHARLEY

I'm sorry.

Stephen sits down in an armchair. Charley turns to him.

What happened? Was he drunk? They say there was whisky all over the car. Was there?

STEPHEN

I didn't notice.

CHARLEY

But you found him.

Anna continues packing.

(*To Anna.*)
How did you hear about it?

He goes to her.

440

What are you doing? Why are you packing?

ANNA

I'm going home.

Stephen in chair, eyes half closed.

Charley stands, bewildered.

Anna bending at suitcase. Charley stands.

CHARLEY

Why?

Anna moves to collect some records, comes back, packs them under dresses.

Why are you going home?

STEPHEN

They were going to be married.

CHARLEY

Rubbish.

STEPHEN

He told me.

CHARLEY

It's rubbish.

Charley moves to Anna.

Look, I know it's . . . terrible. But listen . . . there's no reason for you to go home.

He touches her shoulder.

Her shoulder. She withdraws her shoulder from his hand quickly.

Anna continues packing.

Charley grips her arm. She becomes still.

Stephen, half-closed lids.

STEPHEN

Why don't you leave her alone?

Charley takes his hand away from Anna. She collects books. Charley stands, lost, in the centre of the room.

CHARLEY

How did she hear about it? I've just heard it from the Provost. Wake up.

STEPHEN

I haven't slept. Sorry. I'm a bit tired.

Anna snaps suitcases shut.

ANNA

It was kind of you both to come.

She goes to the mirror and begins to lipstick her mouth. Charley bends over Stephen's chair, whispers.

CHARLEY
(*whispering*)

What's the matter with her? She didn't care anything about him. Nothing. What's she going home for? It's ridiculous.

STEPHEN

There's nothing to keep her here.

CHARLEY

She loves me. What are you talking about?

Anna walks to cases.

ANNA

My taxi should be here.

STEPHEN

Have you got a flight?

442

ANNA

Yes. I've booked a flight.

Charley sits down in a chair.

Stephen stands, goes to cases.

STEPHEN

I'll take these down.

Stephen leaves the room.

CHARLEY
(*to Anna*)
Why don't you stay for the funeral?

Anna goes to Charley, holds out her hand.

ANNA

Goodbye.

Charley looks up at her, grins, does not take her hand.

Anna goes.

Charley sits quite still.

EXT. WOMEN'S COLLEGE. DAY.

Stephen closes taxi door. Anna leans back on the back seat. The taxi drives off.

Stephen looks after it, then glances back, through the gate, into the college grounds.

On the college lawn, in long shot, Charley stands alone.

Stephen standing, from Charley's point of view. Stephen walks away.

NOTE: The following scenes until the end of the film are silent except for:

443

ACCIDENT

The hum of a car growing on the soundtrack. The sound grows. It includes jamming gear changes and sharp braking.

The sound begins very quietly.

EXT. CLOISTER. DAY.

Stephen walks through cloister towards his study slowly.

EXT. HOUSE. DAY.

(Identical shot as at the beginning of the film.)

Clarissa and Ted running over gravel towards front door. Clarissa falls, holds her leg, cries.

The sound of the car draws closer.

Stephen comes out of house, picks her up, comforts her, carries her into house, her arms around him, Ted following. The dog runs after them.

Camera slowly moves back to long shot outside the gate.

It comes to rest.

Sound of the car skidding.

A sudden screech, grind, smash and splintering.

Camera withdraws down the drive to the gate.

The house still, in the sunlight.

Silence.

Sound of ignition, ticking.

The Last Tycoon

The Last Tycoon was first presented in Britain by CIC in 1977 with the following cast:

MONROE STAHR Robert De Niro
RODRIGUEZ Tony Curtis
PAT BRADY Robert Mitchum
DIDI Jeanne Moreau
BRIMMER Jack Nicholson
BOXLEY Donald Pleasence
KATHLEEN MOORE Ingrid Boulting
FLEISHACKER Ray Milland
RED RIDINGWOOD Dana Andrews
CECILIA BRADY Theresa Russell
WYLIE WHITE Peter Strauss
POPOLOS Tige Andrews
MARCUS Morgan Farley
GUIDE John Carradine
DOCTOR Jeff Corey
EDNA Angelica Houston

Produced by Sam Speigel
Directed by Elia Kazan

INT. RESTAURANT. NIGHT. (BLACK & WHITE).

A crowded restaurant. Bustle of waiters, loud conversation and laughter, smoke, etc.

Camera gradually focuses on a couple sitting by a window in a corner booth. The Woman, a blonde, is giggling and snuggling up to a Man. He is whispering in her ear. She suddenly kisses him, reaching for her purse. She goes towards the ladies' room, exchanging a look with Another Man. He stands and, as he does, touches the lamp above his table. It sways.

A group in the next booth stands and leaves the restaurant. The Man signals to the waiter for another drink. The waiter pays no attention, moves away. We gradually realize that other tables near the Man have emptied. For a moment the restaurant is quiet. Suddenly the roar of a car is heard. Grinding of brakes. A flash of headlights into the window. A burst of machine gun fire. The Man collapses at his table, plates and glasses crashing to the floor.

INT. PROJECTION ROOM.

A number of men in shadow.

> STAHR
>
> The signal was much too obvious. It kills the surprise. Cut it out.

> MAN
>
> Okay.

> STAHR
>
> What else?

447

MAN

You wanted to see the beach scene from 'Dark Moonlight'.

STAHR

Right.

MAN

Okay. Jack.

The projector light goes on.

A ROUGH ASSEMBLY ON THE SCREEN.

A woman is walking to the edge of the sea.

A man watches her.

The scene is silent and intercut.

STAHR

(*VO*)

No, no, don't go to him at all. Stay on her. You don't need him. Stay on her all the way down to the edge of the sea. She's the one we're interested in.

EXT. BACK LOT. DAY.

Considerable activity. Technicians, prop men, etc. A studio Guide with a group of college girls.

GUIDE

Remember that scene in 'Reaching for the Moon' when Pola Negri ran out of the house down to the lake? This is where we shot it. No, of course you wouldn't remember, you're too young. I've been here since the silent days. I knew them all.

GIRL

Did you know the Keystone Kops?

448

GUIDE

All of them. What a bunch of guys.

He leads the group through a door.

INT. DRESSING ROOM.

Guide and girls.

GUIDE

This was Minna Davis's dressing room. She was taken
ill for the last time in this room.
                    (*Points to painting.*)
That's her.

GIRL

She was beautiful.

GUIDE

She was a great friend of mine. I remember we had to
call her husband. I called him myself. I remember that
call well. I said, Mr Stahr, I'm afraid your wife has been
taken ill. He said, I'll be right over. Yes, this is where it
all happened. In this very room.

He leads them out of the room.

INT. CORRIDOR.

The Guide and girls.

GUIDE

Shh. We have to be quiet. See that red light? That
means they're shooting.

They continue down the corridor into a sound stage.

INT. EMPTY SOUND STAGE.

GIRL

Gee, it's so big.

GUIDE

It's big, all right. They don't have anything bigger in the whole world.

2ND GIRL

How did they do the earthquake in 'San Francisco'?

GUIDE

The earthquake? Well, there are various ways of doing an earthquake. What you can do first, is rock the camera. You see? Or, if you're in a room you can rock the set, I mean you can rock the room. And you can throw in a lot of dust.

2ND GIRL

And bricks?

GUIDE

Sure. And bricks. Either way you get a great earthquake.

INT. SOUND STAGE.

A foreign actress with red hair (Didi) and an actor (Rodriguez) are completing a take.

Didi is standing in the hall of a Paris apartment with a telephone. She is wearing a negligee.

DIDI
(*on phone*)

No, I wasn't asleep . . . When are you coming home? . . . No, I'm all right. I just miss you, that's all . . . She's fine. She has a new tooth. How did it go? . . . Good. When are you coming home?

Rodriguez, naked to the waist, comes into shot, stands close behind her, touches her, kisses her neck. She responds to his touch.

450

DIDI

(*on phone*)

Oh, that's good. You want me to meet you? . . .
Darling, next time I'm coming with you . . . Well, they
owe me some time off at the club anyway . . . No, it
couldn't be more boring than being without you. Yes.
Me too. 'Bye.

*She puts the phone down, flings Rodriguez away, goes to cabinet,
pours herself a drink. The camera follows her. Rodriguez comes
into shot.*

RODRIGUEZ

You want me to go?

DIDI

Yes.

(*She closes her eyes.*)

No.

*She goes to him, kisses him passionately. Ridingwood, the
director, shouts 'Cut'. Didi and Rodriguez break. She glares up at
the lights.*

RIDINGWOOD

That was really good. Fine. I mean very, very good.
Very good indeed. Give me the finder.

The assistant cameraman hands him the viewfinder.

INT. BACK OF THE STAGE. DOOR.

*The red light is on. The door opens quietly and a figure, Stahr,
slips in and stands in the shadows. In the background we see
Didi's dresser running on with a hand mirror.*

ON THE SET.

DIDI

You think so?

RIDINGWOOD

It was absolutely terrific. It was really wonderful.

DIDI

It was shit.

SILENCE ON THE SET. EVERYBODY LOOKS AT RIDINGWOOD.

ON THE SET.

RIDINGWOOD

Listen, Didi, I have to tell you it was exquisite.

DIDI

It was fake. It was false. Didn't you notice? I want to do it again.

Didi is re-touching her make-up.

RIDINGWOOD

You will never do it better.

DIDI

I can really play that scene. I want to do it again.

Rodriguez slides past Ridingwood and whispers out of the side of his mouth.

RODRIGUEZ

It was good for me.

RIDINGWOOD

Didi. Trust me.

Didi lowers the mirror, stares at him a moment. She goes back to her make-up.

DIDI

I'm ready.

The assistant director approaches Ridingwood.

ASSISTANT DIRECTOR

Chief?

Ridingwood shrugs.

RIDINGWOOD

Let's do it again.

Ridingwood gives the finder back to the assistant, walks away.

BACK OF THE STAGE.

Ridingwood and Didi in background.

Stahr's back in foreground watching.

EXT. THE STUDIO. NIGHT.

A guard sitting in his box by the gate.

A soprano's voice in the distance singing over and over, 'Come come I love you only'. Sounds of a movieola playing back.

A group of technicians emerges from a door. They walk away talking and laughing.

Silhouette of Stahr working in his office. He stands, walks to the sofa, lies down.

INT. BRADY'S OFFICE. NIGHT.

Brady and Fleishacker.

They are drinking coffee.

Numerous awards on walls, statuettes in glass cases.

BRADY

I love him. He's a genius. I've always wanted him to get every credit. You know that. But what about me? New York has forgotten me.

FLEISHACKER

No, no.

BRADY

New York has forgotten me. You know why? Because I'm too generous. It's my nature. I make life easy for him. Do you know what I am? I am the strong base on which Monroe Stahr rests. I'm loyal to him and I'm loyal to New York.

FLEISHACKER

New York knows you're loyal. New York respects you for it.

BRADY

New York should be loyal too.

FLEISHACKER

New York is loyal.

BRADY

To who?

FLEISHACKER

To you.

BRADY

All I want is recognition.

FLEISHACKER

You've got it.

BRADY

I want to see it. I want to see it on this table. I want to feel it!

Outside the window Wylie and Cecilia draw up in a car. Brady turns to look.

Wylie puts his hand on Cecilia's thigh. She pushes it off, gets out of the car, walks towards the building.

454

BRADY

Did you see that bastard touch my daughter?

Wylie whistles after Cecilia.

FLEISHACKER

Who is he?

BRADY

He's a goddamned writer.

FLEISHACKER

I was looking in at the writers' building this morning. I watched them for ten minutes and there were two of them didn't write a line.

INT. BRADY'S OUTER OFFICE.

Rosemary and Birdy at their desks. Rosemary looks up, kicks the kick lock under her desk. Brady's door opens.

ROSEMARY

Go right in.

CECILIA

Thanks.

Cecilia goes into Brady's office.

Birdy yawns, puts her hand over her mouth, rubs her forehead.

ROSEMARY

What's the matter, don't you feel well?

BIRDY

I don't feel so good.

ROSEMARY

Do you want some bicarbonate?

BIRDY

I feel so shaky.

455

Sound of soprano.

INT. BRADY'S OFFICE.

Brady is taking a wad of bills from his wallet and counting them.

> FLEISHACKER
> Are you an actress?

> CECILIA
> No! I'm just daddy's little daughter. What are you?

> FLEISHACKER
> I'm just a lawyer. I'm from New York.

> BRADY
> She's too intelligent to be an actress. She'll be graduating next June from Bennington with honours.

> CECILIA
> I love actors though.

Brady hands Cecilia the wad of bills.

Slight tremor of an earthquake. The chandelier sways. Fleishacker looks up.

> I don't need all this.

> BRADY
> Sure you do.

INT. STAHR'S OFFICE. NIGHT.

Stahr lying on a sofa. His eyes are open.

(In this shot, Stahr's face is seen for the first time.)

Silence except for the sound of the soprano.

Stahr is sweating and breathing heavily.

THE CEILING. STAHR'S P.O.V.

A crack suddenly appears along the length of the ceiling. The overhead light sways. A picture falls from the wall.

STAHR STARING AT THE CEILING.

The room shakes.

INT. BRADY'S OFFICE.

Cecilia skating across the room. Fleishacker nowhere to be seen. Brady clutching the desk.

> BRADY
> (*shouting*)
>
> Are you all right?

INT. OUTER OFFICE.

Rosemary and Birdy on the floor.

They try to reach each other.

> ROSEMARY
>
> Jesus Christ!

INT. CORRIDOR. NIGHT.

All the lights are out. The earthquake ceases. Brady, Cecilia, Fleishacker, Rosemary and Birdy emerge from Brady's office and run along the corridor to Stahr's office.

INT. STAHR'S OFFICE.

Stahr is sitting on the sofa. They all rush in. Cecilia goes to him.

> CECILIA
>
> Are you all right?

                         STAHR
What happened?

                         BIRDY
We just had an earthquake, Mr Stahr.

                         STAHR
It woke me up.

                         BIRDY
I knew something was going to happen. I was shaking all
over.

The telephone rings. Brady picks it up.

                         BRADY
    Yes? Yes?

Brady hands phone to Stahr.

EXT. THE BACK LOT.

A section of the back lot is flooded.

Flood lights, people running, etc.

Stahr, followed by a group of men, approaches the lot.

                       ROBINSON
We'll pump it out into the swamp on 36th Street.

                         STAHR
They're shooting on 17 and 24. See the gates are shut
tight.

                         A MAN
Hey, look at that!

*On top of a huge head of the goddess Siva, Two Women float
along the current of the flood. They are sitting along a scroll of
curls on the bald forehead.*

ROBINSON

We ought to let them drift out to the waste pipe, but De Mille needs that head next week.
(He shouts at the Women.)
Put that head back! You think it's a souvenir?

THE HEAD OF SIVA.

Men wade through the flood trying to stop the progress of the head with poles. The head spins in the water, the Women hang on.

The head is finally controlled and the Women slide down the cheek of the idol to the ground. One of them wears a silver belt.

EDNA

We just followed a truck in through the gate, just to look around. I'm sorry.

ROBINSON AND STAHR.

Robinson and Stahr remain at a distance from the Women.

ROBINSON

They're strangers. What'll we do with them, chief?

The Two Women tread their way out of the water.

What'll we do with them, chief?

CLOSE-UP. STAHR, STARING. NO SOUND.

THE BACK LOT.

The Two Women threading their way to the gate, escorted by a policeman. Robinson makes his way towards them.

Various shouts: '. . . get the big pumps on the tanks on Stage 4 . . . put a cable around this head . . . raft it up on a couple of two by fours . . . get the water out of the jungle first, for Christ's sake . . . that big "A" pipe, lay it down . . . all that stuff is plastic . . .'

459

STAHR ALONE. NO SOUND.

A TRACTOR BUMPING THROUGH THE SLUSH INTO THE BACK
LOT. NORMAL SOUND.

Various men greet Stahr.

KATHLEEN STANDING IN THE WATER. NO SOUND.

INT. STAHR'S HOUSE. NIGHT.

A large room.

The Butler is taking off Stahr's coat.

> BUTLER
>
> Is everything all right at the studio, Sir?

> STAHR
>
> Yes.

*Stahr, unobtrusively, slips a pill into his mouth and drinks a glass
of water. The Butler watches him.*

> BUTLER
>
> Would you like some tea?

> STAHR
>
> No, thank you.

Stahr walks towards the stairs and goes up.

> BUTLER
>
> Shall I turn off the lights?

> STAHR
>
> Yes.

*He walks into his bedroom. From below, we see him pause a
moment in the doorway.*

INT. STAHR'S BEDROOM. NIGHT.

Stahr on the telephone.

> STAHR
>
> Yes . . . yes . . . I told you, one of them wore a silver
> belt. Two women . . . yes . . . that's right . . .

INT. SCREENING ROOM. NEXT MORNING. RUSHES.

*In background voices of actors on screen, repetitive. In shadow,
Stahr on the telephone.*

> STAHR
>
> . . . No, I don't know which one wore the belt. I don't
> know the women . . . Right . . . Yes, find the cop . . .
> And tell Robinson to call me as soon as he wakes up.

He puts the phone down and looks at the screen.

ON SCREEN.

Garbo in scene from 'Camille'.

> MAN
> (*VO*)
>
> Which one, Monroe?

> STAHR
>
> Take six. Let's see it again.

Screen goes blank.

INT. CAR, DRIVING DOWN SUNSET BOULEVARD. DAY.

*Cecilia driving, Wylie beside her. Wylie is stroking her hair and
neck. Cecilia is fiddling with the car radio. Hitler in full flood
suddenly comes on. A barrage of 'Sieg Heil's'. They listen a
moment in silence.*

Wylie turns the knob and gets 'Lovely to Look At'.

WYLIE

There's enough Krauts in Hollywood as it is without
having to listen to that crap.

(*Pause.*)

Listen. Why don't you marry me? I may be a lousy
writer, but I'm a remarkably nice person –

CECILIA

Writer's aren't people.

WYLIE

But I love you. I love you more than I love your money,
and that's plenty. Do you think anyone would look at
you if you weren't Pat Brady's daughter?

CECILIA

Stahr's going to look at me this morning. Don't you
think I look lovely? He's going to look at me and think
'I've never really seen her before'.

WYLIE

We don't use that line this year.

CECILIA

Then he'll say, 'Little Cecilia. I've never noticed you
have become a woman'. He will then kiss me as you
would a child.

WYLIE

That's all in my script, and he's reading it now.

CECILIA

He'll sit down and put his face in his hands and say he
never thought of me like that.

WYLIE

You mean you get in a little fast work during the kiss?

CECILIA

I will have bloomed during the kiss.

WYLIE

Him too, huh?

CECILA

Then he'll say –

WYLIE

I know all his lines. What I want to know is what you
say.

CECILA

What do you think I say?

WYLIE

You wouldn't say a thing like that. You wouldn't dare.
He's old enough to be your uncle.

INT. STAHR'S OFFICE. DAY.

*Stahr is talking into the phone. Behind him on a shelf, a
photograph of Minna is glimpsed.*

STAHR

You found the name? Good. Good boy. Uh-huh . . .
well, divide it between yourselves and try every one in
the book.

He puts the phone down and smiles across the desk.

CECILIA
(*VO*)

Will you go with me to the ball tomorrow night?

INT. STAHR'S OFFICE. STAHR AND CECILIA.

STAHR

What ball?

CECILIA

The Screenwriters Ball down at the Ambassador.

463

STAHR

Oh yes. No, I can't. I might just come in later.

CECILIA

Oh.

Pause.

STAHR

When do you go back to college?

CECILIA

I've just come home.

STAHR

You get the whole summer?

CECILIA

I'm sorry. I'll go back as soon as I can.

STAHR

Don't you want to?

CECILIA

Well, I don't know. I'm pretty well educated. Maybe I should get married.

STAHR

Ah. Well, I'd marry you. I'm lonely. But I'm too old and tired to undertake anything.

CECILIA

Undertake me.

STAHR

What?

CECILIA

Undertake me.

Pause.

STAHR

Oh . . . No. I've known you so long. I've . . . never thought of you that way, Cecilia.

CECILIA

We don't use that line this year.

STAHR

What?

CECILIA

Nothing.

The intercom buzzes.

MISS DOOLAN'S VOICE

Mr Stahr, Mr Rodriguez is still waiting to see you.

STAHR

Oh yes. Send him in. Sorry, Cecilia, these actors . . .

CECILIA

Did you press a buzzer with your foot?

STAHR

Of course not.

CECILIA

All right. Will you dance with me at the ball?

STAHR

Sure.

Rodriguez comes in.

RODRIGUEZ

Hello, Monroe.

(*To Cecilia.*)

Hello!

CECILIA

How are you?

RODRIGUEZ

Wonderful. Really great.

CECILIA

You look wonderful.

RODRIGUEZ

Thank you.

Cecilia goes out.

STAHR

What's the trouble?

RODRIGUEZ

I had to see you, Monroe. I'm through.

STAHR

Through? Have you seen Variety? Your picture's held over at the Roxy and did 37,000 in Chicago last week.

RODRIGUEZ

I know. That's the tragedy. I'm in a tragic mess.

STAHR

What are you talking about?

RODRIGUEZ

It's Esther . . . and me. I love her. She's my wife. But I'm through. I'm washed up. It's gone.

STAHR

What's gone?

RODRIGUEZ

I've gone. I'm ashamed to go to bed. I know 'Rainy Day' grossed 25,000 in Des Moines and broke all records in St. Louis and did 27,000 in Kansas City, but here I am afraid to go to bed with my own wife, with the woman I love. So I came to you, Monroe. I've been to a doctor, I've been to a cathouse. Nothing. So I came to you.

466

STAHR

You did. Yes.

RODRIGUEZ

I mean, we both came from nowhere, from nothing.
Right?

STAHR

Right.

RODRIGUEZ

What were you, a messenger boy?

STAHR

That's right.

RODRIGUEZ

I delivered groceries. This is America. Look where we
are now. I mean, look at this office. Look at you. We
both came from nothing. That's why I can speak to you.

STAHR

Uh-huh.

(*Pause.*)

How's Esther?

RODRIGUEZ

She's the greatest girl in the world. She's my wife.

STAHR

I know that.

RODRIGUEZ

I mean she loves me.

STAHR

I know.

RODRIGUEZ

Five hundred girls marched to my house from the High
School. I stood behind the curtains and watched them. I

couldn't go out. If they knew! If my family knew! I
watch myself on the screen, I want to puke.

STAHR

Uh.

RODRIGUEZ

Look at me. All right, I'm a big star. But what's really
profound about me is that I'm a big star with a big fan
club who actually loves his wife! So what does anyone
want to play these lousy tricks on me? Do you see what I
mean? So I came to you.

STAHR

Yes.

(*He clears his throat.*)

That's right.

They sit in silence.

INT. STAHR'S OUTER OFFICE. DAY.

*Miss Doolan at her desk. The office is empty, except for a Doctor
and his Assistant, who carries an electrocardiograph.*

*The door of Stahr's office opens. Rodriguez stands with Stahr on
the threshold. Rodriguez shakes his hand warmly.*

RODRIGUEZ

Thank you. Monroe, thank you.

STAHR

Just play the part the way I said. Hello, doc. Come in.

INT. STAHR'S OFFICE.

Man setting up electrocardiograph. Doctor examining Stahr.

DOCTOR

When are you taking that vacation?

STAHR

Oh, some time. Six weeks or so.

DOCTOR

Getting any sleep?

STAHR

About five hours.

DOCTOR

Need any more pills?

Stahr pats his pocket.

STAHR

Fine.

DOCTOR

Any pain?

STAHR

Some.

INT. COMPANY DIRECTOR'S DINING-ROOM. DAY.

The Company Directors eating lunch:

Marcus, Brady, Popolos, Fleishacker and others.

BRADY

They'll never get writers unionized. You know why?

Stahr comes into the room.

BRADY

Hello, Monroe. Everything all right?

STAHR

Fine.

He sits at the table.

BRADY

I was saying that they'll never get writers unionized. You know why? Because they hate each other's guts. They'd sell each other for a nickel.

STAHR

This man in New York is pretty set on doing it. The one who's coming out to see me. What's his name?

FLEISHACKER

Brimmer.

BRADY

A Communist.

STAHR

(*to himself*)

Brimmer.

POPOLOS

You mean a real Communist?

BRADY

A real one. Sure.

POPOLOS

I mean some of these guys are just jokers, that call themselves Communists. And mostly they're fairies too.

STAHR

Well, I'll find out – next week.

BRADY

You'd better find out. The last thing we need is a writers' strike. We've got sixteen pictures going into production.

STAHR

I'll handle him.

POPOLOS

Monroe can handle him.

BRADY

Monroe can handle anybody.

POPOLOS

Anyway, mostly they're fairies.

They eat.

(*to Stahr*)

Hey, Monroe, how about this idea of making 'Manon' with a happy ending?

STAHR

It's been making money without a happy ending for a century and a half.

Pause.

BRADY

What about the South American picture?

STAHR

We're going ahead with that.

BRADY

With the same budget?

STAHR

Yes.

Pause.

BRADY

It's out of proportion.

POPOLOS

At that budget we have no chance.

STAHR

What do you think, Mr Marcus?

471

Mr Marcus, a cripple, is being lifted from his chair by a chauffeur. He speaks from the chauffeur's arms.

MARCUS
Monroe is our production genius. I count upon him and lean heavily upon him. The balance sheet last year showed a twenty-seven million dollar profit. It's due to him.

They all watch the chauffeur carrying Marcus out of the room.

BRADY
(*to Stahr*)
You know who first told him were a genius? Guess.

STAHR
You.

BRADY
Right.

STAHR
That was damn good of you, Pat.

BRADY
When I admire a man I say so. I want the world to know. Perhaps it's because I'm Irish. The Irish are warmhearted people.

POPOLOS
The Greeks are warm too. You try to find me a Greek Communist. You couldn't find one.

BRADY
But there's not a two million dollar gross in this country right now. Don't forget – there's a depression.

STAHR
I know that. I think we can count on a million and a quarter from the road show. Perhaps a million and a half. And a quarter of a million abroad.

Pause.

FLEISHACKER

But your budget is seventeen hundred and fifty thousand. You expect less than that in grosses. What about prints, advertising, distribution costs, interest on the money – and some profits?

STAHR

I'm not even sure we'll gross a million.

A Waiter enters the room with a telephone. He plugs it in, puts it in front of Stahr.

WAITER

For you, Mr Stahr.

STAHR
(into phone)
Yes? . . . Hello, Robbie . . . Uh-huh. Good . . . Thank you. Yes, leave the number with Miss Doolan. I'll call later. Good work.

He puts the phone down. The Waiter takes it and leaves the room.

FLEISHACKER

I'm . . . fairly new here and perhaps I fail to comprehend implicitly and explicitly. Do I understand you to say you expect to gross half a million short of your budget?

STAHR

It's a quality picture.

They all look at him.

POPOLOS

A quality picture? What the hell . . .?

STAHR

For two years we've played safe. It's time we made a picture that isn't meant to make money. Pat Brady's always saying at Academy dinners that we have a certain duty to the public. Okay. It's a good thing for the company to slip in a picture that'll lose money. Write it off as good will.

He stands, leaves the room. They all stare after him. Brady shakes his head slowly and smiles.

BRADY
(*murmuring to himself*)

Boy . . .

INT. CORRIDOR. DAY.

Stahr walks down the corridor.

On the walls are large blow-ups of all the stars, including Minna Davis, Didi and Rodriguez. Stahr does not look at them.

Wylie is waiting at the end of the corridor.

WYLIE

Mr Stahr! Sir!

STAHR

Hello, Wylie.

WYLIE

You going somewhere?

STAHR

Stage 17.

They walk to the elevator.

EXT. BUILDING. DAY.

Stahr and Wylie emerge.

The camera tracks with them throughout the scene as they pass through the back lot. The back lot is crowded with extras and technicians. There is a great variety of sets.

WYLIE

Listen. Have you read my script?

STAHR

Ah. Yes.

WYLIE

What do you think of it?

STAHR

It's an interesting script.

WYLIE

Uh-huh. Then how come you have two other writers on it?

Stahr stops, smiles.

In background is the door to stage 21, open. Technicians are hauling equipment through the door.

STAHR

Who told you that?

WYLIE

They're friends of mine! They didn't know I was doing it, I didn't know they were doing it! We all found out this morning.

STAHR

I'm sorry. What can we do? That's the system.

WYLIE

You invented that system.

Stahr does not reply. They walk on.

STAHR

You've distorted the girl. By distorting the girl you've
distorted the story.

WYLIE

How?

STAHR

I'm not interested in your fantasies.

WYLIE

How have I distorted the damn girl?

A group of men pass. Stahr hails one of them.

STAHR

Hey, Eddie!

EDDIE

Hello, Monroe.

Stahr puts his arm round Eddie's shoulder.

STAHR

Two people at the sneak preview complained that
Morgan's fly was open for half the picture.

EDDIE

What!

STAHR

It's probably a couple of seconds, but I want you to run
the picture until you find the footage. Have some people
with you. Someone'll spot it.

EDDIE

Sure.

Stahr pats him on the back, joins Wylie. They walk.

STAHR

You've given her a secret life. She doesn't have a secret

476

life. You've made her a melancholic. She is not a
melancholic.

WYLIE

How do you know?

STAHR

Because I paid fifty thousand bucks for that book and
because that's the way I see it. If I want to do a Eugene
O'Neill play I'll buy one. The girl stands for health,
vitality, love. You've made her a whore. You can work
with Beth and Charlie on this or I'll take you off the
subject. It's up to you.

Wylie stops. Stahr stops.

WYLIE

So how do you want the girl?

STAHR

Perfect.

Wylie grins.

WYLIE

Gee.

INT. STAHR'S OFFICE. DAY.

Stahr picking up phone.

A VOICE

Hello?

Pause.

STAHR

Hello.

VOICE

Hello.

STAHR

I'm glad we found you. We didn't have much to go on.

VOICE

Oh really?

STAHR

Were you wearing a silver belt last night?

VOICE

Yes. I was.

Pause.

VOICE

Who are you?

STAHR

My name is Monroe Stahr.
                    (*Pause.*)
I . . . I'd like to see you.
                    (*Pause.*)
There's a reason.

VOICE

What reason?

STAHR

I can't tell you now.

Pause.

Look . . . it's very simple. I'd just like to talk to you for a
few minutes.

VOICE

To put me in the movies?

STAHR

That wasn't my idea.

Pause.

VOICE

When?

STAHR

Tonight.

VOICE

Where?

STAHR

At your house?

VOICE

No. Somewhere outside.
(*Pause.*)
I'll meet you somewhere at nine o'clock.

STAHR

That's impossible, I'm afraid.

VOICE

Oh. Well, what about tomorrow?

STAHR

No, no. Okay. Tonight. Nine o'clock. On the corner of
Wilshire and Rodeo Drive.

VOICE

Okay. Should I wear the silver belt?

STAHR

Yes.

VOICE

Okay. See you later.

Stahr sits still. The intercom buzzer buzzes. He ignores it.

Silence.

The buzzer again.

INT. SOUND STAGE.

Stahr enters the stage swiftly. Ridingwood leaves the set and walks towards him.

RIDINGWOOD
Hello, Monroe. Jesus, I'm glad you came down.

STAHR
How's it going?

Without waiting for an answer, he strides towards the set. Ridingwood follows.

Rodriguez slides past Stahr and murmurs to him.

RODRIGUEZ
She's too old for me.

Didi is having her hair combed. A make-up man is putting cream on her skin.

Stahr puts his arm around her.

Photographers immediately start taking photographs of Stahr and Didi.

STAHR
How's things?

DIDI
These fucking publicity men!

She turns to the First Assistant.

Get these photographers away from me!

Stahr waves them away, crisply. They withdraw.

STAHR
(gently, to Didi)
How are you?

DIDI

I've got the damn curse and I'm having all this trouble with my fucking hair.

Stahr moves a lock of hair to behind her ear.

STAHR

Don't worry about it.

DIDI

It's like seaweed. They keep using the wrong shampoo. They're trying to screw me, these bitches, on my word of honour.

HAIRDRESSER

We're using her favourite shampoo –

Didi embraces the hairdresser impulsively, turns to walk away with Stahr.

DIDI

Nobody likes me or something.

STAHR

I love you, Didi.

They walk towards a far corner.

DIDI

How do you think I look? How do you think I look on the screen?

STAHR

You're going to be beautiful.

DIDI
(*tearful*)

No, I mean my performance! He doesn't say anything to me! Let's go on! Let's push on! Push on! That's all he says!

CLOSE-UP. STAHR.

> STAHR
>
> You're a great actress.

DIDI LOOKING AT HIM.

STAHR CLUTCHES HER ELBOW AND MOVES AWAY.

> STAHR
>
> Red.

Ridingwood joins him. Stahr leads him towards the door.

> RIDINGWOOD
>
> Thank God you talked to her. She's been driving me crazy.

> STAHR
>
> Come with me.

> RIDINGWOOD
>
> With you? What about –?

> STAHR
>
> Leave it as it is.

EXT. SOUND STAGE.

They emerge from the stage.

> RIDINGWOOD
>
> Isn't she a terrible bitch?

> STAHR
>
> You can't handle her.

INT. STAHR'S CAR.

They get in. The chauffeur drives away.

STAHR

We'll have to call if off, Red.

RIDINGWOOD

The picture?

STAHR

I'm putting Daditch on it.

Pause.

RIDINGWOOD

Oh.

STAHR

We'll try some other time.

The car pulls up. They get out.

EXT. CAR.

RIDINGWOOD

Shall I finish this take?

STAHR

It's being done now. Daditch is in there.

RIDINGWOOD

What the hell –

STAHR

He went in when we came out. He read the script last night.

RIDINGWOOD

You bastard.

STAHR

Listen.

He regards Ridingwood calmly.

> STAHR

You haven't touched what she's able to do.

Pause.

> RIDINGWOOD

How about my coat? I left it on the set.

> STAHR

Here it is.

Stahr takes the coat from the front seat and hands it to Ridingwood.

INT. STAHR'S OFFICE. STAHR AND MISS DOOLAN.

Stahr is turning pages of a script swiftly. He crosses out various pages with a red pencil. He looks at his watch, hands the script to Miss Doolan and stands.

> STAHR

Okay. That's it.

The intercom buzzer buzzes. Miss Doolan answers.

> MISS DOOLAN

It's Mr Brady.

She hands the receiver to Stahr.

Brady's voice on intercom.

> BRADY
> (*VO*)

Monroe, I'm with Fleishacker.

INT. BRADY'S OFFICE. BRADY AND FLEISHACKER.

> BRADY

We've just had a call from New York. Urgent. Do you have a few minutes?

> STAHR
> (*VO*)

No. It'll have to wait till morning.

> BRADY

We'll come in to you. We just need –

> STAHR
> (*VO*)

Not now!

The receiver is slammed down. Brady looks at the receiver, then looks at Fleishacker.

INT. STAHR'S OFFICE. STAHR AND MISS DOOLAN.

> STAHR
> (*to Miss Doolan*)

That's all.

He leaves the room.

EXT. STUDIO. NIGHT.

Stahr jumping into his car and driving out of the studio.

BRADY AT WINDOW WATCHING STAHR DRIVE AWAY.

EXT. STREET. NIGHT. THE BACK OF A WOMAN WEARING A SILVER BELT.

Stahr's car draws up. He opens the door.

INT. CAR. OVER STAHR.

The woman gets into the car. It is Edna. She sits, smiles at him.

> EDNA

Hi.

He stares at her.

Where are we going?

STAHR

I don't know.

EDNA

What about a hotel?

STAHR

No. I'll run you home. Where do you live?

EDNA

Run me home?
                    (*She laughs.*)
There's no hurry. What's the matter? Don't you like
me?
                    (*She puts her hand on his thigh.*)
I thought you liked me.

Stahr is still, at the wheel. He turns to her.

STAHR

I've been stupid. Last night I had an idea you were the
exact double of someone I knew. It was dark and the
light was in my eyes.

EDNA

Really? That's funny.

He starts the car.

STAHR

Which way?

EDNA

Westwood.

He drives.

EDNA

You were married to Minna Davis, weren't you?

486

STAHR

That's right.

EDNA

Well, if you meant . . . your wife . . . well, I'm quite a different type to her, but the girl who was with me, now she's . . . something like her. Are you sure you're not talking about her?

STAHR

No. I remember the silver belt you wore.

EDNA

That was me all right.

They approach an area of lighted bungalows.

I live just over the top of the hill.

They drive in silence, approach the hill.

I'm an actress . . . I'm going to be an actress.

No response from Stahr.

Listen, could you stop here a minute?

STAHR

You said over the hill.

EDNA

Yes, but I'd like to stop here a minute, please.

He stops the car.

EXT. CAR.

They both get out.

EDNA

Could you wait a second?

She goes towards a small house and rings the bell.

487

Stahr stands by the car.

The door of the house opens. Stahr looks up. Kathleen is at the door.

KATHLEEN
Edna.

She looks beyond Edna at Stahr.

CLOSE-UP. STAHR.

CLOSE-UP. KATHLEEN.

EXT. THE HOUSE.

Stahr and Kathleen still. Edna looks from one to the other.

EDNA
I think it was you he wanted to see. He telephoned me –

Stahr steps forward.

STAHR
I'm afraid we were rude at the studio.

KATHLEEN
The studio?

STAHR
Yes. Last night.

KATHLEEN
Oh. We had no business there.

Pause.

STAHR
I hope you'll both . . . come and make a real tour . . . of the studio.

KATHLEEN

Who are you?

EDNA

He's a producer. He got us mixed up.
(*Pause.*)
Phone me, will you? Good night. Mr Stahr.

STAHR

Good night.

*Edna walks away, towards the top of the hill. Stahr walks
towards Kathleen, and stands with her on the porch.*

You're Irish.

KATHLEEN

I've lived in London a long time. I didn't think you
could tell.

STAHR

Oh yes.
(*Pause.*)
You . . . lived in London?

KATHLEEN

Yes. I came out here a few months ago.
(*Pause.*)
Was it me you wanted to see, or Edna?

STAHR

I made a silly mistake. I thought you were wearing the
silver belt.

KATHLEEN

Oh. Well, I wasn't.

STAHR

No. But it was you I wanted to see.

489

KATHLEEN

Yes? Why?

STAHR

You reminded me of someone.

Pause.

KATHLEEN

So you're Mr Stahr, the producer? I suppose the girls
are all after you to put them on the screen.

STAHR

They've given up.

KATHLEEN

You didn't want to put me in pictures?

STAHR

No.

KATHLEEN

Good. I'm not an actress.

Pause.

STAHR

I feel as if I had my foot in the door – like a collector.

She smiles.

KATHLEEN

I'm sorry I can't ask you in.

STAHR

Well . . .

They walk to his car. He turns to her.

Is this all?

She smiles uncertainly, holds out her hand.

490

KATHLEEN

I do hope we'll meet again.

STAHR

I'd be sorry if we didn't.

He gets into the car, turns it, waves, drives off.

She remains standing.

His car goes down the hill.

She walks back to the house, goes in and closes the door.

Sound of a lawn mower in the distance.

INT. STAHR'S HOUSE. NIGHT.

Stahr climbing stairs to landing. The Butler appears below.

BUTLER

Will you be running a movie tonight, sir?

STAHR

No.

BUTLER

Shall I turn out the lights?

STAHR

Yes.

INT. STAHR'S OFFICE. DAY.

Boxley, a distinguished English writer, recently brought to Hollywood, is walking up and down the office. He is in a state of great agitation. Stahr is still, at his desk, in his shirtsleeves. Jane Meloney and Harry Sachs lounging heavily in chairs.

BOXLEY
(*explosively*)
I can't go on! It's a waste of time.

STAHR

Why?

BOXLEY

You've stuck me with two hacks. They can't write and they bugger up everything I write.

Meloney smiles. Sachs laughs.

STAHR

Why don't you just write it yourself?

BOXLEY

I have. I sent you some.

STAHR

That was just talk. We'd lose the audience.

BOXLEY

Talk! I don't think you people read things. The men are duelling when the conversation takes place. At the end one of them falls into a well and has to be hauled up in a bucket.

STAHR

Would you write that in a book of your own?

BOXLEY

Of course I wouldn't! I inherited this absurd situation.

Stahr studies him.

STAHR

Do you ever go to the movies?

BOXLEY

Rarely.

STAHR

Because people are always duelling and falling down wells?

BOXLEY

And talking a load of rubbish.

Stahr stands.

STAHR

Listen . . . has your office got a stove in it that lights
with a match?

BOXLEY

Er . . . yes I think so.

STAHR

Suppose you're in your office. You've been fighting
duels all day. You're exhausted.

He sits.

This is you.

He stands.

A girl comes in.

He goes to the door, opens it, comes back in, shuts it.

She doesn't see you. She takes off her gloves, opens her
purse and dumps it out on the table.

He mimes these actions.

You watch her.

He sits.

This is you.

He stands.

She has two dimes, a nickel and a matchbox. She leaves
the nickel on the table, puts the two dimes back into her
purse, takes her gloves to the stove, opens it and puts
them inside.

493

He mimes all this while talking.

> She lights a match. Suddenly the telephone rings. She picks it up.

He mimes this.

> She listens. She says, 'I've never owned a pair of black gloves in my life'. She hangs up, kneels by the stove, lights another match.

He kneels, mimes lighting another match, then quickly jumps up and goes to the door.

> Suddenly you notice there's another man in the room, watching every move the girl makes . . .

Pause.

BOXLEY
(intrigued)

What happens?

STAHR

I don't know. I was just making pictures.

BOXLEY

What was the nickel for?

STAHR
(to Jane)

Jane, what was the nickel for?

JANE

The nickel was for the movies.

Boxley laughs.

BOXLEY

What do you pay me for? I don't understand the damn stuff.

494

STAHR

Yes you do. Or you wouldn't have asked about the nickel.

INT. SCREENING ROOM.

The lights go up. There are four people in the room. Brady stands, Fleishacker stands. The assistant editor, Jeff, stands. The editor, Eddie, remains seated.

BRADY

Monroe's right. It needs twenty minutes out of it. Twice it just lays there, goes to sleep. Okay, I've got to go to this damn Writers' Ball. I'll talk to you tomorrow, Eddie.

He turns towards Eddie, who remains seated.

What's Eddie, asleep? Christ, the goddamn movie even sends the editor to sleep.

Jeff goes to Eddie, bends over him, looks up.

JEFF

He's not asleep, Mr Brady.

BRADY

What do you mean, he's not asleep?

Pause.

JEFF

He's dead, Mr Brady.

BRADY

Dead?

JEFF

He's not breathing.

BRADY

What do you mean, he's dead?

JEFF

He must have died during the . . .

BRADY

How can he be dead? We've just been watching the
rough cut!

He looks at the screen to confirm this.

Jesus!
                    (*He turns to Fleishacker.*)
I didn't hear anything. Did you hear anything?

FLEISHACKER

Not a thing.

JEFF

Eddie . . . probably didn't want to disturb the
screening, Mr Brady.

INT. BALLROOM. WRITERS' BALL.

*A large ballroom. Crowded. A Glen Miller type orchestra. Many
tables.*

*Stahr enters the ballroom, pauses on the stairs, looks about, goes
towards his company table.*

He suddenly sees Kathleen at a table with others.

*He stops, turns, goes to her table, passing a table at which
everyone is speaking German, stops at her chair, asks her to
dance. She gets up.*

STAHR AND KATHLEEN DANCING.

The camera pans with them. They slow the dance.

STAHR

What are you doing here?

KATHLEEN

I'm with Martha Dodd's party.

STAHR

What's your name?

KATHLEEN

Kathleen Moore.

STAHR

Kathleen Moore? How do you know her?
(*Indicating Martha Dodd's party.*)

KATHLEEN

Oh, I met her . . . recently.

Cecilia and Wylie are dancing in background.

Cecilia glances at them.

STAHR

Are you married?

KATHLEEN

No. I must go back now. I promised this dance.

STAHR

Can we have lunch or dinner?

KATHLEEN

No. It's impossible.

She stops dancing and laughs.

I must go back. Thank you for the dance.

She goes. He stands, looking after her. Rodriguez and his wife dance up to Stahr.

RODRIGUEZ

Monroe!

497

STAHR
(*abstractedly*)

Hi, Rod. Hello, Esther.

RODRIGUEZ

Doesn't she look wonderful? Isn't she beautiful?

Stahr looks at Esther.

STAHR

How are you, Esther?

ESTHER

Really great.

THE COMPANY TABLE AT THE BALL.

POPOLOS

This is the greatest country in the world. Everybody stands a chance in this country. There ain't gonna be no revolution. The only people who want a revolution are the Communists.

BRADY

And the fairies.

FLEISHACKER

What kind of revolution do the fairies want?

POPOLOS

A Communist one.

BRADY

What else?

FLEISHACKER

Do you think Stalin likes homosexuals?

POPOLOS

Homosexuals? I'll tell you something. Do you know what the word 'homo' is? It's a Greek word. I come from Europe. I'm Greek.

BRADY

That's why he knows all about Stalin.

FLEISHACKER

Stalin ain't Greek.

POPOLOS

You're damned right he ain't.

BRADY

He's a fairy.

POPOLOS

He's a bastard Communist Russian fairy.

FLEISHACKER

That's why he hates homosexuals.

BRADY

Fleishacker, let me tell you something. After the revolution, you'll be the only safe one. You know why? Because they always need lawyers after a revolution to straighten out the legal side.

He laughs.

Stahr sits down.

What do you think, Monroe?

STAHR

I think so too.

BRADY

Listen, I saw 'Highway to Tomorrow' today. I agree with you. Take twenty minutes out and you got a fine movie.

STAHR

Possibly. The shape's not too bad though.

BRADY

The shape's good. You know why? Eddie's one of the best cutters in the business.

STAHR STARING AT BRADY.

THE BALLROOM.

Kathleen gets up from her table and moves towards the door. The camera tracks after her, stopping at the table where Cecilia and Wylie are sitting. In background, Stahr seen rising from his table.

CLOSE-UP. CECILIA, WATCHING STAHR'S EXIT.

LOBBY OF BALLROOM.

Stahr catches up with Kathleen. Middle-aged women cluster behind a rope, watching the ballroom entrance.

> STAHR

Why are you going? It's early.

> KATHLEEN

It's late.

She moves towards the elevator. He follows.

They talked as if I'd been dancing with the Prince of Wales.

> STAHR

Meet me tomorrow.

> KATHLEEN

I've said I can't. Isn't that enough?

> STAHR

Look, it's Sunday tomorrow. Would you like to see the studio? I'll show you around the studio.

> KATHLEEN

No, I wouldn't like to see the studio.

> STAHR

You wouldn't? Well, we can go anywhere. Where would you like to go?

Pause.

> KATHLEEN

I'm a weak woman. If I meet you tomorrow will you leave me in peace? No, you won't, will you? So I'll say no and thank you.

The elevator arrives. She gets in, he follows.

INT. ELEVATOR.

They descend in silence. He smiles at her. She smiles back. The elevator arrives at the lobby. They get out.

INT. LOBBY.

At the main door, heads and shoulders of a crowd, held back by the police.

> KATHLEEN

They looked so strange when I came in as if they were furious at me for not being someone famous.

> STAHR

I know another way out.

He takes her towards a side door.

EXT. ALLEY. NIGHT.

They emerge from a door into the alley and walk towards the car park.

> KATHLEEN

How old are you?

> STAHR

I've lost track. About thirty-five I think.

> KATHLEEN

Where do you come from?

STAHR

I was born on the East Side of New York.

KATHLEEN

They said at the table you were the boy wonder.

STAHR

Yes? Listen, where shall we meet tomorrow?
                    (*She stops.*)
I'll come and pick you up at two o'clock.

KATHLEEN

No.
                    (*She looks at him.*)
I'll meet you here. This same spot.

She walks to her car. A loud cheer comes through the night from the crowd outside the hotel. She drives away.

EXT. CAR PARK. DAY.

Stahr standing on the same spot in day clothes. Her car arrives. He helps her out.

KATHLEEN

Have you been here all night?

STAHR

Yes.

KATHLEEN

I'd like some tea, if it's a place you're not known.

STAHR

There's a place on the coast where they have a trained seal. He knows me pretty well – he bit me once – but he won't say a word unless you're rude to him.

Pause.

STAHR

What do you want to hide?

KATHLEEN

Nothing.

EXT. A ROADHOUSE. DAY.

Stahr and Kathleen sitting with tea on the terrace. The seal and his Trainer approach. The seal slips over to Stahr and nuzzles him.

TRAINER
(*to Kathleen*)

He remembers him.

STAHR

This seal has the memory of an elephant.

TRAINER

He likes him, because he's a charming guy.

KATHLEEN
(*smiling*)

Really?

TRAINER

Sure. This seal's got taste.

STAHR

How long have you known him?

TRAINER

I've known him for years. His father was an old friend of mine.

STAHR
(*to Kathleen*)

But the family history ain't so good.

TRAINER

His mother ran away with another seal.

STAHR
(*to Kathleen*)

All this happened before you were born, lady.

Kathleen giggles.

STAHR

Is he good to you?

TRAINER

He's good to me on the whole.
(*to Kathleen*)
I only got one problem.

STAHR

He won't ride in the back seat.

TRAINER

That's right. He climbs over the back and rides up front.
I know he's a good driver –

STAHR

But who owns the car?

Stahr gives the Trainer a dollar.

Give him this.

TRAINER

Thanks.
(*To the seal.*)
Say thanks.

The seal growls.

EXT. MALIBU HOUSE. SEA SHORE. MID AFTERNOON

*Stahr and Kathleen walk down towards the house. The house is
slowly disclosed. It is a skeleton. No roof. Great boulders rise to the*

504

unfinished terrace. A concrete mixer, yellow wood, rubble. The sea in background.

> STAHR
>
> Well, this is it. I don't know why I'm building it. Maybe it's for you.

> KATHLEEN
>
> I think it's great of you to build a big house for me without even knowing what I look like.

> STAHR
>
> I didn't know what kind of roof you wanted.

They walk under the scaffolding into a large room. Built-in bookshelves, curtain rods, a raised platform with two holes in the wall. She looks up at the sky.

> KATHLEEN
>
> I don't need a roof.

She looks at the platform and the holes in the wall.

> What's that for?

> STAHR
>
> For the projector. The movie projector.

They walk out on the porch. Cushioned chairs, ping pong table. Another ping pong table on newly laid grass beyond.

> Last week I gave a luncheon out here, so I brought out a few props, and some grass, to see how the place felt.

> KATHLEEN
>
> Is that real grass?

> STAHR
>
> Sure.

> KATHLEEN
>
> Is it from a film set?

He laughs.

STAHR

No.

KATHLEEN

Can I walk on it?

STAHR

Walk. I'll watch you.

She walks on the grass. He watches her.

KATHLEEN

Are you going to live here alone?

STAHR

Oh yes.

KATHLEEN

Alone with your movie projector.
(*Pause.*)
Where do you live now?

STAHR

I live in my old house.

She walks to an excavation. Seagulls.

KATHLEEN

What's this?

STAHR

A swimming pool.

KATHLEEN

You'll need a constant supply of nereids, to plunge and gambol.

STAHR

Nereids? What's that?

KATHLEEN

Sea nymphs.

STAHR

Oh no. I'll come out here to read scripts. No
distractions.

*He looks at her, walks towards her. She makes an almost
imperceptible move, which stops him.*

KATHLEEN

I lived with a man, for a long time. Too long. I wanted
to leave but he couldn't let me go. So finally I ran away.

Pause. She smiles at him.

I must go now. I have an appointment. I didn't tell you.

STAHR

That's not true. But it's all right.

KATHLEEN

Thank you. It's been nice.

STAHR

We'll do it again.

KATHLEEN

No. I'm sorry. I'll write you a letter. I must go now.

They walk to his car.

STAHR

Do you ever go to the movies?

KATHLEEN

Oh . . . not much.

STAHR

Why not?

KATHLEEN

Should I?

STAHR

Millions of people do.

KATHLEEN

Why?

STAHR

Because movies are necessary to them. I give them what
they need.

KATHLEEN

What you need.

They stand still.

STAHR

It's my life.

*She smiles, glances towards the house. He remains looking at her.
She looks back at him quickly, then gets into the car. He closes her
door, gets in. The car drives off.*

EXT. PARKING LOT. NIGHT.

*Stahr and Kathleen walking towards her car. She opens her bag,
looks for her car keys.*

STAHR

Have you got them?

KATHLEEN

Yes.

*She unlocks the car door, turns to look at him. She looks at him
for a little too long. He kisses her. She sighs. They part. He moves
a lock of hair behind her ear.*

They kiss again.

This wasn't my idea.

She opens the car door. He holds the door, seizes and kisses her.

Let's go back . . . to your house, on the beach.

INT. MALIBU HOUSE. NIGHT.

Stahr looking out to sea.

In background, in shadow, Kathleen appears, naked. He turns towards her.

KATHLEEN

Come here.

STAHR TREMBLING.

KATHLEEN WALKS TOWARDS HIM.

She unties his tie.

KATHLEEN LYING ALONE, HER FACE THOUGHTFUL, RELAXED. SHE IS NAKED.

Candlelight flickers over her face.

STAHR
(VO)

Lift your head.

He comes into shot with a cushion, places it under her head. He too is naked.

THE ROOM.

He has lit one candle in the room and attached an electric heater to the light fitting.

He pulls the mattress towards her, helps her on to it, settles a cushion again under her head, wraps her coat around her. She laughs.

STAHR

Comfortable?

509

She smiles at him, looks away.

KATHLEEN

I wonder when it's settled.

STAHR

What?

KATHLEEN

I mean there's a moment when you needn't, and then there's another moment when you know nothing in the world could keep it from happening.
(*Pause.*)
I know why you liked me at first. Edna told me.

STAHR

What did she tell you?

KATHLEEN

That I look like Minna Davis.

STAHR

Yes.

KATHLEEN

You were happy with her?

Pause.

STAHR

I don't remember.

KATHLEEN

You don't remember?

STAHR

No.
(*Pause.*)
I remember her face, but I don't remember what we were like. She . . . became very professional. She was very successful. She answered all her fan letters. Everyone loved her.

(Pause.)

I was closest to her . . . when she was dying.

Kathleen stands.

KATHLEEN

I'm warm now.

She takes off the coat. She goes to a closet, looks in, feels about in it, brings out an apron, looks at it, puts it on.

Does the maid live in? Or just come for your breakfast?

She brings a tablecloth from the closet and covers him with it. She looks down at him.

There'd be lots for a maid to do – looking after Mr Stahr.

He laughs, stops.

STAHR

Are you going to stay in California?

She does not reply.

Are you going to stay? Can't you tell me? What's the mystery?

KATHLEEN

Not now. It's not worth telling.

STAHR

Come here then.

She goes to him. He sits up on the mattress, presses his cheek against her thighs.

KATHLEEN

You're tired.

STAHR

No I'm not.

KATHLEEN

I meant you work too hard.

STAHR

Don't be a mother.

KATHLEEN

What shall I be?

STAHR

I'll show you.

He takes off her apron.

KATHLEEN

You've taken off my apron.

She touches her cheekbones, distorting her cheeks slightly.

It's here I look like Minna Davis.

CAMERA BEHIND STAHR'S HEAD.

Stahr lies her down, bends over her, obscuring her face.

STAHR

No. It's here.

THE SHORE.

Kathleen comes into shot and walks down to the edge of the sea.

STAHR
(*VO*)

What was he like?

KATHLEEN

He was a very learned man. He could have taught all
sorts of subjects. He taught me. We travelled. He was
very attractive, and he was also . . . well, he was a king. I
mean he really was, a real one . . . but he was out of a
job. That's what he used to say. I went everywhere with

512

him. I belonged to him. We were too close. We should probably have had children – to stand between us. He wasn't really much like a king. Not nearly as much as you. None of them were. Then . . . he started to drink, he tried to force me to sleep with all his friends. I should have left him . . . long before.

She glances at him, then away.

I want a quiet life.

STAHR
(*VO*)
I can't stop looking at you.

She turns to him. His hand touches her face. Close up. Stahr.

I don't want to lose you.

Close up. Kathleen.

KATHLEEN
I want a quiet life.

INT. CAR. STATIONARY. PARKING LOT. NIGHT.

Kathleen probing behind seat cushions.

STAHR
Lost something?

KATHLEEN
It might have fallen out.

STAHR
What?

KATHLEEN
An envelope.

She feels through her purse.

513

STAHR

Was it important?

KATHLEEN

No. It doesn't matter.

EXT. PARKING LOT. NIGHT.

They stand by his car.

STAHR

I'll call you.

KATHLEEN

I haven't got a phone. What's your real address?

STAHR

Just Bel Air. There's no number.

KATHLEEN

Bel Air.

They stand apart. Constraint.

KATHLEEN

Well, Mr Stahr, goodnight.

STAHR

Mr Stahr?

KATHLEEN

Stahr. Is that better?

STAHR

As you like.

They remain apart. Suddenly she goes to him. He folds her in his arms and kisses her.

STAHR

Goodnight.

She walks to her car, gets in. He watches her a moment, gets in his own car. The cars drive away, in separate directions.

INT. STAHR'S HOUSE. STUDY. NIGHT.

List of names on pad:

Marcus
Harlow
Fairbanks
Brady
Coleman
Skouras
Fleishacker

Stahr's hand puts pad down. He pours himself a glass of water. The Butler comes in with an envelope.

BUTLER

This fell out of the car.

STAHR

Oh, thanks.
(*Pointing at pad.*)
Did any of these people want to speak to me urgently?

BUTLER

All of them.

STAHR

Oh yes? Okay. Goodnight.

Stahr looks at the envelope in his hand. It is addressed to himself. He starts to open it, stops, puts it down.

He picks up a script from a pile of scripts, a pencil, and starts to read the script.

LATER.

Stahr still reading.

He pours a glass of water and swallows a pill.

LATER.

Stahr still reading.

He suddenly puts the script down, picks up the envelope, opens it and reads.

He puts it in his pocket, sits still.

He stands, goes up the stairs, switches off lights.

Night light in room.

Over his retreating figure Kathleen's voice:

> **KATHLEEN**
> (*VO*)
>
> In half an hour I will be seeing you. When we say goodbye I will hand you this letter. It is to tell you that I am to be married soon and that I won't be able to see you after today. I should have told you last night but it didn't seem to concern you. And it would seem silly to spend this beautiful afternoon telling you about it and watching your interest fade. Let it fade all at once – now. I am very flattered that anyone who sees so many lovely women – I can't finish this sentence. And I'll be late if I don't go to meet you straight away. With all good wishes.
>> Kathleen Moore

The bedroom door closes.

INT. WRITERS' BUILDING. DAY.

Door to Boxley's office.

Wylie is trying the handle and knocking.

> **WYLIE**
> George! Come on. Open up.

                              BOXLEY'S VOICE
You're all mad.

                              WYLIE
I know that. But why don't you open up?

                              BOXLEY'S VOICE
Because you're all mad.

                              WYLIE
Let's get you out of there and we'll go and have a drink.

INT. BOXLEY'S OFFICE.

*Boxley is sitting at his desk with a three-quarter empty whiskey
bottle.*

                              BOXLEY
I don't drink in the middle of the day because the Holy
Roman Catholic and Apostolic Church . . . because the
Holy Roman . . . Church . . . says it's a bad habit.

                              WYLIE'S VOICE
You're not Catholic, Boxley.

                              BOXLEY
You're all so on the *nose* over here, you're all so *literal*,
you know nothing about subtle and refined references to
our fine old European traditions and heritage . . .
heritages-es – or syllogisms, for that matter. Wouldn't
know a damned syllogism if you say one. Cheers.

*A key turns in the door. The door opens. Stahr comes in, followed
by Wylie, behind him a superintendent.*

                              STAHR
Hello, Mr Boxley.

Boxley stares at him.

What's the trouble?

BOXLEY

I'm dangerous when I'm drunk. Watch your step.

STAHR

I heard you were writing a script.

BOXLEY

That's right. Here it is.

He picks up sheets of blank paper from the desk, lets them slip on to the floor. He takes a coin from his pocket, flips it at Stahr.

And here's the nickel.
                    (*He laughs.*)
It's for the movies.

STAHR

Get him home.

He leaves the room.

Boxley gets up, staggers to the door, shouts after him.

BOXLEY

I want copyright protection for that scene I just wrote!
About the drunken writer and the producer!

WYLIE

You didn't write that scene. You just think you're John
Barrymore or someone.

Boxley leaves the room.

EXT. BALCONY.

Boxley leaning over the balcony.

Wylie and other writers come on to the balcony.

Boxley shouts.

BOXLEY

Stahr! Did you hear what I said?

The writers applaud ironically.

STAHR DISAPPEARS ROUND A CORNER WITHOUT LOOKING
BACK.

INT. STAHR'S OUTER OFFICE. DAY.

Stahr comes in. Miss Doolan, at a filing cabinet, turns, sees him.

MISS DOOLAN

Oh, Mr Stahr –

Stahr ignores her, enters his own office.

INT. STAHR'S OFFICE. DAY.

*Stahr enters the office, slamming the door. He stops still upon
seeing Cecilia, who is standing by the window.*

STAHR

Hello.

CECILIA

What's the matter?

STAHR

Nothing. Drunks.
(*Pause.*)
How are you?

CECILIA

I have a terrible grudge.

STAHR

What's that?

CECILIA

You forgot to dance with me at the ball.

Pause.

CECILIA

STAHR

The ball. Oh God.

CECILIA

One moment you were there, and the next moment you were gone. And you never came back.

STAHR

I'm sorry. I just slipped out for some air, and then I met a man, a man I hadn't seen for years. We went for a drive. I hadn't realized how that part of Hollywood had changed. You could see it very clearly at night. Then it was late . . . you know. So I went home to bed.

CECILIA

So that part of Hollywood has changed?

STAHR

Unrecognizable.

CECILIA

What about the man?

STAHR

What about him?

CECILIA

Did he think that part of Hollywood had changed?

STAHR

Yes, he thought so too.

CECILIA

Well, that must have been a nice drive, both of you just driving around, thinking the same thing.

STAHR

Yes.

Pause.

CECILIA

Listen, I want to ask you a question.

STAHR

What is it?

CECILIA

Had the man changed?

STAHR

No, he was exactly the same.
             (*He chuckles.*)
Old Gus.

INT. CORRIDOR.

Cecilia running down the corridor towards Brady's office half crying.

INT. BRADY'S OUTER OFFICE. DAY.

Rosemary on phone. Cecilia comes in.

ROSEMARY
             (*on phone*)
No. He's in conference at the moment –

Cecilia presses the clicker under the desk and goes towards the opening door.

             (*hand over phone*)
Your father's in conference –

INT. VESTIBULE LEADING TO BRADY'S OFFICE.

Cecilia passes through, opens door to Brady's office, goes in.

INT. BRADY'S OFFICE. DAY

Brady is in his shirtsleeves, sweating, trying to open a window.

CECILIA

God, it's like a steam room in here. Why don't you open a window?

BRADY

I am.

CECILIA

I don't know how you can stand it.

He opens the window. She regards him. He is trembling.

Hey, are you all right? Your shirt is soaked.

BRADY

I'm fine, I'm fine. I'm just bothered, that's all.

CECILIA

What is it?

BRADY

It's Stahr! That goddamn little Vine Street Jesus! He's in my hair night and day.

CECILIA

Oh, what are you talking about?

BRADY

He sits like a goddamn priest or rabbi and says what he'll do and what he won't do. I'm half crazy. Look, why don't you go along. I've got some thinking to do.

CECILIA

You're coming with me. You're going to wash your face and put on a clean shirt and come and do your thinking outside. It's beautiful out.

She moves to him, clutches his arm.

(*intensely*)

Do you know how long it is since we had lunch together?

522

Pause.

He looks at her for the first time.

Have you been drinking?

BRADY
(quietly)
Okay, I'll come out. You go and get some air. I'll be
with you.

*He goes into bathroom, taking off his shirt. Cecilia opens two
more windows.*

Get some air. I'll be there in a minute.

*A long low moan comes from somewhere in the room. Cecilia looks
about the room and finally at a small closet. She goes to the closet
and opens it.*

*Birdy tumbles out, stark naked, flops on to the floor, one hand
clutching some clothes, remains on the floor bathed in sweat.*

Brady comes in from the bathroom.

CECILIA
Cover her up.

*She takes a rug from the sofa and throws it over the body. She
looks down at the body, laughs, looks at Brady, stops laughing,
goes out.*

INT. KATHLEEN'S HOUSE. DAY.

The room is bare, clean, still. Flowers.

A knock on the screen door. Silence. Another knock.

The screen door squeaks open. Footsteps.

*Cecilia enters the room, walks to the centre table and stands,
looking at the room.*

There is clear evidence in the room that two people live in the house: a man and a woman.

A curtain shifts in the breeze. Silence.

Cecilia stands still.

EXT. KATHLEEN'S HOUSE. DAY.

Cecilia comes out of the house, walks to the gate, gets into her car.

ON SCREEN: NIGHT CLUB. DAY.

(This scene is in the form of a rough assembly.)

The night club is empty. Chairs on the tables.

Rodriguez sits in the shadows at the piano. Didi enters from side door, dressed in a trench coat. She carries a suitcase.

She sees Rodriguez and stops. He begins to play.

When they first speak, they are clearly quoting from the past.

                    RODRIGUEZ
Can I buy you a drink? I don't usually drink with the talent.

                      DIDI
I don't usually drink with the boss.

They smile.

                    RODRIGUEZ
One before you go.

                      DIDI
I'll get it.

She goes to the bar and pours.

Bourbon. One cube of ice.

She gives him the drink and pours one for herself.

524

RODRIGUEZ

You're quite a girl, Lucienne.

DIDI

Yes. Everybody likes Lucienne.

RODRIGUEZ

Here's to you.

They drink.

He picks out a melody on the piano.

She begins to sing, is unable to finish the song.

It's too bad. I thought you were coming away with me.

DIDI

I can't. You know I can't. I owe it to him. I must go to him.

RODRIGUEZ

Don't you owe me something too?

DIDI

He's my husband.

Rodriguez continues to play.

RODRIGUEZ

I won't forget you, kid.

DIDI

Nor I you.

She picks up her case, goes towards the kitchen door.

RODRIGUEZ

Remember me to your husband. Tell him he'll never know you . . . the way I know you.

She turns and looks at him.

CLOSE-UP. DIDI.

> DIDI
> I lied. I will forget you. I'll forget you by tonight.

She goes out.

INT. KITCHEN.

Didi stands in the kitchen, her eyes brimming with tears.

INT. NIGHT CLUB.

The kitchen door swings backwards and forwards. The piano continues to play.

Screen goes to black. Lights up.

> STAHR
> (*VO*)
> Make-up and Hair here?

> VOICES
> Yes, Mr Stahr.

> STAHR
> (*VO*)
> You've made her look like an angel. I don't know how you've done it. Congratulations.

GROUP IN THE SCREENING ROOM.

> MAKE-UP MAN and HAIRDRESSER
> Oh, thank you, Mr Stahr.

> BRADY
> These French girls, you know, they really . . . they've really got depth, they really know what it's all about.

> A MAN
> Yes, I think they've got depth.

STAHR
(*sharply*)

Who wrote that scene?

ANOTHER MAN

The English writer, Mr Stahr. Boxley. It was the last
thing he wrote before . . . before he left.

STAHR

What a great going away present. Whoever heard
anyone say 'Nor I you'? Has anyone ever said 'Nor I
you' to you?

FIRST MAN

Never.

STAHR

'Nor I you'. We'll have to re-write the scene and re-shoot
it. It's crap. People don't speak like that. Do I have any
writers around who understand the way people talk? Jake.

JAKE

Yes, Monroe.

STAHR

Put four writers on that scene tonight and I want to see
the re-write before they shoot it.

JAKE

Sure, Monroe.

BRADY

How much would it cost to re-shoot?

JAKE

Well . . . the set's already been struck.

BRADY

So how much would it cost?

JAKE

Oh . . . about fifty thousand dollars.

SECOND MAN

And we have a preview next week.

STAHR

I don't care how much it costs. Make it.

He leaves the room.

Silence.

FIRST MAN

What was so wrong with the scene? I thought it was a
pretty touching scene.

They sit in silence.

Brady sits hunched.

INT. STAHR'S OFFICE. DAY.

Stahr lying on the sofa looking at the ceiling.

STAHR ON THE SOFA.

The intercom buzzes.

*Stahr stands, with effort. He takes a pill from his pocket, slips it
into his mouth. The intercom continues to buzz. He answers it.*

MISS DOOLAN
(*VO*)

Do you know a Miss Kathleen Moore?

STAHR

What do you mean?

MISS DOOLAN
(*VO*)

A Miss Kathleen Moore is on the line. She said you
asked her to call.

STAHR AND KATHLEEN. MALIBU HOUSE. LATE AFTERNOON.

STAHR

Who is he?

KATHLEEN

He's an American.

Pause.

He took me away. He brought me here. I live in his
house.

STAHR

Where is he?

KATHLEEN

He's away. He's an engineer. He'll be back . . . next
week.

Pause.

We're getting married.

STAHR

Are you in love with him?

KATHLEEN

Oh yes. It's all arranged. He saved my life.

Pause.

I just wanted to see you once more.

Pause.

It's all arranged.

*She moves away from him and walks along the terrace, looking
out to the sea.*

STAHR

Stop walking.

529

She stops.

Come back.

She turns, is still. She walks slowly towards him, stops.

Closer.

She comes closer to him. She looks at him.

Open your coat.

She hesitates, and then slowly opens her coat.

Close your eyes.

She does so. He extends his arm, traces her cheek. His hand goes down over her throat, her breasts, her belly.

She looks at him.

He takes her into his arms.

INT. CAR. NIGHT.

Stahr is driving. Kathleen sits apart from him. Silence.

> KATHLEEN
> I can never get used to the way . . . night falls here. So fast. There's no twilight. Is there?

> STAHR
> Not really . . . no.

> KATHLEEN
> It's so sudden.

Pause.

> I suppose some parts of America are gentle.

> STAHR
> Sure.

Pause.

Are you leaving California?

KATHLEEN

We might . . . I might . . . I don't know.

Pause.

Are you going away . . . for a holiday?

STAHR

No.

He stops the car, suddenly.

Listen –

KATHLEEN

What?

Pause.

STAHR

Nothing.

They drive on in silence, approach Kathleen's house.

KATHLEEN

Can you drop me here, at this corner?

Stahr stops the car.

She looks at him, swiftly, and away.

Goodbye.

She gets out of the car and walks towards her house. Stahr reverses the car and drives away.

INT. OUTER OFFICE. MORNING.

Miss Doolan at her desk. Two other secretaries answering telephones, which ring continuously. To all enquiries they reply, 'Sorry, Mr Stahr won't be available today.'

The office is filled with people. A Lady Casting Director is talking to Miss Doolan.

LADY CASTING DIRECTOR
I tell you, she's just flown in from New York. I mean, Christ, she's a very important actress. We have an appointment.

MISS DOOLAN
Sorry. There's nothing I can do about it.

LADY CASTING DIRECTOR
Well, what the hell am I going to do with her?

Robinson comes to Miss Doolan's desk.

ROBINSON
Listen. We've got to get this set approved by two o'clock. Otherwise we're way behind.

MISS DOOLAN
There's nothing I can do.

The Doctor with the cardiograph sits, looking at his watch. Other people sit around the room, some with their heads in their hands.

Rodriguez sits apart, forlornly.

INT. STAHR'S OFFICE.

Stahr is at his desk. He is writing, very slowly, on a piece of blue notepaper. Around his desk are crumpled pieces of the same notepaper.

INT. OUTER OFFICE.

Cecilia with Miss Doolan.

CECILIA
We have to make arrangements for the preview on Friday. He's escorting me.

Miss Doolan looks at her unhappily. Cecilia moves to the buzzer.

I'll do it.

She kicks the buzzer and moves towards Stahr's door.

INT. STAHR'S OFFICE.

Stahr looks up as Cecilia comes in.

Without haste, he puts the piece of notepaper into his desk drawer. She walks towards him. Silence.

CECILIA

We have to make arrangements for the preview. What time shall I pick you up?

He leans back in his chair and regards her.

Don't say you're not going. Because you must go. You've no alternative. You're the head of the studio.

Stahr smiles faintly.

You understand what I mean, don't you? What time shall I pick you up?

Pause.

STAHR

Any time.

CECILIA

I'll be here at seven.

She looks at the crumpled pieces of paper, looks back at him. He stares at her coolly.

Okay.

She leaves the room. Stahr gets up, goes to the door and locks it. He goes back to his desk, takes out the notepaper and continues to write.

533

THE LAST TYCOON

INT. LOBBY OF THEATRE. PREVIEW.

Stahr, Cecilia, Brady, Didi, Daditch, Rodriguez and Esther,
Fleishacker, police, photographers, etc. Stahr stands slightly
apart, with Cecilia. She is holding his arm.

> DIDI
> *(to Stahr)*
>
> Are you happy?

> STAHR
> *(expressionless)*
>
> It went very well.

> CECILIA
>
> A really beautiful performance.

> DIDI
>
> You really think so?

> BRADY
>
> Listen! You were terrific.

> DIDI
>
> It's thanks to you all. To you all.
> *(She turns to Stahr.)*
> And to you for changing that fucking director.

Didi walks towards the entrance, and acknowledges loud cheers
from the waiting crowd.

Stahr remains still. Cecilia holds his arm.

INT. CAR. NIGHT.

Stahr and Cecilia sitting still.

> STAHR
>
> Let's go to the beach.

534

CECILIA

What about the party? They're expecting you at the party.

STAHR

Drive me to the beach.

EXT. HOUSE ON MALIBU BEACH. NIGHT.

Stahr and Cecilia in evening dress walk from the car towards the house.

Stahr lights a few candles.

They look out to sea.

CECILIA

Are you ever going to finish it, so you can live in it?

STAHR

I'll finish it.

Pause.

CECILIA

I think you like it as it is.

Pause.

You like it without a roof.

STAHR

Do you think it needs a roof?

CECILIA

If you don't want one, it doesn't need one.

Pause.

It's your house.

THE LAST TYCOON

STAHR
(*distantly*)
When do you go back to college?

CECILIA

Any time.

They stand, silent.

INT. STAHR'S HOUSE. STUDY. AFTERNOON.

At the far end of the room, by the window, Stahr is sitting in an armchair, unshaven, in his bathrobe. The study door is open. Silence. The telephone rings. The Butler answers it, in the hall.

BUTLER
Yes . . . I see . . . Will you hold a minute, please?

The Butler approaches the study door.

Miss Kathleen Moore.

He shuts the door.

Stahr picks up the phone on his desk.

STAHR

Hello.

KATHLEEN'S VOICE
I got your letter.

STAHR

Yes.
(*Pause.*)
Listen. I must see you.

Pause.

KATHLEEN'S VOICE
It's very difficult.

STAHR

It's essential. You know that. Look. We have the
weekend. Come away for the weekend.

KATHLEEN'S VOICE

I can't.

STAHR

You must. We must have time . . . to talk.

KATHLEEN'S VOICE

I'll tell you tomorrow.

STAHR

No. You must say yes now.

CLOSE-UP. KATHLEEN, IN HER HOUSE.

KATHLEEN
(*into phone*)

Yes.

INT. STAHR'S HOUSE. MORNING

*Stahr running down the stairs with a suitcase. He opens the front
door and goes out into sunlight.*

INT. PROJECTION ROOM.

Stahr looking at rushes. Miss Doolan enters.

STAHR

I'm going away this afternoon, for the weekend. For a
break. I'll be unreachable. Cancel all my appointments.

MISS DOOLAN

You're meeting with Mr Brimmer at Miss Brady's
tonight, for drinks.

STAHR

Cancel it. I'll see him on Monday.

MISS DOOLAN

Fine. This just came for you.

She gives him a telegram and leaves. He stands, opens the telegram, holds it in the flickering light from the projector, reads.

TELEGRAM IN FLICKERING LIGHT.

'I was married at noon today stop. Goodbye'. On sticker attached: 'Send your answer by Western Union telegram'.

STAHR SITTING.

STAHR
(*muttering*)

Keep going.

He stares at the screen, immobile.

INT. BRADY'S HOUSE. LEATHER ROOM.

CECILIA

Sugar, Mr Brimmer?

BRIMMER
(*VO*)

No thank you, Miss Brady.

Camera pans with Cecilia to discover Brimmer. Cecilia gives coffee to Brimmer.

CECILIA

Sugar, Monroe?

STAHR
(*VO*)

No thank you.

Camera pans with Cecilia to discover Stahr. Cecilia gives coffee to Stahr.

538

I've never been in this room before. Who designed it?
                    (*With a smile.*)
Your father?

CECILIA

My father asked a designer to design it.

STAHR
                    (*laughing*)
Well, he designed it, all right.

CECILIA

I thought it would be a quiet place for you two to meet.

STAHR

It is.

BRIMMER

It's a very nice room.

Pause.

STAHR

Know California well, Mr Brimmer?

BRIMMER

No. I spend most of my time in New York.

STAHR

Busy?

BRIMMER

Oh yes.

STAHR

Your name is well known here.

BRIMMER

Yours is well known in New York, Mr Stahr.

539

CECILIA
(*to Stahr*)
You have done well by water.
(*To Brimmer*.)
And you by land.

STAHR
Sorry?

CECILIA
Antony and Cleopatra. Did you recognize it?

STAHR
Shakespeare? No. I didn't get much Shakespeare at school. How about you, Mr Brimmer?

BRIMMER
Oh, a little.

STAHR
Where do you come from?

BRIMMER
Tennessee. Baptist.

STAHR
I'm New York. Jewish.

BRIMMER
I know.

STAHR
At least we're all Americans.

BRIMMER
We sure are, Mr Stahr.

Pause.

STAHR
Well, I'm glad you came out. I wanted to talk to you. You've got my writers all upset.

540

BRIMMER

That keeps them awake, doesn't it?

STAHR

I want them awake but I don't want them crazy.

BRIMMER

We're simply concerned that they have proper
protection, that's all.

STAHR

From me?

BRIMMER

You're a very good employer, Mr Stahr, but we still
think the position could be rationalized.

STAHR

I'll tell you three things. All writers are children. Fifty
percent are drunks. And up till very recently writers in
Hollywood were gag-men. Most of them still are gag-
men, but we call them writers.

BRIMMER

Uh-huh. But they're still the farmers in this business.
They grow the grain but they're not in at the feast.

STAHR

It looks to me like a try for power. I'll give them money
but I won't give them power. Anyway, they're not
equipped for authority.

CECILIA

More coffee, Mr Brimmer?

BRIMMER

No thank you.

CECILIA

Monroe?

Stahr waves his hand. He stares at Brimmer.

STAHR

I don't get to meet Reds very often. Are you a real Red?

BRIMMER

A real one.

STAHR

I guess some of you believe in it.

BRIMMER

Quite a few.

STAHR

Not you.

Brimmer frowns.

BRIMMER

Oh yes.

STAHR

Oh no.

Brimmer laughs.

BRIMMER

Oh yes.

INT. HOLLYWOOD RESTAURANT. EVENING.

Cecilia, Brimmer and Stahr at table. Stahr drunk.

CECILIA

All the stars come here to eat.

BRIMMER

Oh really? Is Greta Garbo here?

CECILIA

No.

BRIMMER

What a pity.

A photographer, Bernie, approaches the table.

BERNIE

Good evening, Mr Stahr. Okay, Mr Stahr?

STAHR

Want your photograph taken, Brimmer?

BRIMMER

If you don't mind, I'd prefer . . . not.

Stahr laughs.

STAHR

Okay, Bernie.

Bernie turns away.

Wouldn't they have liked that photograph back in New York? The two of us happy and smiling?

BRIMMER

They'd have been tickled pink.

CECILIA

The three of us happy and smiling.

STAHR

Of course. With the beautiful boss's daughter.

BRIMMER

They'd have liked her.

STAHR

Did I say beautiful boss's daughter? I meant the boss's beautiful daughter.

BRIMMER

Is Mr Brady your boss?

STAHR

No he's not. And he's not beautiful either.

CECILIA

What's not beautiful about him?

STAHR
(*to Waiter*)

The same again. Listen. I like writers. I understand them.

BRIMMER

Sure you like them.

STAHR

I don't think I've got more brains than a writer. I just
think his brains belong to me. I know how to use them.

BRIMMER

You know yourself very well, Mr Stahr.

The drinks arrive.

CECILIA
(*lightly*)

Now I know you've been disappointed in love.

STAHR

What?

CECILIA

That's your fourth scotch.

STAHR

Don't be silly. I never drink.

CECILIA

I know you don't. But that's your fourth scotch.

STAHR

Is it? I haven't tasted any of them.

544

BRIMMER

This is my first drink in a week. I did my drinking in the Navy.

Stahr winks at Cecilia.

STAHR

This soapbox son-of-a-bitch has been working on the Navy.

Brimmer smiles faintly. He looks at his watch.

BRIMMER

Well, thanks for dinner, and the meeting. I must go along now. I have to meet some people.

STAHR

You mean you have friends out here?

BRIMMER

That's right.

STAHR

No. You've got time.
                    (*To Cecilia.*)
We'll go back to your little room, we'll have one game of ping pong, and we'll have one more drink –
                    (*He turns to Brimmer.*)
– and then I'll tell you what I really think.

Brimmer stares at him.

BRIMMER

You good at ping pong, Mr Stahr?

INT. CECILIA'S HOUSE: BAR. NIGHT.

Cecilia pouring whiskey. She takes the tray through the leather room out on to the terrace.

EXT. TERRACE. NIGHT.

Stahr and Brimmer at the ping pong table. Stahr is batting a box of new balls across to Brimmer, one after the other, taking careful aim with each one. Brimmer ducks or turns them aside.

CECILIA

Is this ping pong?

Stahr takes the bottle.

STAHR

He can't play.

BRIMMER

Test me.

Stahr sits down with the bottle.

STAHR

Saturday is a night to relax.

Cecilia and Brimmer begin to play ping pong. Stahr watches them.

STAHR

What do you think you're doing?

CECILIA

What does it look like?

BRIMMER
(*to Cecilia*)

Hey, you're pretty good.

They continue playing. Stahr watches. He drinks.

STAHR

I'm going to beat up Brimmer. I'm going to handle this thing personally.

BRIMMER

Can't you pay someone to do it?

STAHR

I do my own dirty work. I'm going to beat hell out of
you and put you on a train.

He stands. They stop playing. Cecilia goes to him, holds his arms.

CECILIA

Now stop this!

STAHR

This fellow has an influence over you. Over all you
young people. You don't know what you're doing.

CECILIA
(*to Brimmer*)

Please go home.

*Stahr slips out of her grasp and goes towards Brimmer. Brimmer
retreats around the table. Stahr follows him, lurches towards him.
Brimmer holds him off.*

Stahr swings, misses.

Brimmer hits him.

Stahr collapses under table.

Cecilia walks around the table.

EXT. HOUSE. WINDOW. NIGHT.

Brady looking down on to the terrace.

EXT. TERRACE.

Brimmer stands looking down at Stahr's body.

BRIMMER

I always wanted to hit ten million dollars.

CECILIA

Please go home.

BRIMMER

Can I . . . do anything?

CECILIA

No. Really.

Brimmer looks down at Stahr, turns and goes.

CECILIA AND STAHR.

Cecilia kneels and touches Stahr.

He sits up suddenly, stares at Cecilia.

STAHR

What happened?

CECILIA

He's gone.

STAHR

Did I hit him?

CECILIA

Oh yes. Quite badly.

She stands, goes out of shot.

Stahr gets to his feet, goes out into the garden, to behind a bush. Sound of him retching.

EXT. GARDEN. NIGHT. P.O.V. UPPER WINDOW OF HOUSE.

Stahr among the bushes, retching.

EXT. HOUSE. WINDOW.

Brady looking down into garden.

He pulls the blind down.

EXT. TERRACE. NIGHT.

Cecilia returns to the terrace with a wet towel.

Stahr slowly walks back to the terrace. She supports him. He sits down.

She wipes his face.

> STAHR
>
> I didn't want to hurt him. I just wanted to chase him out. I guess he got scared and hit me.

> CECILIA
>
> Do you hold it against him?

> STAHR
>
> Oh no. I was drunk.

He looks at her.

> How would you like to go out to Doug Fairbanks' ranch with me and spend the night? I know he'd love to have you.

INT. BRADY'S HOUSE. SPARE BEDROOM. NIGHT.

The door opens. Cecilia leads Stahr into the room. She switches on a lamp with a soft light.

> CECILIA
>
> There.

Stahr sits heavily on the bed.

Cecilia goes out, leaving the door open.

Stahr reaches into his jacket pocket. He finds the telegram, brings it out, looks at it, crumples it, puts it back in his pocket. He finds his pills, keeps one in his hand. He begins to take off his shoes, with difficulty.

Cecilia returns with a pitcher of water, places it on the bedside table, pours him a glass.

Here.

He sips the water, slipping the pill into his mouth.

The bathroom's through there.

Stahr has one shoe off. Cecilia unlaces the other and takes it off. She stands.

Sleep.

STAHR

Yes.

CECILIA

Just sleep.

She goes out.

Stahr remains sitting on the bed.

INT. SPARE BEDROOM. MORNING.

Stahr asleep in bed.

There is a knock on the door.

Brady comes in, immaculately dressed. He stands by the bed and looks down at Stahr.

BRADY
(*quietly*)

Monroe.

Stahr suddenly looks up. He has a black eye.
(*gently*)

Monroe. I've called an emergency meeting of the board at twelve o'clock. My office at the studio. We'd be glad if you'd come along.

INT. HALL: BRADY'S HOUSE.

Brady comes out of the spare bedroom, comes into the hall and collects his coat.

Cecilia comes into the hall.

> **BRADY**
>
> Morning, darling.
> > (*He puts on his coat and smiles at her.*)
>
> Your Monroe was in great form last night. See you later.

He kisses her on the cheek and leaves the house.

The camera remains on Cecilia.

EXT. STUDIO. SUNDAY MORNING.

The studio is empty.

Four cars are parked outside the production building.

A chauffeur stands by one.

Stahr's car arrives at the building.

He gets out. He is wearing dark glasses.

INT. BRADY'S OFFICE. DAY.

Brady, Popolos, Fleishacker and Marcus are sitting at a table. Coffee cups, cigar butts in ashtrays.

Stahr comes in.

> **BRADY**
>
> Ah, come in, Monroe. Sit down.

Stahr sits in the chair offered him.

> I've been speaking to New York. They've instructed me
> to tell you that they no longer hold you competent to
> negotiate with the writers. They've asked me to be the
> spokesman of this board in all further discussions.
> > (*He sips his coffee and smiles.*)
>
> They don't consider that trying to beat up the writers'
> representative is in the best interests of the company. I

just want to tell you that this board endorses these views. We also recommend that you go away for a long rest. Take a break. Go to Tahiti or somewhere.

Stahr stares at Brady.

STAHR

This studio will fall without me.

BRADY
(*sympathetically.*)
Take a break, Monroe.

Stahr stands.

STAHR

This is a waste of time. I'll be talking to New York.

BRADY

They'll be glad to speak to you. Any time. Oh, they said be sure to go see a doctor about your eye.

Stahr goes to the door.

FLEISHACKER
Mr Stahr.

Stahr stops.

We'll see the studio doesn't fall.

INTERIOR. CORRIDOR.

Stahr walks down the corridor, passing the photographs of stars on the walls.

He swallows a pill.

A watchman is testing locks.

Stahr passes him, gets to his office, goes in.

INT. STAHR'S OFFICE.

Stahr standing in the middle of his office.

Sudden cuts of:

A COWBOY RIDING INTO A WESTERN TOWN.

A CARTOON.

DIDI.

> DIDI
> Nobody likes me or something.

TWO MEN FIGHTING IN A STORM.

BRIMMER, LAUGHING.

> BRIMMER
> Oh yes.

HUNDREDS OF NEGROES PLAYING WHITE PIANOS.

CECILIA.

> CECILIA
> We don't use that line this year.

GARBO IN 'CAMILLE'.

DOCTOR.

> DOCTOR
> Any pain?

THE SAN FRANCISCO EARTHQUAKE.

STAHR IN HIS OFFICE. HE IS STANDING.

This set-up is exactly the same as that in the scene with Boxley, except that Stahr is talking directly into the camera.

> STAHR
>
> Suppose you're in your office. You've been fighting duels all day. You're exhausted.

He sits.

> This is you.

INT. KATHLEEN'S HOUSE. DAY.

Kathleen comes into the room. She puts her purse on the table.

> STAHR
> (*VO*)
>
> A girl comes in.

Kathleen opens her purse.

> (*VO.*)
>
> She doesn't see you.

Kathleen takes a blue envelope out of her purse.

STAHR INTO CAMERA.

> STAHR
>
> She takes off her gloves, opens her purse and dumps it out on the table.

He mimes these actions.

> You watch her.

He sits.

> This is you.

554

He stands.

> She has two dimes, a nickel and a matchbox. She leaves the nickel on the table, puts the two dimes back into her purse, takes her gloves to the stove, opens it and puts them inside.

He mimes all this while talking.

> She lights a match. Suddenly the telephone rings. She picks it up.

He mimes this.

> She listens. She says, 'I've never owned a pair of black gloves in my life'. She hangs up –

INT. KATHLEEN'S HOUSE.

Kathleen is kneeling in front of the fireplace, which is full of ashes. She picks up a box of matches.

STAHR
(*VO*)
– kneels by the stove, lights another match.

Kathleen lights the envelope. She places it on the ashes. It burns.

A Man's back comes into foreground. His hair is blond.

> Suddenly you notice there's another man in the room, watching every move the girl makes.

Kathleen looks up, sees the Man, stands, goes to him, smiles, embraces him.

BOXLEY
(*VO*)

What happens?

555

STAHR
(*VO*)

I don't know. I was just making pictures.

Kathleen stands back to look at the Man.

The camera becomes the Man.

She looks into the camera.

The Man's hand touches her face.

STAHR INTO CAMERA.

STAHR

I don't want to lose you.

EXT. STUDIO. OVER STAHR'S BACK AT WINDOW.

Brady, Fleishacker, Popolos and Marcus getting into four black limousines. They drive out of the studio.

EXT. STUDIO. LONG SHOT.

Stahr walking. The studio silent. He stops.

EXT. SOUND STAGE. OVER STAHR.

The door to the sound stage is open. Black inside.

Stahr walks into the blackness.

He disappears. The sound of his steps.

Over this, the echo of 'I don't want to lose you'.

Langrishe, Go Down

Note. The camera directions in this screenplay are particularly detailed as I originally wrote it with the intention of directing it myself.

Obviously, David Jones did not observe every direction in the shooting of the film. The structure of the film, however, remained the structure as written.

HAROLD PINTER

Langrishe, Go Down was first screened on BBC-2 television on 20 September 1978 with the following cast:

OTTO BECK Jeremy Irons
HELEN LANGRISHE Annette Crosbie
FIRST MAN ON BUS John Molloy
SECOND MAN ON BUS Niall O'Brien
LILY LANGRISHE Susan Williamson
IMOGEN LANGRISHE Judi Dench
JOSEPH FEENEY Arthur O'Sullivan
MAUREEN LAYDE Margaret Whiting
BARRY SHANNON Harold Pinter
MR LANGRISHE Liam O'Callaghan
MRS LANGRISHE Joan O'Hara
PRIEST Michael O' Briain

Produced and directed by David Jones

The main action of this film takes place in 1932 – THE PAST, and 1937/8 – THE PRESENT.

In 1932 IMOGEN is thirty-nine, HELEN forty-three and OTTO thirty-five.

EXT. SPRINGFIELD HOUSE. SUMMER. EARLY EVENING. LONG SHOT. PAST.

The camera looks through trees at the Lodge gate cottage. The door is open.

Silence.

During titles Otto emerges from the cottage. He leans against the cottage wall and lights a pipe. He smokes, puts a hand in his pocket, and looks up at the evening sky, relaxed. He wears corduroy trousers and a black sweater.

The camera begins to track in towards Otto. Sharp cut to:

EXT. COUNTRY ROAD. WINTER. NIGHT. LONG SHOT. PRESENT.

A singledeck bus, lights on, slowly approaches.

INT. SPRINGFIELD HOUSE. HELEN'S BEDROOM. SUMMER. DAY. PAST.

A gramophone turning. John McCormack singing 'I hear you calling me'.

The camera pans slowly from the gramophone to Helen's face. She sits still, listening to the music.

EXT. SPRINGFIELD HOUSE. SUMMER NIGHT. PAST.

The house dark, but for one light in an upper room.

'I hear you calling me' dimly heard.

Suddenly sound of footsteps, close.

561

A woman's voice: 'Ssshhh'.

EXT. COTTAGE DOOR CLOSING. SUMMER NIGHT. PAST.

A shadow in the window. A curtain pulled.

EXT. TENNIS COURT AND ORCHARD. FROM AN UPPER WINDOW AT THE BACK OF THE HOUSE. DAY. PAST.

The tennis court is overgrown but the net is still up.

The camera pans. Otto's back glimpsed moving through the orchard, carrying a shotgun.

INT. BUS. NIGHT. WINTER. PRESENT.

Profile Helen. A man seated next to her.

The bus jogs up and down. Helen bends her eyes to the evening paper on her lap, the bus jogs, she raises her head, takes a spearmint from her bag, chews it. Cigarette smoke drifts across. She tightly chews the spearmint.

Voices behind her:

> ###### FIRST MAN
> You'll be the right ram when you get started. Oh ho ho yes. The right ram, I'm telling you.

> ###### SECOND MAN
> Ah, now, I'd be too shy.

> ###### FIRST MAN
> Shy! Get away out of that!

> ###### SECOND MAN
> I'd be mortified.

> ###### FIRST MAN
> Ah, get away out of that, for God's sake!

The man next to Helen yawns widely.

INT. BUS. P.O.V. OF THE TWO MEN.

The back of the yawning man's head, bald, creasing with the yawn.

> FIRST MAN
> And you'll feel the better for it after. And begob so will she. Tip her a sup of the blood while it's warm. In like a lion and out like a lamb.

INT. BUS. CLOSE-UP. SECOND MAN.

He looks swiftly at the back of Helen's head, and then down.

> SECOND MAN
> Ah, for God's sake.

INT. BUS. PROFILE HELEN.

She looks down at her paper. The camera follows her eyes and glimpses the headlines, bus jogging: 'Madrid bombed again.'

> FIRST MAN
> Oh the right ram. Oh God the right ram.

EXT. BRIDGE. CELBRIDGE VILLAGE. WINTER NIGHT. PRESENT.

Sound of a bus going away.

Two men walking towards a bar. They enter, brief light, door shuts, silence.

EXT. CLANE ROAD. NIGHT. LONG SHOT. PRESENT.

In the distance the stationary bus. In the buslight a figure descending. The bus draws away.

EXT. LODGE GATE. SPRINGFIELD HOUSE. NIGHT. PRESENT.

Helen opens the white barred gate and walks past the dark shape of the lodge gate cottage.

EXT. DRIVE. SPRINGFIELD HOUSE. NIGHT.

Helen walking slowly in darkness down curving drive under trees through mounds of fallen leaves.

Camera tracks with her. She emerges from trees to see the house dark against the sky.

Sudden sprinting feet.

MID-SHOT. HELEN.

She stops, gasps sharply, looks down.

CLOSE SHOT. ALSATIAN DOG.

The dog is old and skinny. He jumps up. Helen's hand grasps his muzzle.

HELEN.

> HELEN
> Be good. Be good now. Go down.

HELEN'S HAND CLUTCHING DOG'S MUZZLE.

The dog whimpers, breaks away.

EXT. THE HOUSE. STUDY WINDOW.

Helen's hand tapping on the window. Light behind the blind.

Scuffle of feet and whispering from within.

> IMOGEN'S VOICE
> Who's there?

EXT. SIDE OF THE HOUSE. LONG SHOT.

Helen standing by window, clasping her arms. Wind.

IMOGEN'S VOICE

Who's there, please?

HELEN

Who do you think?

INT. THE HOUSE. SIDE DOOR.

Lily lifting the heavy wooden bolt. Imogen behind her. The door opens. Helen enters.

INT. STUDY.

Helen enters. She takes off her coat and gloves, catches sight of herself in the mirror, pauses briefly, throws coat down and sits by the fire, stretching her hands towards it.

Sound of bolt being put back into place, with effort.

HELEN'S P.O.V. THE FIRE AND FENDER. HER HANDS REACHING.

Ovaltine, a saucepan of milk, odd cups and saucers, a packet of biscuits, stand by the fender.

INT. STUDY.

Imogen and Lily in the doorway, looking at her.

HELEN
(*off-screen*)

Will you two come in and close the door there? For God knows I'm cold enough as it is.

They close the door and stand.

LILY SITTING.

LILY

Did you see the solicitors?

HELEN

Well, what do you think I've been doing all day?

WIDE SHOT. STUDY. FAVOURING HELEN.

Lily sitting. Imogen standing.

HELEN

And there's no bones about it. The house has to be sold and that's all there is to that.

INT. COTTAGE. SUMMER. NIGHT. PAST.

In foreground a woman's shoulder. Otto standing by fireside in background.

OTTO

Irishwomen are so pure and clean. So pure – and that's not to be found any more in Germany – that great purity – but here you have it. You yourself possess it. That look in the face, the eyes, and one knows that such women are not corrupted. One knows it *here.*

He thumps his chest.

A man might sometimes have filthy thoughts about girls. That's natural enough. But when I meet Irish girls and can recognise at once their essential purity, then I am touched, incapable of a base thought. I have a great reverence for Irish women.

INT. HELEN'S BEDROOM. WINTER. MORNING. PRESENT.

The ceiling. A frieze of donkey at the seaside. The camera, from the bed's P.O.V. pans down the wall to the dressing table, silver crucifix, finally reaching the bedrail.

A cat cries.

MID-SHOT. THE BED.

Helen lies in bed. Two cats at her feet, clawing the eiderdown.

HELEN
Stop that! Get away! Get away out of that!

INT. IMOGEN'S BEDROOM. WINTER. MORNING. PRESENT.

Low shot of the bed. A humped shape under the bedclothes, still.

A sharp knock on the door.

Silence.

The door opens. The camera eases to see Helen in background at the door. In foreground empty Guinness bottles on the floor, Imogen's clothes over the bed rail. Helen walks into the room and looks down at the bed.

HELEN
Imogen.

OVER HELEN TO THE BED.

Imogen's head slowly appears from under the bed clothes.

HELEN
What ails you?

IMOGEN
Nothing ails me. Why?

Imogen sits up. She wears a shapeless brown cardigan over a nightdress.

HELEN
You don't look so well.

IMOGEN
Do I ever look well?

Silence.

I didn't sleep very well last night, that's all.

Helen moves to the bed. Her shoe kicks a bottle.

TWO SHOT.

HELEN
I'm going to visit the graves today. It's after the anniversary.

Pause.

IMOGEN
Why not?

The camera remains on them for some moments in silence.

EXT. CELBRIDGE VILLAGE. THE BRIDGE.

Helen stands by the parapet looking down the river.

THE RIVER. HER P.O.V.

INT. IMOGEN'S BEDROOM. MORNING. CLOSE SHOT.
PRESENT.

A leg emerging from the bedclothes. Hands reach for a stocking and pull it on the foot, up to the knee and out of sight under the bedclothes. The other stocking is pulled on in the same fashion.

Imogen pushes the bedclothes aside, slips into her shoes and sits on the bed fully dressed.

EXT. THE BRIDGE. AFTERNOON. PRESENT.

Helen turns to face the opposite parapet. A cinema poster is flapping on the wall. She steps off the footpath.

Sound of a motor horn. A vehicle approaching. Helen hesitates in the middle of the bridge.

EXT. BREAD VAN. FLY BLOWN WINDSCREEN.

The driver brakes and stares, waves Helen across the bridge.

EXT. THE BRIDGE. LONG SHOT.

Helen crosses to the other side of the bridge. The van drives on.

CLOSE SHOT. TORN CINEMA POSTER ON THE BRIDGE WALL.

Helen bends to lift the torn piece and read the poster. The poster reads: 'Forbidden Heaven, featuring Charles Farrell and Charlotte Henry at the Electric Picture House, Newbridge. Romance and pathos among four human derelicts. Prices of admission 4d, 9d, 1/ 4d, Wednesday and Thursday, March 10 and 11.'

Helen bends lower to read the supporting film: Strike it Rich, with George Gee and Gina Malo.

EXT. DONYCOMPER CEMETERY. WINTER. EARLY EVENING. HIGH SHOT. PRESENT.

Helen walks down a lane of the cemetery on a carpet of leaves. She bends to read the headstones, and passes on. Eventually she stops.

CLOSE-UP. HELEN.

A PLAIN MONUMENT. HELEN'S P.O.V.

On it is written: Louisa Kathleen Langrishe, died 9th May, 1924. Robert Langrishe, died 17th September, 1923. And their beloved daughter, Emily, died 3rd March, 1929. RIP.

HELEN TURNING HER HEAD FROM THE HEADSTONE.

The camera follows her gaze. An old man approaches along the avenue of cypresses, carrying a gardening fork.

Leaves dance between them on the lane.

He approaches very slowly.

He raises his head, sees her, stops, takes off his hat.

> ### HELEN
> Grand evening.

> ### FEENEY
> 'Tis indeed grand, thanks be to God.

He stares at her.

> ### HELEN
> Do I trespass here at this hour?

> ### FEENEY
> Not at all. Yarra, not at all. Sure you have it all to yourself.

The old man moves a few steps forwards her.

The camera settles into a closer two shot.

The old man stares at her.

> ### HELEN
> Don't let me interrupt you, if you have work to do.

> ### FEENEY
> Oh faith I have that. I'm on my way to a grave needs attention, for an anniversary tomorrow, and that's why I'm carrying this fork.

SHOT OVER HELEN TO FEENEY.

Feeney looks at her keenly. Helen, uncertainly, turns away.

> ### FEENEY
> Do you not know me?

Helen turns back to him.

> You don't mean to say you've forgotten me?

570

HELEN

I don't know. Who are you?

FEENEY

Don't you remember Josey Feeney, your old gardener and boilerman?

HELEN

Are you Joseph?

FEENEY

I am, Miss Helen.

CLOSE-UP. HELEN.

HELEN
(*blankly*)

Yes, I remember you.

CLOSE-UP. FEENEY.

FEENEY

I well remember her sitting out on the summer seat with a big bowl of eating apples. When I came into the yard with a fine jack rabbit for her dinner she didn't say a word but took a hold of him by the hind legs and handed me an apple. An apple! Oh, I'm telling you she was the right haro!

CLOSE-UP. HELEN.

HELEN

Who?

CLOSE-UP. FEENEY.

FEENEY

Miss Emily.
(*Pointing.*)

Her beyond.

TWO SHOT. FAVOURING HELEN.

> FEENEY
> Many's the time I heard your poor Daddy, God rest his
> soul, singing and laughing to himself above in the fields.
> Oh a grand smart hardy little man.

EXT. ROAD. ALONGSIDE GRAVEYARD. DUSK.

*Workmen on bicycle past. In background, behind the hedge,
Feeney and Helen, turning.*

> FEENEY
> 'Night, men.

*The workmen cycle by, unhearing. The camera pans to follow the
lights of the bicycles disappearing.*

INT. HELEN'S ROOM. EARLY EVENING. PRESENT.

The blinds are half drawn.

Imogen moves swiftly to the desk. A cat slips out from under it.

*Imogen sits at the desk. A book lies open upon it. She pushes it
away, retrieves it, places it carefully in former position, studies the
position and the position of other objects on the desk, and then
carefully moves the book.*

CLOSE SHOT. IMOGEN'S HAND OPENING A DESK DRAWER.

*She takes a bundle of letters tied together from the drawer. She
unties the bundle. The letters slip apart and fall on the desk.*

*We see briefly that they are all addressed in the same handwriting
to the same person: Herr Otto Beck, at a Munich address, and
that they are unstamped and unsealed.*

MID-SHOT. IMOGEN AT DESK.

She opens a letter and reads quickly, her eyes darting over the page.

EXT. HOUSE. TENNIS COURT. EARLY EVENING.

Lily stands with a basket of cooking apples by a garden roller which is half buried in the long grass. The tennis net sags along the ground, soaked and torn.

Lily whistles.

> **LILY**
> Oscar!
> *(Whistles.)*
> Oscar!

HELEN'S ROOM.

Imogen at desk. Faint calls of 'Oscar' and whistling. They stop. Imogen opens another letter.

She squints, turns, sees small bicycle lamp on mantelpiece, collects it, sets it on desk, turns it on.

CLOSE-UP. IMOGEN.

She reads intently, her lips moving silently.

Sound of a bicycle below on the gravel.

INT. HELEN'S ROOM.

A cat jumps on the bed.

Beyond the bed, Imogen hastily thrusts pages into the envelope, binds the bundle with a rubber band, pushes it into the drawer, stands, turns over the cushion on the chair, puts the book back into position, adjusts other objects, takes lamp, moves to the door.

A door shuts below.

The light goes out. The bedroom door closes softly.

The camera remains on the cat, staring in the darkness.

INT. HELEN'S ROOM. NIGHT. HIGH SHOT. PRESENT.

Helen in bed.

Helen lies on her back, her eyes open. A paraffin lamp is alight.

She mutters to herself:

HELEN

Poking about again. Poking about as usual.

Pause.

I've eyes in my head.

Pause.

Camera descends slowly into a close shot of Helen in bed.

I won't go out again. I won't go down again. I'll stay where I am. I'll stay here. In my bed.

Helen reaches under her pillow and brings out an envelope. She studies it, almost opens it, throws it onto the floor.

The camera draws nearer her face.

She smiles thinly.

Huh!

She murmurs quietly, but with a mild scepticism.

I am no good without you.

Pause.

Your lovely body.

Pause.

Love of all my life and all my senses.

A CAT JUMPS ON THE BED. HELEN'S P.O.V.

OVER CAT, WHICH SETTLES TO SLEEP, TO HELEN.

Helen looks at the cat.

HELEN
Days are passing, years could go by, oh my love.

Pause.

The happiness we had.

Pause.

Your lovely body.

Pause.

Love of all my life . . . and all my senses.

EXT. THE HOUSE. THE FRONT PLANTATION. SUMMER. LATE
AFTERNOON. PAST. OTTO.

OTTO
Otto Beck, student.
            (*A slight bow.*)
How do you do.

MID-SHOT. IMOGEN.

She wears a light belted raincoat.

IMOGEN
Ah yes. You're the person who's staying at the back
lodge.

TWO SHOT.

OTTO

Yes. I've rented the back lodge – for five shillings a week
– in order that I can complete my thesis.

IMOGEN

Ah yes.

OTTO

You are Miss Imogen Langrishe, I think.

IMOGEN

I am, yes.

She looks away.

What star is that?

Otto looks up.

OTTO

Venus.

IMOGEN

I thought it was Hesper.

OTTO

Hesper? No, no. Unmistakably Venus, the brightest of
the planets. A planet, in fact, not a star.

OVER OTTO TO IMOGEN.

IMOGEN

I thought they were the same.

OTTO

The same? The same as what?

IMOGEN

The same as each other. Planets and stars.

CLOSE-UP. OTTO.

> OTTO
>
> Decidedly not. Planets are closer than stars, for one
> thing. And nine of them revolve around the sun, against
> a background of constant stars which do not move. How
> does one know it's Venus, you ask. Well, because it's
> the brightest of planets, and because it's in the position
> it should be, if it is Venus, moving in the direction
> Venus ought to move in. How then can it be anything
> else but Venus?

MID-SHOT. IMOGEN.

> IMOGEN

I see.

Imogen leans her arms on the paling between them, looking about her.

The camera withdraws to regard them both.

> What country do you come from?

> OTTO

I come from Bavaria.

> IMOGEN

You speak English very well.

> OTTO

Thank you. I learnt to speak it as a child. My mother
was a great Anglophile.

Sound of a donkey and cart on the road.

> IMOGEN

I have never travelled very much. I was at school in
France, near Poitiers, many years ago.

OTTO

You speak French?

IMOGEN

I get no opportunity to . . . practise.

OTTO

Let me hear your pronunciation.

IMOGEN

Je sens toujours les houblons mouillés des pluies.

CLOSE-UP. OTTO

OTTO

First class.

EXT. THE PLANTATION.

Bats dipping, squealing.

IMOGEN LOOKS UP.

The sound of Galli-Curci on a gramophone record floats from the house.

TWO SHOT.

OTTO

Who is playing that record?

IMOGEN

My sister, Helen.

OTTO

It's very beautiful.

The record stops abruptly.

IMOGEN

Would you care for some tea, perhaps?

OTTO

That is very kind of you.

IMOGEN

Not at all.

They walk towards the house in which some rooms are lit in the growing dusk.

OTTO

That was Galli-Curci singing.

IMOGEN

Yes, I think it was.

INT. HOUSE. HALL.

Through the open front door Otto and Imogen are seen approaching the front steps.

She enters first and indicates a room to her right.

IMOGEN

Please go in. I won't be long.

INT. HALL. REVERSE SHOT.

Imogen walks to the kitchen stairs. She disappears down the stairs. Otto looks to his right, into the drawing-room. He goes in, the camera behind him.

INT. DRAWING-ROOM.

The camera follows Otto's gaze as he examines the paintings, prints and the open door. He walks back to the door, and looks into the hall, then pads quickly across the hall to a closed door.

INT. EMPTY ROOM. DINING-ROOM.

Otto opens door, looks in, closes it.

INT. HALL. EVENING.

Imogen comes down the stairs, wearing an attractive dress. She glances at herself in the hall mirror and goes into the drawing-room.

INT. DRAWING-ROOM.

Otto rises from the sofa.

IMOGEN
Please sit down. The tea won't be long.

Otto sits. Imogen walks to the other end of the long sofa and sits, settling herself to face him. He watches her.

OTTO
Charming room.

INT. HELEN'S BEDROOM. NIGHT. PAST.

Helen sitting reading. McCormack on record. Voices rise from the front door.

OTTO
Thank you very much. Goodnight.

EXT. FRONT DOOR.

Otto going down the steps. Imogen at the door.

IMOGEN
Goodnight.

She closes the door.

OTTO WALKING AWAY.

HELEN READING. MCCORMACK SINGING.

EXT. PLANTATION. NIGHT. PAST.

Otto at the foot of a laurel tree. He climbs up it for some fifteen feet and then swings onto the adjacent pine. He climbs steadily up the pine until he can climb no higher. He settles and looks about him. It is a clear night.

THE HOUSE AND ESTATE. OTTO'S P.O.V.

The house is dark. A candle moves at the top of the house, goes out. Light behind the blind in Helen's room.

MID-SHOT. OTTO IN TREE.

He reaches for a cluster of pine cones. He pulls one away. The bunch comes away and falls.

HIGH SHOT PINE CONES FALLING.

MID-SHOT. OTTO.

He examines his cone and then flings it. As he does so he starts and stares.

EXT. THE PLANTATION. OTTO'S P.O.V.

A white flickering shape runs out of the shadow of the trees and across the meadow.

CLOSE-UP. OTTO, STARING.

THE PLANTATION AND MEADOW.

Stillness. The shape has vanished.

Suddenly it appears again; a swift blur of white, then gone.

CLOSE-UP. OTTO.

LONG SHOT. OTTO SITTING IN TREE.

INT. IMOGEN'S BEDROOM. NIGHT. PAST.

A raincoat is thrown to the floor.

The camera pans to the bed to see Imogen flinging herself on her stomach onto the bed, naked.

EXT. SPRINGFIELD BACK LODGE GATE. AFTERNOON. PAST.

In foreground Otto standing. In background the road stretching.

A bus comes into view and draws nearer. He puts out his hand. The bus stops.

INT. BUS.

He takes a seat. The bus is half empty. The bus moves and then draws to a halt again as we see Imogen step out from front lodge gate and raise her hand. The camera remains behind Otto as we hear the concertina doors open and close. Imogen passes Otto and sits near the front.

The bus moves.

EXT. CONYNGHAM ROAD TERMINUS, DUBLIN. EARLY EVENING. PAST.

The bus stops. Imogen gets off.

She begins to walk up the street. The bus passes her. In the distance we see the bus stop and Otto get off. He waits until the bus moves away and then walks back towards her.

EXT. STREET.

Imogen and Otto meet.

OTTO

How do you do.

They smile.

That worked very well, didn't it?

INT. LOUNGE BAR. DUBLIN. EVENING.

Otto and Imogen sitting at a table with drinks. A sherry for her, a gin and tonic for him. They face each other. They drink.

OTTO

I am making investigations into seventeenth century Ireland and Irish customs.

IMOGEN

Oh. Are you?

OTTO

Yes. Such investigations of course involve philological studies into the story of Ossian, with reference to Goethe's time, the brothers Grimm, Hebbel and Hamann.

IMOGEN

Oh, is that so?

OTTO

That is so.

He drinks.

I will show it to you one day.

IMOGEN

I would love to see it.

OTTO

Of course I will have to translate it for you first. I write in my native language, German.

Imogen sips her drink.

583

IMOGEN

This is . . . quite exciting for me. I haven't been to the
theatre for ages.

OTTO

I'm looking forward to it. It will be interesting for me to
take an intelligent Irishwoman to see a Swedish play
performed by an Irish company in English.

He sits back, grinning, and looks around the room.

INT. RESTAURANT. DUBLIN. NIGHT. PAST.

*Otto and Imogen eating fish. Otto pouring hock. They sit facing
each other, in reverse positions to previous scene.*

OTTO

The man possessed a certain ferocity, I grant you, but
his performance remained tentative. As for the woman,
it seemed to me she lacked totally true depth and a
proper understanding of her role. It was much inferior
to a production of the piece I remember seeing in
Dusseldorf, where the values of the play, I must confess,
were properly embodied in the characterisation and the
polarities inherent in the work understood.

IMOGEN

Oh, really?

OTTO

Yes. A disappointing production. I apologise.

IMOGEN

Oh, not at all.

Otto takes a forkful of fish and holds it to his mouth.

OTTO

What exactly did you think of the play yourself?

IMOGEN

It didn't mean very much to me.

Otto regards her.

OTTO

Interesting.

EXT. DUBLIN. BUS STOP BY THE LIFFEY. NIGHT.

*Imogen and Otto hurry along towards it from a side street. They
slow when they see no bus.*

The camera moves in to them as they stop.

IMOGEN

It's gone.

OTTO

Is there no other?

IMOGEN

No, there is not.

Pause.

OTTO

A taxi is outside my range, I'm afraid.

Pause.

IMOGEN

Well, what now?

OTTO

Now, now, wait. I have just remembered.
            (He looks about.)
Yes, we're very near. There is a place I sometimes stay
in. A friend of mine. You can certainly have a bed there
for the night. He is away, I happen to know. There will
be no problem.

585

> **IMOGEN**
> And what about you?

> **OTTO**
> I will make other plans. Please. There is no other answer. Come.

He takes her arm and leads her along the quay. Her voice floats back.

> **IMOGEN**
> They won't know what's happened to me.

EXT. METAL FOOTBRIDGE OVER LIFFEY. DUBLIN. NIGHT.

Long shot along the Liffey. They cross the bridge.

EXT. DUBLIN. ANGLESEA ST. NIGHT. LOOKING TOWARDS LIFFEY.

They appear from the Liffey and walk up the street. Otto stops at a dark house amid other dark houses. By the plaques on the walls they are clearly office buildings.

EXT. HOUSE. ANGLESEA ST.

Otto trying to fit the key into the dark lock. In background Imogen stands on the pavement, watching.

INT. HALL. ANGLESEA ST. HOUSE.

The hall is dark. The heavy front door is flung open. Otto switches on a light and holds the door open for her. She hesitates, and then climbs the steps and passes through into the hall. Otto closes the door, switches on the landing light and switches off the hall light.

> **OTTO**
> It's right at the top.

CLOSE-UP. IMOGEN. HER FACE IN THE SHADOWS.

FIRST LANDING.

They ascend. Dusty passages and office doors. She stops by a board: Sean Brett, Collector of Taxes.

SECOND LANDING.

They ascend.

> OTTO
> Just a minute.

He runs up the remaining stairway to the top landing, which is dark.

She remains.

The top light goes on.

She goes up.

TOP LANDING.

She arrives, to find Otto standing at an open door, leading to a light low-ceilinged studio.

INT. STUDIO. NIGHT.

Otto and Imogen stand inside the closed door.

> OTTO
> Make yourself at home.

Imogen walks into the room, taking off her gloves, and examines two potted plants.

> IMOGEN
> What kind are these?

OTTO

Tropical blooms, stolen from the Botanic Gardens. My
friend wanted them for details in a painting.

IMOGEN

He's a painter?

*She watches as Otto bends down behind a very large easel in a
corner to a stack of unmounted canvases.*

IMOGEN

What a big easel.

INT. STUDIO.

Imogen through the easel from Otto's P.O.V.

*Otto rises from the corner with a few canvases and comes into shot
to place one on the easel.*

THE PAINTING. IMOGEN'S P.O.V.

A dark gypsylike nude, in an attitude of repose.

The camera eases to find Otto.

OTTO

Well?

MID-SHOT. IMOGEN.

IMOGEN

Yes . . .

Sound of Otto changing canvases.

OTTO
(*off-screen*)

And this?

Imogen scrutinizes the painting.

THE PAINTING.

The same model, crouching, her breasts heavy in foreground.
Otto's head comes into the frame.

> OTTO

Mmmmm?

MID-SHOT. IMOGEN.

> IMOGEN

Mmmmm . . .

Sound of Otto changing canvases.

> OTTO
> (*off-screen*)

And this?

THE PAINTING.

The same model, in an attitude of abandon.

MID-SHOT. IMOGEN.

She smiles.

> IMOGEN

She's bursting out of her skin.

Imogen moves away and takes off her coat. The Camera
withdraws. Otto comes out from behind the easel dusting his
hands.

> OTTO

Would you like a drink?

> IMOGEN

Oh yes, please.

He goes out the door.

INT. STUDIO. WIDE SHOT.

Imogen sitting alone on sofa. She places her handbag on the seat beside her. She lights a cigarette and looks about her.

Noise from the kitchen.

Otto enters with a tray. A bottle of gin and tonics. He pours drinks.

> OTTO
>
> Yes, an interesting painter. He's away all summer. Until he returns, the place is ours.

> IMOGEN
> (*laughing*)
> Ours? What on earth do you mean?

IMOGEN ON SOFA.

Otto bends over her to give her her drink. He stays standing above her and raises his glass.

> OTTO
>
> Prosit! Your health!

REVERSE SHOT.

> IMOGEN
> (*faintly*)

Yours.

She sips her drink. He draws up a chair and sits close to her.

> IMOGEN
>
> I suppose you'd call this an attic.

> OTTO
>
> Attic! I've lived in attics. One in Swiss Cottage London I shall never forget. I had started working on my thesis and was starving.

IMOGEN

When?

CLOSE-UP. OTTO.

OTTO

When? Years ago. One long wet winter and one long
hot summer. A hencoop. In winter I closed the skylight
and kept the gasring on. By the end of the winter my
face was bluish grey, even a kind of green. Terrible.

TWO SHOT.

IMOGEN

How awful.

OTTO

In summer it was a furnace. And there I was writing my
thesis! The only solution was to prop the skylight open,
drag my table under it, set a chair on top of that,
arrange my books on another chair alongside of that,
and work with my head stuck out of the roof. That was
an attic!

He drinks.

But of course the rent was only four shillings a week.

IMOGEN

What a dreadful existence.

CLOSE-UP. OTTO.

OTTO

The life of a scholar . . . is lived within a very narrow
compass, in mute abstraction and solitary drudgery.
The wonder is that Swiss Cottage didn't kill me. But no,
here I am, as you see, sound in mind and limb.

591

CLOSE-UP. IMOGEN.

>IMOGEN

I'm glad.

>OTTO
>(*off-screen*)

Sound in mind and limb.

WIDE SHOT.

Otto and Imogen sitting, he bending, knees almost touching.

>OTTO

To go no further than that.

Silence.

The door bell rings.

They stiffen. Otto drains his drink. They wait for the bell to ring again. It does. Otto sighs, stands, goes to the window and looks out and down.

>(*calling*)

Have you no scruples, waking people up at one o'clock in the morning?

A laugh and shout from below.

Otto takes a key from his pocket, wraps it in his handkerchief and throws it out of the window.

>IMOGEN

Who is it?

>OTTO

Shannon and his trollop.

He stands, thoughtful.

Excuse me.

He turns and leaves the room.

Imogen sits. She picks up her drink, drinks, puts the glass down. A pause. She pours another gin and another tonic. She drinks.

Raised voices and laughter ascending. Otto's voice, low and urgent. A sudden silence. A woman's sharp laugh. Silence. Various footsteps. The door opens. Otto comes in.

IMOGEN

Who are they?

OTTO

They've gone to eat, in the kitchen.

THE STUDIO. IMOGEN PROFILE FOREGROUND.

Otto in background disappears behind the easel, reappears with a reading lamp.

He approaches the sofa and plugs the lamp in to a socket to its side. He switches it on.

MID-SHOT. IMOGEN TURNING TO LOOK AT LAMP.

OTTO AT DOOR. HER P.O.V.

He switches off main light and comes to the sofa.

OTTO

More intimate.

CLOSE-UP. IMOGEN'S HANDBAG ON SOFA NEXT TO HER.

Otto's hand places it on the floor. His buttocks sit in its place.

CLOSE TWO SHOT.

Otto's face moving towards her.

IMOGEN

Wait.

HIS ARM AROUND HER WAIST, LIFTING TO HER BREAST.

> IMOGEN
> (*off-screen*)

Wait!

CLOSE-UP.

> IMOGEN

Those people . . .

CLOSE-UP. OTTO.

> OTTO

Eating.

TWO SHOT FAVOURING IMOGEN.

> IMOGEN
> (*softly*)

Wait.

She takes out her hairpins. Her hair falls loosely.

She is still, looking at him.

He kisses her.

Her eyes remain open.

REVERSE SHOT.

Otto's eyes open.

TWO SHOT.

They look at each other.

> OTTO

What is it?

Silence.

Do you not trust your Otto?

CLOSE-UP. IMOGEN.

Otto's hand strokes her cheek.

QUICK CUT. OTTO'S LEG STEADYING ITSELF ON THE FLOOR.

CLOSE-UP. HER FACE.

Otto's hand stroking her temples, her eyelids, the sides of her nose.

QUICK CUT. IMOGEN'S EYES.

OTTO'S LIPS KISSING HER THROAT.

> OTTO
>
> I long for you.

OTTO'S HAND DIVING THROUGH BURSTING BUTTONS INTO
HER BLOUSE.

OTTO'S OTHER HAND SPEEDING UNDER HER SKIRT.

IMOGEN'S HEAD, PULLING BACK VIOLENTLY, STRIKING
THE WOODEN END OF THE SOFA.

TWO SHOT.

> IMOGEN
>
> Please. We've gone far enough.

> OTTO
>
> I want your clothes off. I want to see you naked.

> IMOGEN
>
> No.

OTTO

Will you give me nothing but your mouth?

CLOSE-UP. IMOGEN.

IMOGEN

Don't *harass* me!

LONG SHOT.

Otto eases from her. She arranges herself, looks at him, is still.

CLOSE-UP. IMOGEN. STARING.

Suddenly she clenches her eyes.

OTTO
(*off-screen*)

Permit me.

OTTO'S HANDS FEELING HER BREASTS.

Imogen's breasts accept this briefly.

CLOSE-UP. IMOGEN.

IMOGEN

No!

OVER OTTO TO IMOGEN.

His hands remain on her breasts, but still.

IMOGEN

I'm not well. It's my time.

OTTO

Your time?

IMOGEN

It's my time! I'm not well.

OTTO

Is that all?

IMOGEN

All? Isn't it enough? It's my condition, my time.

CLOSE-UP. OTTO'S HAND DARTING UP HER SKIRT.

Her hand seizes his.

OTTO
(*off-screen*)

Permit me.

IMOGEN
(*off-screen*)

No!

TWO SHOT.

She clutching his hands.

IMOGEN

You're naughty. You're a naughty man.

CLOSE-UP. OTTO, STARING AT HER.

IMOGEN
(*off-screen*)

You're a very naughty man.

Pause.

OTTO

Would you like some coffee?

IMOGEN
(*off-screen*)

Now that's a good idea.

WIDE SHOT. ROOM.

Otto and Imogen sit on sofa.

His left hand roams over her breasts, gently.

His right hand slides up her skirt, slowly and gently.

She is still.

CLOSE-UP. OTTO'S HAND SLOWLY WITHDRAWING FROM UNDER HER SKIRT.

INT. LANDING. STUDIO DOOR.

The door opens.

Otto.

Imogen seen still sitting.

She stands and walks towards the door.

INT. LANDING. REVERSE SHOT.

Imogen joins Otto on the landing. They walk up a short flight of steps to the kitchen.

> **MAUREEN LAYDE**
> (*off-screen*)
> And then the nurse said try that. And it was green
> blancmange. God I said I couldn't touch that.

Otto pushes open the kitchen door.

INT. KITCHEN. NIGHT.

The kitchen is very cramped. Dirty gas stove, stone sink full of unwashed plates. A table. On the table the remains of a meal. Guinness bottles and whiskey. Maureen Layde sitting, Barry Shannon standing. Maureen wears a leather eyepatch.

Maureen turns in her chair in foreground into the camera.

MAUREEN

And who have we here?

SHOT OF ROOM FROM GAS STOVE.

OTTO

Maureen Layde. Barry Shannon. Imogen Langrishe.

They all murmur 'hello'. Shannon offers Imogen a chair. She sits. Shannon pours whiskey and Guinness for all.

SHANNON

Have a drink now.

Shannon goes to lean against the sink. Otto leans against the dresser. The women sit opposite each other.

MAUREEN
(to Otto)

Did you hear I've just come out of the fever hospital?

THE KITCHEN. OTTO'S P.O.V.

MAUREEN

A bout of scarlet fever laid me low. Didn't it, Barry?

SHANNON

It did.

MAUREEN
(to Otto)

But did you hear this? There I was lying there with a temperature of a 102 in the shade and then I heard this voice, you see, from down the ward. 'Martha, Martha, I'm not well a-tall.' And then I heard this other, you see, say: 'What's the matter, Dolly dree-am?' And then Dolly Dree-am said: 'Oh, Martha, I can't feel in me toes an' feet.'

599

Maureen, Shannon and Otto laugh. Imogen smiles.

CLOSE-UP. MAUREEN.

Her one eye stares quickly at Imogen.

> OTTO
> (*off-screen*)
> We've just been to the play at the Gate.

OVER IMOGEN TO MAUREEN.

Imogen picks up her whiskey and drains the glass.

> MAUREEN
> What's that one like who plays the wife?

> OTTO
> (*off-screen*)

Bad.

Shannon comes into shot with whiskey bottle, fills Imogen's glass. Imogen raises her hand sharply to stop him.

> SHANNON
> (*pouring*)
> It'll do you no harm.

> MAUREEN
> Even if it kills you.
> (*She lifts her glass.*)
> Will you top me up too, my darling?

> SHANNON
> (*pouring*)
> All the way, all the way.

> MAUREEN
> What's that one like who plays the wife? Oh yes, you
> said. Bad. And I'll tell you another thing she is.
> (*To Imogen.*)

Drink up, sweetheart, and here's to you.
(*To Otto.*)
Do you know what else she is? She's a bloody pain in
the arse. The last time I saw her she was going on about
the Sole Meuniere she'd had the night before at the Red
Bank and how the day after she was down with stomach
cramps and Christ knows what else – all told in great
detail. Well, those are not matters of much interest, fish
and flatulence, what?

SHANNON
(*off-screen*)
The Irish theatrical tradition –

Maureen turns to him.

MID-SHOT. SHANNON, SLIGHTLY SWAYING.

SHANNON
– was once a very great theatrical tradition.

LONG SHOT. ROOM. OTTO IN FOREGROUND.

MAUREEN
What the hell do you know about the Irish theatrical
tradition?

SHANNON
God Almighty!

He moves suddenly and bends under the table.

UNDER THE TABLE.

Imogen's legs withdraw quickly under her chair.

Shannon lifts up a crate of Guinness.

*The camera rises with him, to see him set it with a bang on the
table.*

SHANNON

I know every damn thing there is to know about it.

MAUREEN

Why don't you take that stinking crate off the table?
There's a lady present.

*Shannon pulls open a few bottles and places one in front of
Imogen. He looks down at her.*

SHANNON

Do you know Lord Fordham?

LONG SHOT. KITCHEN.

Silence.

IMOGEN

No, I don't actually.

MAUREEN

Why not?

Pause.

IMOGEN

I hear he's very stout.

MAUREEN

Is that why you don't know him? You refuse to make his
acquaintance because he's stout? What a remarkable
attitude.

SHANNON

She didn't say that, you bloody eejit!

CLOSE-UP. MAUREEN. DRINKING.

MAUREEN

At least she can talk. I was beginning to think she
couldn't talk.

CLOSE-UP. OTTO.

Otto swallowing a glass of Guinness.

MID-SHOT. SHANNON COUGHING VIOLENTLY.

TWO SHOT. MAUREEN AND IMOGEN.

Sound of coughing.

> MAUREEN
> (*wincing*)

Oh Christ!

Imogen swallows her whiskey.

Maureen lights a cigarette.

MAUREEN FROM IMOGEN'S P.O.V. CONSUMED IN SMOKE.

The following sequence is constructed in order to indicate a passage of time passing and, with it, the effect of drink on the characters. Each shot will concentrate on its object to such a degree that the characters will appear suspended in time, encased in themselves. Time, although dislocated, has progressed by the end of the sequence.

CLOSE-UP. SHANNON.

> SHANNON
> They can't hide it anymore . . . you can see it on every street corner . . . in this country. Insanity . . . that's what's under the skin. All the brave words and all the brave faces . . . are unable to keep it from bursting out . . . and that's a fact.

CLOSE-UP. OTTO.

> OTTO
> It was a German who discovered parthenogenesis in bees. Dzierzon, a clergyman.

CLOSE-UP. SHANNON. STARING.

CLOSE-UP. MAUREEN.

MAUREEN

All this stuff about the right season and the wrong season . . . never ending rubbish and pub-chat and claptrap. What do they know about women?

CLOSE-UP. IMOGEN.

She is vaguely pulling her unbuttoned blouse together.

CLOSE-UP. SHANNON.

SHANNON

This fellow told me he had two brothers monks. And fine great monks they are too. Fine damn great monks.

CLOSE-UP. MAUREEN.

MAUREEN

The wrong bloody season and the right bloody season. Makes us all sound like bitches on heat.

CLOSE-UP. OTTO.

OTTO

Among bats which have connection in the autumn, the sperm can remain dormant in the uterus throughout the winter and impregnate the ova in the spring.

CLOSE-UP. SHANNON.

SHANNON

Parthenogenesis.

THE ROOM.

CLOSE-UP. IMOGEN.

CLOSE-UP. MAUREEN.

> MAUREEN
> . . . another one of nature's bastards and it's only a fool like you will tolerate him . . .

THE TABLE.

Bottles, glasses, plates, crates of Guinness, hands. Silence.

CLOSE-UP. MAUREEN.

> MAUREEN
> I'm an exception. I look lovely in the morning.

CLOSE-UP. OTTO.

> OTTO
> I myself am indifferent to politics, absolutely indifferent.

CLOSE-UP. MAUREEN.

> MAUREEN
> I've played Jane Eyre, for Christ's sake!

CLOSE-UP. SHANNON.

> SHANNON
> Take the Sacre Coeur for example . . .

CLOSE-UP. IMOGEN. STARING VACANTLY.

CLOSE-UP. OTTO.

OTTO

My professors were Edmund Husserl, lecturing on
philosophy and phenomenological investigations, and
Martin Heidegger, lecturing on philosophy. University
of Freiburg.

WIDE SHOT. KITCHEN.

*Shannon in foreground, gripping a bottle of Guinness between his
knees, straining to pull the cork. Maureen staring at Imogen, who
sits smiling vaguely. Otto leaning against dresser.*

OTTO

Take the case of Mohammed the Second.

MAUREEN

Why doesn't *she* say something?

Shannon looks up.

MAUREEN

Why doesn't she say something? She's not opened her
mouth yet, except to inform us that Lord Fordham's too
bloody stout! That's an insolent piece of information for
a start! And now she just sits there sulking!

SHANNON

Nobody's sulking. Shut your mouth.

*Maureen stands and leans across the table. Imogen looks up at her
weakly.*

MAUREEN

It's you I'm talking about. Wake up and say something,
for Christ's sake. Condescend to that much, will you?

Shannon pulls the cork. He drinks from the bottle.

MAUREEN

You bloody Anglo-Irish shit! That's the sum of it.
Coming over here and ruining the bloody country. Do

you think we don't know? Coming here tonight and boring the knickers off the lot of us. Full of arrogance and hens! You haven't even got the guts to milk a bloody cow!

Imogen collapses on the table, crying.

A glass falls and smashes.

Shannon stands, swaying.

INT. STUDIO. NIGHT.

Imogen lying on studio bed whimpering.

Otto comes into the room with a cup of black coffee. He sits on the bed and strokes her head.

OTTO

Come on. Drink this.

He helps her to sit up. She sips the coffee. She drops down again on the pillow. He puts the cup on the floor and tucks her up.

HER P.O.V.

Otto tucking her up. He stands and looks down at her. He crosses the room to an armchair, sits in it wrapping a blanket around him.

INT. STUDIO. NIGHT. CLOSE-UP. OTTO IN ARMCHAIR. HIS EYES OPEN.

INT. STUDIO. MORNING.

Otto is asleep. Light floods into the room. The camera pans to find Imogen standing looking at him. She then, with her handbag, moves carefully out of the room. Before she reaches the door at the rear of the studio she passes another door, half open, and looks in.

INT. STUDIO BEDROOM.

Shannon and Maureen, asleep in the bed.

INT. STUDIO BATHROOM. MORNING.

Imogen, blouse off, washing. She dries herself, and pats perfume on herself.

A sound from outside window. She looks out.

EXT. COURTYARD. HER P.O.V.

A groom leading a roan mare through a double doorway. He turns her about. He commences to comb her mane with a currycomb. The mare moves its legs. The groom slaps her flank.

GROOM

Whoa there, my beauty.

EXT. THE LIFFEY. SUMMER. MORNING. PAST.

Imogen walking slowly across the metal footbridge.

INT. ANGLESEA ST. HOUSE. KITCHEN.

The door opens sharply.

Otto stands a moment and then closes the door sharply.

EXT. THE LIFFEY.

The metal footbridge. Empty.

EXT. ANGLESEA ST. MORNING. HIGH SHOT.

Otto standing by cross roads. Bright sunlight.

CLOSE-UP. OTTO. LOOKING RIGHT AND LEFT.

LONG SHOT FROM THE LIFFEY.

Otto in the far distance standing.

EXT. CLANE ROAD. BACK LODGE GATE. DAY.

The bus slowly draws near the gate and stops. Otto descends. The bus moves on. Otto goes through the gate.

EXT. COTTAGE.

Otto approaches the door, unlocks it, goes in.

EXT. SPRINGFIELD HOUSE. THE PLANTATION.

Imogen standing still among the trees.

INT. COTTAGE.

Otto naked to the waist, goes to the open door, hangs a mirror on a hook.

EXT. PLANTATION.

Imogen still.

EXT. COTTAGE.

Otto shaving at open door.

He suddenly stops, stares.

INT. COTTAGE.

Otto slams the door shut, wipes his face with a towel.

The camera pans to the open bedroom door.

Imogen can be seen lying on the bed, on the edge, moving a matchbox with her finger on the floor, hair dangling. A brick supports one leg of the bed. Hen dirt over the floor.

She speaks into the sheet.

> **IMOGEN**
> Vous êtes un homme ou quoi?

INT. COTTAGE.

Otto standing by the door. He moves out of shot. The camera stays on the door.

> **IMOGEN**
> *(softly off-screen)*
> Help me. Please. Help me.

INT. SPRINGFIELD HOUSE. LANDING. SUMMER. DAY. PAST.

The camera looks down into the hall, which is empty. Helen comes into view from the kitchen, carrying tray which contains a teapot, etc. and some thin slices of bread and butter.

She ascends the stairs.

The camera follows her to her bedroom door, which is open. She goes in.

INT. HELEN'S BEDROOM.

Helen places the tray on a small table.

She picks up a piece of bread and, chewing it, walks to the window and looks out.

EXT. THE PLANTATION. HELEN'S P.O.V.

INT. HELEN'S ROOM. HELEN AT THE WINDOW.

Helen returns to the tray. She pours tea. She sits down and sips it.

EXT. THE PLANTATION. DAY.

The camera moves along trees and shrubs to find Otto and Imogen sitting at the foot of a chestnut tree.

OTTO

And you? Are you well off? Rich Irish heiresses?

Imogen laughs.

IMOGEN

Irish heiresses! Do we look it?

OTTO

Well, certainly your manner . . . the house . . . leads
one . . .

IMOGEN

No. If it's money you're after you're wasting your time.

Pause.

We had it once. At least Dada had it. But I'm afraid
we've come down in the world considerably . . . since
those palmy days.

OTTO

I'm sorry? Palmy days?

IMOGEN

Oh you know, when we were well-to-do.

CLOSE-UP. OTTO.

OTTO
(*reflectively*)
Palmy days. Curious expression.

TWO SHOT.

Otto buries his face in her lap.

She strokes his head, moves her fingers up and down his back.

OTTO

That's good. Go on doing that.

MID-SHOT. IMOGEN. HIS HEAD ON HER LAP.

She strokes him.

> OTTO
> (*muffled*)
> All right. That's enough.

She stops. He turns and looks up at the trees.

> IMOGEN
> I want to tell you a secret. About myself. Something no
> one knows.

Pause.

> Shall I tell you?

> OTTO
> Very well.

> IMOGEN
> At one time . . . I took airbaths in my skin.

> OTTO
> Airbaths?

> IMOGEN
> Yes. I would get out of bed and take off my nightdress
> . . . and put on a raincoat. I would slip out of the house
> and over the meadow into the plantation. Here. I'd take
> off my coat. I'd walk around, in my shoes. Sometimes I'd
> keep my coat on, and walk about opening and closing it.

Pause.

> It was wonderful on a hot night. But I loved it when it
> rained, too. I lay on the grass in the rain.

Pause.

> I liked it when men on bicycles went by. They didn't
> know . . . how close I was to them.

Pause.

> Once a drunk went by. He kept stopping, muttering. I was crouching in the ditch, by the hedge. I could have touched him.

TWO SHOT.

Otto sits up and looks at her.

OTTO

Tell me, that first time we met, had you anything on then, under your raincoat? That crepuscular hour when first I heard your angel footsteps.

IMOGEN

Not a stitch.

OTTO

Hmmnn.

Pause.

IMOGEN

Imagine . . . I got up in such a hurry this morning that I forgot to put on my bra.

CLOSE-UP. OTTO.

OTTO

Show me.

CLOSE-UP. IMOGEN.

IMOGEN

I will not.

OTTO
(*off-screen*)

Just for me.

Imogen looks away. Her fingers (unseen) begin to undo her blouse.

IMOGEN

Don't look.

She looks slowly at him. Her gaze stays on him.

Look now.

CLOSE-UP. OTTO. EYES SHUT.

His eyes open. He gazes at her.

CLOSE-UP. IMOGEN.

Otto's hands, unseen, feeling her breasts.

LONG SHOT.

Both sitting quite still. Otto feeling her breasts. Her head turning.

INT. HELEN'S ROOM. DAY.

Helen with empty teacups on her lap.

IMOGEN
(*VO*)

Oh, Otto . . . Beck! What are you doing to me?

EXT. THE MEADOW AND PLANTATION. DAWN. IMOGEN'S P.O.V. PAST.

In the distance the Dublin Hills. From Imogen's bedroom window.

Early morning mist.

INT. IMOGEN'S BEDROOM. DAWN.

The bed in disorder.

Imogen dressing. Clock on table shows 5.30.

INT. HOUSE. HALL.

The hall is empty.

Imogen appears on landing. She walks carefully down the stairs.

EXT. HOUSE. DAWN.

Birds.

The front door opens. Imogen comes out.

The camera watches her walk to the meadow and disappear under the trees.

EXT. LODGE. DAWN.

Imogen taps on window.

Silence. She looks towards the hedge.

EXT. CLANE ROAD. DAWN.

Silence.

EXT. LODGE.

Otto opens the door, wrapped in an overcoat, hair ruffled. She goes in.

INT. LODGE. BEDROOM.

Otto gets back into his bed. Imogen goes into the kitchen.

INT. LODGE. BEDROOM.

Otto in bed. A cup of coffee is placed at his side. He stirs, sips. Imogen's lower half in frame. He drinks, slowly, revives, looks up at her. He puts cup down, reaches for her buttocks, caresses them.

INT. DOOR OF LODGE. DAY.

The sun streams through the door. Hens.

Camera pans into room to find Otto typing at the table, books open beside him.

Camera pans from him to Imogen tidying his papers and books on the shelves, and dusting.

Camera pans back to Otto typing, stopping, thinking, typing.

INT. LODGE KITCHEN. DAY.

A mop thrown on the floor.

Imogen gets down on her knees and begins to wash the floor.

INT. KITCHEN. HOUSE.

Lily, with a bucket of cooking apples, enters the back door into the kitchen.

INT. KITCHEN. HOUSE.

Lily in foreground. Helen boiling kettle background.

Lily moves to empty apples into the sink. She turns the tap on.

Helen pours water into teapot, sets pot on a tray, leaves kitchen with tray.

Lily washes the apples.

CLOSE-UP. LILY, WASHING APPLES.

INT. COTTAGE. DAY. KITCHEN.

Imogen washing Otto's hair.

IMOGEN
You're as lousy as all hell.

OTTO

Irish lice.

IMOGEN

They've had their last great times with you.

INT. HOUSE. HALL.

Helen walking through the hall to stairs with her tray.

INT. LODGE.

Mid-shot. Otto.

A plate of macaroni pudding placed on the table in front of him.

Camera eases to see Imogen sitting with her plate.

Otto tastes the macaroni, turns to Imogen and kisses his hand.

INT. HOUSE. IMOGEN'S ROOM. NIGHT. PAST.

The door closing softly.

INT. HOUSE. KITCHEN.

Lily sitting at the table eating bread and butter.

INT. HALL.

The front door closing softly.

INT. HELEN'S ROOM.

Helen in bed, eyes open.

INT. LODGE.

A plate of cream meringues.

Imogen's hand takes the cream out of the meringues.

INT. LODGE. NIGHT.

In foreground Otto's shadowed figure, seated in the firelight.

Imogen standing, naked to the waist.

She dabs the cream on her nipples, regarding Otto seriously.

INT. LODGE. NIGHT.

Otto and Imogen in bed.

Otto moans in his sleep. Imogen strokes his head and his hands. He quietens.

Sound of turf-carts on the road.

EXT. CLANE ROAD. NIGHT.

Cottage dimly discerned behind the hedge.

Donkeys pulling turf carts along the road, very slowly. Carriage lights fixed to the carts. Uneven heaps of sacks on the carts.

From under one of the sacks a man suddenly sits up, scratches his head, draws the sack over him.

INT. COTTAGE. DAY.

Imogen fixing new cover onto new armchair. Otto at the table studying a map.

> OTTO
> Ah. This village here for instance – Killashee. Do you know the origin of the name?

> IMOGEN
> I do not.

> OTTO
> It comes from Bishop Auxilius, coadjutor to St. Patrick. The Cill – or church – of the same. Thus you have: Cill Auxuli. Or Killashee.

IMOGEN

Fancy that.

OTTO

I must get to Rathcoffey.

IMOGEN

Why?

OTTO

It was formerly the residence of Chevalier Wogan, a
Jacobite and member of Dillon's regiment in the Irish
Brigade. He was the man who rescued Princess
Clementina Sobieski from Innsbruck and conducted her
back to Bologna to marry the Old Pretender.

IMOGEN

Good gracious.

OTTO
(*studying map*)

Hazelhurst has a very interesting derivation. It's from
the Old English hyrst and the Middle Dutch horst.
Hazel-hyrst. Or horst.

Imogen goes to Otto, turns him from the map and kisses him.

INT. HOUSE. LANDING. SUMMER. PAST.

Imogen knocks at Helen's door. Helen's voice: Come in.

INT. HELEN'S ROOM.

*Imogen enters. Helen is at her desk, writing. She looks round
briefly, looks back to her paper.*

IMOGEN

What are you doing?

HELEN

Writing.

IMOGEN

What?

HELEN

Nothing of any importance.

Pause.

IMOGEN

How are you?

HELEN

Perfectly well.

Imogen walks to the window and looks out.

IMOGEN

Isn't the weather beautiful?

Pause.

I'm thinking of making a blackberry pie.

Pause.

Shall I?

HELEN

Why not?

IMOGEN

I mean . . . would you like some of it?

HELEN

Me? What have I got to do with it?

Pause.

HELEN

Food doesn't interest me.

Pause.

IMOGEN

I'll make it anyway.

Pause.

Perhaps you'll like it.

Pause.

HELEN

Yes, I might. I might like it.

Pause.

IMOGEN

All right then.

She walks to the door.

INT. COTTAGE. NIGHT.

Otto's hand banging a bottle of gin on the table. The camera pans up to them both.

OTTO

A bottle of gin! To celebrate!

IMOGEN

To celebrate what?

Otto throws a copy of the London Fortnightly Review on the table. The camera with Imogen bends to look at the cover. Among the list of contributors is: O. B. Beck, Symbolism in Grimm.

CLOSE-UP. IMOGEN.

IMOGEN

It's you!

CLOSE-UP. LILY BEHIND WINDOWPANE.

IMOGEN

It's your name!

The camera withdraws from Lily's face to a view of Springfield House. Night.

INT. COTTAGE. NIGHT.

Gin bottle, half empty, slams on the table. A glass lifted.

INT. COTTAGE.

Imogen and Otto sitting by the fire.

IMOGEN

But they printed it. They liked it. They admired it. Why else would they print it?

OTTO

It's worthless. It's superficial. It's nothing. But I can do better.

IMOGEN

You are doing better. You're working all the time.

OTTO

Yes, I am. I shall complete my thesis, of course. I shall complete it.

He drinks.

IMOGEN

And you have me.

OTTO

Yes. I have you indeed. A great solace.

He drinks.

Archery in ancient China was played traditionally to the

beat of music. The contestants were allowed four arrows
but could only fire at the proper beat of the music. The
Chou dynasty, in fact.

She goes to him and kneels by him.

IMOGEN

Listen . . . it's high time you had a bath.

OTTO

A bath?

IMOGEN

Can you climb?

OTTO

Of course. Where?

IMOGEN

To the bathroom. But you must be quite sure which
window you're at. Otherwise you might end up on top
of Lily.

EXT. HOUSE. NIGHT.

*Otto treading gently along the dairy roof to the bathroom window.
He taps. The window opens.*

INT. HOUSE. LANDING. NIGHT.

Silence.

A light under Helen's door.

INT. BATHROOM.

Otto and Imogen in bath.

They stare at each other.

Otto washes his armpits.

INT. IMOGEN'S BEDROOM. WIDE SHOT.

Otto and Imogen in bed.

THE BED.

He leans over her.

> **OTTO**
> *(whispering)*
> Do not close your eyes. They are remarkable.

CLOSE-UP. IMOGEN IN BED.

> **IMOGEN**
> *(whispering)*
> You are so gentle.

INT. KITCHEN. NIGHT.

Lily sitting sipping tea. The dog asleep.

EXT. HOUSE. NIGHT.

Otto shinning down ivy to the ground.

EXT. PLANTATION. DAY.

An ash tree falling.

Men scatter and then gather around and proceed to cut the branches.

INT. COTTAGE. MORNING. KITCHEN.

Imogen kneading dough.

The cottage door opens. She turns.

INT. COTTAGE DOOR.

Otto at door swinging dead pheasant, his gun in his other hand.

OTTO

Dinner.

INT. HOUSE. NIGHT. HALL. LILY IN FOREGROUND.

LILY

Helen!

Helen appears on the landing.

HELEN

What is it?

LILY

There's flames out there.

HELEN

They're burning the branches. We're selling some of the trees.

Lily looks down. Camera pans down. The dog looking up. Lily pats him.

INT. COTTAGE. NIGHT. THE TABLE.

Plates with pheasant bones. Otto rises.

OTTO

Excuse me. I must attend to nature.

He goes out of shot. Imogen remains drinking hock. Sound of splashing.

INT. COTTAGE. OTTO'S BACK AT DOOR. HE TURNS.

OTTO

One of the heresies of Johannes Scotus Erigena was that the sexual organs would not be resurrected on the Last Day.

CLOSE-UP. IMOGEN.

OVER IMOGEN TO OTTO STANDING, FILLING HIS PIPE.

> OTTO
>
> His students, so the story goes, alarmed by the boldness
> of his thought, stabbed him to death with their pens.

CLOSE-UP. IMOGEN.

> IMOGEN
>
> Not with their penises?

Otto lights pipe.

> OTTO
>
> How much do you get for a tree, may one ask?

INT. HELEN'S BEDROOM. NIGHT.

Helen sitting. McCormack on record.

> IMOGEN
> (*VO*)
>
> Two pounds.

INT. COTTAGE.

Imogen and Otto.

> IMOGEN
>
> Well, you see . . . we couldn't go on running the place
> at a loss and pay the men their wages. So all but Feeney
> had to be dismissed. Galvin and Flynn drove the
> remains of the herd to the cattle-market in Dublin.
> Feeney went . . . sometime after . . .

EXT. THE PLANTATION. NIGHT. LONG SHOT.

A fire burning. Shadows of men.

OTTO
(*VO*)

You have a nice nature. A nice kind nature. And very
white skin.

IMOGEN
(*VO*)

Goat.

OTTO
(*VO*)

Most white.

IMOGEN
(*VO*)

Oh darling.

OTTO
(*VO*)

Most white. Most . . .

Indrawn breath from Imogen.

Most . . .

EXT. PLANTATION. NIGHT.

Men sitting round the fire smoking.

INT. HELEN'S ROOM. NIGHT.

*Helen's chair. Empty. The camera moves slowly along the carpet,
past cats, to Helen's feet, which move quickly out of shot. Camera
pans up slightly to look at desk. Books, papers, pen.*

IMOGEN
(*VO*)

I love you. I love you.

INT. COTTAGE. NIGHT.

Imogen lying on couch. Otto with his feet on the table, smoking.

>   OTTO
> Husserl was Heidegger's teacher, and his philosophy
> had a detrimental influence on the latter, who
> succeeded him at Freiburg University in 1928. After a
> while Heidegger would not greet him, much less argue
> with him, much less agree with him.

INT. COTTAGE. DAY. DOOR OPEN. SUN.

Otto and Imogen in the same positions.

*Otto is watching a wasp crawling on the table. He picks up a pair
of scissors.*

>   OTTO
> Do you recall Maureen Layde?

>   IMOGEN
> I'm not likely to forget her.

>   OTTO
> She tried to kill herself. Almost did this time. They had
> to use a stomach pump to get about a hundred aspirins
> out of her. At least she has the grace to try it on only
> when there are people about.

He leans forward and cuts.

CLOSE-UP. WASP. CUT IN HALF.

EXT. KILLADOON ESTATE. DAY. PAST.

*Otto and Imogen walking through the trees. He carries a gun and
game bag.*

OTTO

Your sister, Helen, is what one could call a recluse, is she not?

IMOGEN

She lives her own life.

Pause.

She has her own thoughts.

OTTO

What are they?

IMOGEN

She doesn't tell me.

OTTO

About you, some of them, perhaps? About your life?

IMOGEN

She probably thinks I'm a total fool, but she can't change that, so she doesn't try.

Otto stops, looks up into a tree, raises gun. She watches him.

OTTO

And Lily, what does she think about?

IMOGEN

Nobody knows that.

OTTO
(*murmuring*)

Very interesting.

He shoots. She covers her ears.

IMOGEN

What was it?

A squirrel drops at her feet.

629

Why the hell did you shoot that?

EXT. RIVER. KILLADOON. LATE AFTERNOON.

Otto in foreground fishing from the bank. Imogen in background wading in the water, naked.

Silence.

IMOGEN

Otto!

She jumps and slaps the water.

Otto! I'm being eaten alive by these damn minnows!

Otto grimaces in irritation. She splashes about.

These minnows! Help! I'm being devoured!

OTTO

God damn you! Quiet! Shut up! How do you expect me to catch fish!

EXT. RIVERBANK. LATE AFTERNOON. MID-SHOT. IMOGEN.

She is sitting on the bank, a towel around her, drying herself.

Otto's shadow falls upon her. She looks up.

The camera eases to see him standing above her, looking down.

He places his foot under her thighs and prods her.

She slowly falls back and turns on her stomach to lie in the grass, the towel around her.

LONG SHOT. OTTO AND IMOGEN ON BANK.

Otto places his foot on her buttocks and stands, gently moving her, in the growing dusk.

INT. COTTAGE. DAY.

Otto at the table typing. The door opens. Imogen enters.

> IMOGEN
>
> What happened to the apples on the apple tree?

> OTTO
>
> Apples?

> IMOGEN
>
> You didn't take them, by any chance?

> OTTO
>
> I took some, yes.

Pause.

> IMOGEN
>
> You might have asked me first. It's my father's orchard.

> OTTO
>
> I took one when I was cutting the hedge. I was hungry, so I took two more. I took three. There were eight on it.

> IMOGEN
>
> Nine. There were nine.

> OTTO
>
> One was bad.

> IMOGEN
>
> Eight or nine, what does it matter? They've gone. You were underhand about it.

> OTTO
>
> Even you must appreciate that after twelve hours of abstinence the lower intestine stands severely in need of solace.

> IMOGEN
>
> Don't be impertinent.

631

OTTO

Am I being impertinent? I'm not conscious of it, I assure you.

IMOGEN

You say you took three. What happened to the other five? I suppose they walked off the tree by themselves?

OTTO

You are an imbecile.

IMOGEN

You haven't paid any rent for ages. We don't ask you for it. Don't I give you enough? Are you never satisfied?

INT. DINING-ROOM. THE HOUSE. NIGHT. CLOSE-UP. IMOGEN SEATED. PAST.

She raises her glass.

IMOGEN

Happy Birthday.

CLOSE-UP. LILY, SEATED, RAISING GLASS.

LILY

Happy Birthday.

CLOSE-UP. HELEN, SEATED.

HELEN

This is a great surprise.
                    (*Raising glass.*)
Thank you.

INT. DINING-ROOM. WIDE SHOT.

The three sitting at the dining-room table. Helen at one end, Lily and Imogen facing each other. A leg of pork, bowls of potatoes and brussel sprouts, etc. Wine. Candlelight.

They eat.

LILY

Imogen cooked the whole dinner herself.

HELEN

It's very good.

LILY

Oh, it is.

Pause.

IMOGEN

I've made a cherry pie. You like that.

HELEN

When I was a girl I did. Yes, I remember that.

LILY

Ah sure, we're not all that old.

Pause.

But what a long time since we all had such a grand
dinner together.

Pause.

CLOSE-UP. LILY.

LILY

When Imogen carved the joint it reminded me of Dada
carving the joint. Do you remember how Dada carved
the joint?

CLOSE-UP. HELEN.

HELEN

He was very serious about it.

633

CLOSE-UP. IMOGEN.

>IMOGEN
Ah well, it was a serious matter.

THREE SHOT. HELEN'S HEAD FOREGROUND.

>LILY
Biddy used to bring round the gravyboat on a wooden tray.

>IMOGEN
She did.

INT. COTTAGE. BEDROOM. NIGHT.

Imogen lies in bed, her face turned to the wall.

Otto comes into shot, throws the bedclothes back, climbs onto the bed. He studies Imogen's curled body for a moment and then clasps her roughly from behind.

INT. BEDROOM. NIGHT.

Imogen foreground. Otto leaning over her feeling her body.

>IMOGEN
I want to sleep. I want my rest.

Her body tightens. Her eyes close. Otto stares down at her.

INT. DINING-ROOM. THE HOUSE. NIGHT.

>LILY
How long was Biddy with us?

>HELEN
All her life.

Pause.

LILY

Do you remember Dada laughing when that very stout
gentleman – what was his name – in his braces – chased
the ball in the tennis match and fell with such a crash?

IMOGEN

All nineteen stone of him.

HELEN

Bill Odlum was his name.

LILY

Bill Odlum. Ah, that's right. My goodness he was a big
man.

IMOGEN

They shouldn't have let him play tennis anyway.

*They all continue to eat, and talk, spasmodically, but the sound
ceases.*

Imogen's voice heard over:

(VO)

Looking for compliments from you, honest to God, it's
like boring down a mine.

OTTO
(VO)

I am expected to make you pretty speeches?

IMOGEN
(VO)

What is it? Have I done something wrong? Tell me what
I've done wrong.

OTTO
(VO)

Nothing at all.

IMOGEN
(*VO*)

Do I no longer excite you? Is that what it is?

OTTO
(*VO*)

Oh you excite me, certainly. It's only . . .

IMOGEN
(*VO*)

Only what?

OTTO
(*VO*)

You grind your teeth at night.

IMOGEN
(*VO*)

Oh is that a fact? Well, what about you? What about all
the lousy filthy degrading disgusting things I have to put
up with from you? What about then?

*During the preceding, Lily has brought a birthday cake from the
sideboard and lit the candles. Helen blows them out. Imogen and
Lily begin to sing Happy Birthday.*

EXT. HOUSE. AUTUMN. NIGHT. PAST.

Rain sweeping across the meadow.

EXT. COTTAGE. AUTUMN. NIGHT. PAST.

Rain dripping on the cottage roof.

INT. COTTAGE. NIGHT. AUTUMN. PAST.

*Imogen foreground combing her wet hair by the fire, sitting on a
stool.*

In background Otto, with his back to her at the table, writing. A

636

paraffin lamp by him. A bottle of whiskey. Imogen is singing softly a ballad to herself. Otto turns with a piece of paper, brings it to her.

OTTO

The revised title. For my thesis.

THE PAPER IN IMOGEN'S HANDS. OTTO'S HAND-WRITING. IT READS:

Das Ossianische Problem und die tatsächlichen Volksmythen und Gebräuche Irlands im siebzehnten Jahrhundert unter besonderer Berücksichtigung des Werkes Goethes und der Gebrüder Grimm: Eine sozial-philologische-kritische Studie. Herr Dr Otto Bernhardt Beck, phil, et rer. pol. et habil.

IMOGEN

Read it.

Otto reads the title aloud.

TWO SHOT. SHE SITTING. HE STANDING.

IMOGEN

Good gracious. What does it all mean?

OTTO

The Ossianic problem and the actual folk sagas in seventeenth century Ireland, with special reference to the work of Goethe and the Brothers Grimm. A sociological-philological-critical study.

IMOGEN

What a mouthful. When will it be finished?

He looks at her.

OTTO

I hope to bring it to a satisfactory conclusion in about two years time.

637

IMOGEN
(*holding out her glass*)
Pour me a drop more.

Otto goes to the table with the glass and pours.

I didn't know you had a second name, Bernhardt.
Bernhardt. I like it.

Otto returns with her glass. She takes it.

INT. COTTAGE. MID-SHOT OTTO.

He takes wooden pipe rack from mantelshelf.

ACROSS OTTO TO IMOGEN.

*In foreground Otto approaches table with pipe rack, places it on a
sheet of newspaper and arranges his pipes and cleaners. Imogen at
fire in background.*

IMOGEN
Do you ever miss Germany?

Otto unscrews the stem of a pipe and begins to clean it, sitting.

OTTO
I do not look back. I am contented, as things stand.

IMOGEN
But you must miss it sometimes. You're not a machine!

*Otto continues an elaborate cleaning and polishing system on his
pipes.*

OTTO
Look at my position. Here am I, a poor scholar, with
free lodging, free fuel, peace and quiet, all my bodily
needs attended to, so that I can get on with my work.
Why should I miss Germany?

Pause.

638

OTTO

Besides, I am not young.

Pause.

I am thirty-five. I am getting on.

REVERSE SHOT. IMOGEN PROFILE.

She looks down a moment, then looks up.

IMOGEN

But if you had the *means* – would you not go back? After all, you're so cut off here, aren't you? You have no friends. You only have me, and I'm poor enough company.

OTTO

Ah! If I had the *means*, that would be different. I'd go back to Freiburg University and study under Husserl. Oh nothing would stop me if I had the means.

The camera tracks into Otto and stays on him.

Higher education in Germany is beyond criticism. Excellent, really excellent.

Pause.

Better still, to study under Heidegger at Marburg. Philosophy. Comparative psychology. Phenomenological investigations. That would indeed be wonderful.

Pause.

You are quite right, of course. I am cut off here. There is no music. None whatever. One feels its absence. Even the mattresses are of inferior quality, hard and uncomfortable.

OTTO FOREGROUND. IMOGEN BACKGROUND.

Imogen stands, comes to the table and pours herself another drink.

IMOGEN

What do you miss apart from the mattresses?

OTTO

(*involuntarily*)

Die Schnall'n.

Imogen looks down at him.

IMOGEN

I beg your pardon?

OTTO

What?

IMOGEN

What does that mean?

OTTO

What?

IMOGEN

What does *that* mean?

OTTO

What does it mean?

Pause.

It means whores. Munich whores.

CLOSE-UP. IMOGEN.

IMOGEN

Whores? Munich whores? But why do you miss them?
You have me.

SHOT FROM FIRE.

Otto rises from table, comes to fireside, throws handfuls of fir cones onto the fire, pokes it. Imogen stands in background.

> IMOGEN
>
> What do they do that I can't . . . or don't . . . or won't?

> OTTO
>
> This is a futile line of enquiry.

Imogen bears down on him.

> IMOGEN
>
> You miss your Munich whores? Well, I'm the bloody best whore you'll get in this part of the bloody emerald isle, I'll tell you that!

OVER IMOGEN TO OTTO.

> OTTO
>
> No, no, you're quite wrong. Irish women are in fact remarkably pure and clean. Remarkably pure. And that's not to be found any more in Germany – that great purity. But here you have it. You yourself possess it. That look in the face, the eyes, and one knows that such women are not corrupted. One knows it *here*.

He thumps his chest.

> A man might sometimes have filthy thoughts about girls. That's natural enough. But when I meet Irish girls and can recognise at once their essential purity, then I am touched, incapable of a base thought. I have a great reverence for Irish women.

> IMOGEN
>
> What about Molly Cushen?

Pause.

OTTO

Who?

IMOGEN

Molly Cushen.

OTTO

What are you talking about?

CLOSE-UP. IMOGEN.

IMOGEN

I'm talking about that snottynosed shortarsed bitch from
the village. Molly Cushen! I'm talking about that
nonentity, that prostitute!

OTTO

You can't call anybody a nonentity.

IMOGEN

I can call her anything.

CLOSE-UP. OTTO

OTTO

Any human being has his, or her, innate dignity.

CLOSE-UP. IMOGEN.

IMOGEN

That slut! That –

QUICK CUT. INT. DARK DINING-ROOM. HOUSE. NIGHT.

Brief shaft of light from door opening. Helen goes out.

IMOGEN'S VOICE

– dirty bitch!

Dining room door closes. Dark. Silence.

EXT. RIVER BANK. AUTUMN. AFTERNOON. TWO SHOT. PAST.

Imogen and Otto sit on the bank on rugs looking at the river. Imogen plucks at something in the grass.

Silence.

OTTO

What are you thinking?

IMOGEN

I was just thinking what a boring autumn I'm having. This is you . . .

She opens her hand to show a withered seed pod and brushes the seeds from her palm.

. . . going to seed.

THEIR BACKS, SITTING. THE RIVER BEYOND.

IMOGEN

What was the name of that fellow we met in Dublin? Doonan . . . or Noonan . . . or Sheehan . . .

OTTO

Shannon!

TWO SHOT.

OTTO

SHANNON!

Silence.

You're so soft. A soft spineless insect. I can feel you beginning to curl up at the sides.

They sit still, looking out to the river. The camera stays with them for some moments.

INT. HELEN'S ROOM. NIGHT. PAST.

Helen sits in an armchair. She is reading a book. Her face is not seen.

Galli-Curci on record.

She turns a page.

INT. IMOGEN'S BEDROOM. HOUSE. NIGHT. AUTUMN. PAST.

Imogen lies in her bed. Her eyes are open.

Faint Galli-Curci.

EXT. STABLE AREA. BACK OF HOUSE. MORNING. PAST.

Lily and Imogen beating carpets. Dog barking. Hens.

> **LILY**
> God save it doesn't rain now we have these carpets out.

EXT. ROAD TO VILLAGE.

A line of schoolgirls led by a nun walking, in pairs. They are chattering. Gradually they stop talking.

THEIR P.O.V.

Otto cycling towards them.

MID-SHOT. OTTO ON BIKE, SEEING THEM.

OTTO PASSING THEM.

They giggle and whisper. One or two look after him.

THE NUN, OBLIVIOUS.

OTTO TURNS INTO A LANE AND CYCLES DOWN IT.

INT. COTTAGE. NIGHT. AUTUMN. PAST.

Imogen enters, looks about. It is empty and untidy. No fire. A few hens.

She puts roses and honeysuckle in two vases.

CLOSE-UP. IMOGEN DOING THIS.

INT. COTTAGE. NIGHT.

Imogen sits silently by the fire, which she has made. She hears steps. The door opens.

MID-SHOT. OTTO AT DOOR.

>   OTTO
> Ah. My dear.

THE ROOM.

Otto takes off his boots.

>   OTTO
> I've been to Breens for a few drinks.

She stands.

>   IMOGEN
> I'm going to bed.

>   OTTO
> Which bed?

>   IMOGEN
> Ours.

645

OTTO

Ah.

IMOGEN

Will you come and hold me?

Pause.

Will you hold me?

Pause.

OTTO

Of course.

INT. COTTAGE. MORNING. AUTUMN. PAST.

Imogen is lying on couch.

Otto stands by the window, smoking a pipe.

Silence.

IMOGEN

Can I help it if I'm not feeling well?

Pause.

It must have been the rhubarb I had last night.

Pause.

Could you at least look at me?

Otto turns to her.

OTTO

Can I get you something?

IMOGEN

Could you pour me a drop of that cordial in the kitchen, in some water? It might relieve it.

Otto goes into the kitchen. He can be seen through kitchen door pouring the cordial. He returns to the room and hands her the glass.

Thank you.

She drinks.

THE ROOM. LONG SHOT.

IMOGEN
Ah, that's good.

OTTO
You need rest. I'll leave you for a little bit. I have an appointment with some people.

Imogen finishes her drink.

Try and get some sleep. You'll feel better for it.

Pause.

IMOGEN
If you leave me now, you needn't come back.

Pause.

OTTO
I told you, I have an appointment.

Pause.

IMOGEN
You need never come back. You can get your meals elsewhere.

OTTO
I have an appointment, with some friends.

IMOGEN
You have no friends.

Pause.

OTTO

I do have friends.

Pause.

Fishing friends.

Silence.

Imogen stands and goes into the kitchen.

Otto stands still. He then goes quickly to the shelf, from which he takes his manuscript and notebooks.

INT. COTTAGE. BEDROOM.

Otto enters. He pulls out a haversack from under the bed, wraps his manuscript in a shirt, knots the sleeves, puts it in the haversack.

INT. KITCHEN.

Imogen dusting the range. She hears the front door close, looks up.

OVER IMOGEN TO OPEN KITCHEN DOOR.

Otto comes through the room into kitchen. He watches her dusting.

OTTO

You should be in bed.

IMOGEN

Ah no. I'd be better doing things.

Pause.

Would you ever set the fire for me?

He remains still, and then goes into the room. The camera shifts to watch him in background bend to the grate and clear the ashes. Imogen comes in and out of shot in foreground, dusting. Otto sets a new fire, does not light it, rises, stands still in the centre of the room. Imogen, coughs out of shot. Otto moves to front door.

EXT. COTTAGE. YARD.

Otto comes out of door, glances quickly at his haversack, which is propped by the wall, and stands looking out at the sky.

The door opens.

> IMOGEN
> I thought you had an appointment.

Pause.

> Can't you make up your mind?

> OTTO
> No.

> IMOGEN
> Will I make it up for you?

Pause.

Imogen goes in.

Otto looks at the ground.

Suddenly she reappears at the door with a basin. He turns.

OTTO'S P.O.V.

A spreading sheet of dishwater comes towards him.

MID-SHOT. OTTO. JUMPING.

He jumps. His trousers and shoes are drenched.

THE BASIN HURTLING TOWARDS HIM.

CLOSE-UP. OTTO.

He ducks.

Sound of basin hitting wall.

EXT. COTTAGE.

Imogen standing at the door.

Otto brushes his trousers.

He walks to the wall and picks up his haversack. He walks towards the outhouse, stops and turns.

> OTTO
> I'll send for the rest of my things, if you would be so kind.

> IMOGEN
> You're not needed here. Don't come back. You're not needed here.

Otto walks to the outhouse.

INT. OUTHOUSE.

Otto enters. Hens. His bicycle is against the wall. He fits the bicycle clips and wheels the bicycle out. The camera follows him through the yard. Imogen is no longer at the door.

EXT. LODGE GATE.

Otto wheels bicycle to gate, opens it, goes out, closes it.

EXT. ROAD.

Otto, whistling, climbs on bicycle, and begins to cycle. He glances towards the hedge, freezes, nearly loses his balance.

HIS P.O.V.

Through gap in hedge the cottage window, open. A shotgun muzzle trained directly at him.

EXT. WINDOW. IMOGEN WITH GUN, FIRING.

BIRDS SCURRYING IN BUSH. LEAVES BLOWN.

LONG SHOT. ROAD.

Otto pedalling at top speed.

INT. COTTAGE. LONG SHOT.

Imogen sitting on floor by window, with gun, trembling.

EXT. HOUSE. DUSK. OCTOBER. PAST.

Lily walking across overgrown tennis court from orchard. She calls 'Oscar! Oscar!' The dog eventually appears. They move toward the house. Lily looks up at the house.

A light through the dusk in Imogen's window.

EXT. HOUSE. OCTOBER. NIGHT. PAST.

The plantation. Camera looks up at the house. Imogen's light burning.

Helen comes into shot and looks up at the light.

INT. HOUSE. LANDING. NIGHT. OCTOBER. PAST.

A light shining from under Imogen's door. The camera pans to see Helen's shoes moving away.

INT. HOUSE. KITCHEN. MORNING. OCTOBER. PAST.

Lily and Helen at kitchen table eating breakfast.

Silence.

LILY

Are you going to rent the cottage?

Helen looks at her.

HELEN

Rent the *what*?

LILY

We've been a month without rent.

HELEN

For God's sake, we've been half a year without rent.

Helen stands and leaves the kitchen.

INT. HOUSE. IMOGEN'S DOOR. MORNING. OCTOBER. PAST.

Helen knocks on the door and goes in.

Imogen, at the table by the window, turns quickly, her left forearm covering a piece of paper, a pen in her right hand.

IMOGEN

Yes?

HELEN

What are you doing?

IMOGEN
(*sharply*)

Nothing at all. Why?

Pause.

HELEN

Are you going to eat breakfast?

IMOGEN

No I'm not. I'm not obliged to, am I?

652

Pause.

I'll eat when I'm hungry.

                    HELEN
Yes, you'll do that, surely.

Pause.

I'll leave you, then.

Imogen stares at her. Helen withdraws and closes the door.

*Imogen takes an envelope, folds the paper into it, writes quickly on
the envelope, rises.*

INT. IMOGEN'S ROOM. WINDOW.

*Imogen pulls away the curtain. In the corner on the windowseat a
pile of envelopes. She places the last upon it.*

*The camera observes, quickly, that the letters are all addressed to
Herr Otto Beck, at a Munich address.*

EXT. HOUSE. DAY. OCTOBER. PAST.

*High shot in plantation sees Imogen walking slowly down the
avenue.*

EXT. HELEN'S WINDOW. DAY. PAST.

Close up. Helen looking down at the avenue.

INT. IMOGEN'S ROOM. DAY. PAST.

*Helen at Imogen's table, looking at blotting paper. She replaces it
carefully, in exact position.*

HELEN DELVING IN DRAWERS OF CHEST OF DRAWERS.

HELEN LOOKING UNDER BED.

WIDE SHOT.

Helen standing in the room, still. She notices one curtain at window is pulled slightly across. She moves towards it. She lifts the curtain.

EXT. KILLADOON ESTATE. DAY. PAST.

Imogen walking.

Far shouts from a field a distance away. She turns to look. In a meadow over a hedge a game of Gaelic Football is in progress.

She walks down towards it, stops at a hedge and watches.

The camera goes with her, staying behind her.

The goalkeeper slaps his hands, gloved. He wears a cap back to front. Five players leap up for the ball.

CLOSE-UP. IMOGEN WATCHING.

IMOGEN FOREGROUND. GAME BACKGROUND.

Three men in a small crowd turn to look at her over the hedge. One of them raises his cap. The others smile. Imogen turns away.

INT. IMOGEN'S BEDROOM. DAY. OCTOBER. PAST.

Curtain pulled away. Pile of letters gone.

INT. IMOGEN'S ROOM. SHOT FROM DOOR.

Imogen at the window, her back to camera.

INT. HOUSE. LANDING AND STAIRS. DAY. PAST.

Helen is ascending the stairs. Imogen comes into shot on the landing.

IMOGEN

Oh Helen . . .

Helen stops.

HELEN

Yes? What is it?

IMOGEN

Could I have a word with you?

HELEN

Surely.

Helen walks up towards her.

TWO SHOT. LANDING.

HELEN

What is it?

Pause.

IMOGEN

I was just wondering . . . why you . . . I mean . . . if
you . . .

Pause.

HELEN

If I what?

Pause.

IMOGEN

Well, I just wondered . . .

HELEN

You wondered what?

Pause.

IMOGEN

Have you been in my room?

Pause.

HELEN

For what purpose?

Pause.

IMOGEN

Well, it's of no importance, really. It's really of little
importance.

Pause.

So.

Imogen turns out of shot. Helen turns, in opposite direction.

The camera remains looking down the empty staircase.

EXT. GARDEN. THE HOUSE. SUMMER. DAY. 1903.

*In background a tennis match (mixed doubles) in progress on the
court.*

*Four girls appear suddenly in foreground. Emily 16. Helen 14.
Lily 12. Imogen 10.*

They whisper and chatter together, swiftly. A call:

MRS LANGRISHE

Girls.

They stop whispering and turn. The camera shifts.

*In the distance Mr and Mrs Langrishe walk towards them from
the house, arm in arm.*

INT. HELEN'S ROOM. NIGHT. PRESENT.

Helen in bed, eyes open.

EXT. HOUSE. STABLE AREA. SUMMER. EVENING. I903.

FROM P.O.V. OF BACK UPPER WINDOW:

Two cowmen and Tommy Flynn, the foreman, appear from the harness room with a bucket. They dip it into the open tank, wash their face and necks. They bring out pint bottles of Guinness, sit down to drink them and smoke. Tommy Flynn takes a concertina from a nail and plays old airs. He looks up.

TOMMY FLYNN
You girls get to bed, you girls, or I'll tell your da.

He laughs. In the dim light the men laugh and talk softly. Tommy Flynn plays.

FOUR GIRLS AT WINDOW, GIGGLING.

INT. HOUSE. HALL. PRESENT.

Imogen passes through the hall and up the stairs with a tray.

EXT. GARDEN. I900.

Three men and two ladies put down their cucumber sandwiches as Mr and Mrs Langrishe walk towards them. The men rise.

INT. HELEN'S BEDROOM. NIGHT. PRESENT.

Helen in bed, eyes closed, the tray on a table by the bedside, a teacup full, untouched.

INT. DRAWING-ROOM. DAY. I903.

Mrs Langrishe sitting knitting. Imogen 10 sitting beside her, with a book. A man's legs in shot.

MR LANGRISHE
After all, they were my father's tenants also. There are ten in the family. They've nowhere to go. On the other

hand I can't afford to be soft, or for that matter daft.
You decide for me, Louisa. Come on now. You decide.

Mrs Langrishe continues knitting.

Imogen looks from one to the other.

LONG SHOT. DONYCOMPER CEMETERY. DAY. PRESENT.

A crowd of people in the graveyard. A line of villagers by the wall, some lifting children. Sound of priest reading the Office for the Dead. He stops. Two children discerned going to the grave with bouquets. The coffin glimpsed between figures being lowered into the grave.

THREE SHOT. CEMETERY.

Imogen and Lily, in black, walking away with the priest.

EXT. SUMMER HOUSE. SPRINGFIELD HOUSE. 1919.

Mr Langrishe seen through glass, seated.

INT. SUMMER HOUSE.

Mr Langrishe lifting a glass of whiskey to his lips. An open book upside down on the table in front of him. His eyes are vacant.

EXT. DONYCOMPER CEMETERY. PRESENT.

A group of mourners whispering together. Gravediggers filling in the grave.

In the distance Imogen and Lily walking away with the priest.

EXT. TENNIS COURT. DAY. SUMMER. 1900.

A lady on the far side of the net lobs the ball high. A very stout man, Bill Odlum, runs backwards for it. He falls.

The camera pans to Mr and Mrs Langrishe and others, watching.

Mr Langrishe and the others laugh. Mrs Langrishe does not.

BILL ODLUM GETS UP AND CLOWNS, BOUNCING ABOUT AND
SLAPPING HIS BUTTOCKS.

*The camera pans to find Emily, Helen, Lily and Imogen
laughing.*

INT. HELEN'S BEDROOM. LATE AFTERNOON. PRESENT.

*Imogen, in black, picks up a newspaper and sits down. She looks
at the front page.*

HER P.O.V. THE PAPER.

ANSCHLUSS!
FINAL DOWNFALL OF AUSTRIA
GERMAN TROOPS POUR IN

She turns to the stop press:

MAJOR FEY 'STRONG MAN'
OF AUSTRIA, FOUND SHOT DEAD
*Suicide in Vienna flat. Wife and son also die from
gun wounds. Other prominent Austrians kill themselves.
Two Dictators speak today.*

Imogen turns the pages until she reaches:

DUBLIN ENTERTAINMENTS:
and (in boxes)
Grand Central:
DR SYN
with George Arliss.
Pillar Picture House:
THE GOOD EARTH
with Paul Muni.

Imogen throws the paper to the floor.

WIDE SHOT. HELEN'S ROOM. NIGHT. PRESENT.

*Imogen standing looking at makeshift altar on mantelpiece.
Dozens of Mass cards surround it.*

HER P.O.V.

*Camera pans along the Mass cards, propped up. They are
elaborate both in design and language.*

IMOGEN, IN BLACK, LYING ON HELEN'S BED.

MID-SHOT. IMOGEN. SEATED AT HELEN'S DESK.

*She opens a drawer and takes out a bundle of envelopes, takes off
the band, lets the letters drop onto the desk. She picks up an
envelope, takes out a letter.*

LONG SHOT. IMOGEN AT DESK. READING. HER BACK.

PROFILE IMOGEN READING.

HIGH ANGLE IMOGEN READING.

CLOSE-UP. IMOGEN READING, HER LIPS MOVING SILENTLY.

LONG SHOT. IMOGEN AT DESK.

She puts letter back in envelope and opens another.